life BEYOND CRIME

life BEYOND CRIME

What do those at risk of offending, prisoners and ex-offenders need to learn?

Edited by Paul Crane

Lemos&Crane

First published in 2017 by Lemos&Crane with the support of The Monument Trust and in association with the member organisations of The Monument Fellowship.

Lemos&Crane
Kings Place Music Base, 90 York Way, London N1 9AG
www.lemosandcrane.co.uk

ISBN: 978-1-898001-77-5

Designed by Tom Keates/Mick Keates Design
Printed by Parish Print Consultants Limited

CONTENTS

PART 2: ADULTS IN PRISON

FOREWORD

MARK WOODRUFF
The Monument Trust

After Simon Sainsbury founded The Monument Trust over five decades ago, the trustees soon reached the conclusion that philanthropy is concerned not only with donations to great causes, but also the means towards people's assured place in the world and its aspirations, for now and into the future, from good health, to fulfilment and life chances, purposeful opportunities to work, decent homes to live in, and access the country's rich tradition of musical, artistic, horticultural and architectural creativity.

This is not least true of Monument's focus on young people found by public services as hard for them to reach: young people at risk of homelessness, disaffected from education and without motivation or prospects, those caught up in substance and alcohol abuse, violence and abusive settings, those drawn into offending with little hope of a better future. Well known for its support to arts and heritage, these social causes began as a small part of Monument's grant-making. All through its history, it has supported health and welfare, as well as a constantly pressing need for their response: social renewal. Health, welfare and social renewal have amounted to almost half of the Trust's grant-making. When, therefore, the trustees decided ten years after Simon's death to devote the remaining resources to investment in the future of the arts and heritage that Monument has supported, they wanted to be sure that their long-standing efforts towards social renewal would also have a lasting effect.

We invited eight organisations to form a Monument Fellowship, covering each turn in the journey of an offender, to draw together what we had seen over many years truly diverts people from offending, prevents crime getting worse, mitigates its harm, stands to restore people free of crime to their place in the world. We wanted our work in this field not to be a past achievement, but a forward movement. The Monument Fellowship members funded to work together over the next five years towards a cumulative, sustained and transformative effect are:

- Restorative Solutions CIC, for community dispute resolution
- Centre for Justice Innovation, towards problem-solving courts
- The Good Prison, ideas for action by Lemos&Crane, with staff training, and involving organisations from the wider world so that prisons play a successful part in rehabilitation
- Khulisa UK, addressing violence and disaffection through rebuilding people in relation to their communities
- Diagrama Foundation UK, with its expertise in the care, and the re-upbringing of troubled young offenders
- Clinks, the vital support network serving community organisations working with prisoners and ex-offenders
- Koestler Trust, for its year-round encouragement to creative arts among prisoners and young offenders
- National Criminal Justice Arts Alliance, for all working with prisoners and ex-offenders because of the power of arts, music and drama to change lives and outlooks.

To this we add more of Monument's legacy. Turning Point in the West Midlands police has now shown that triaging those arrested, on the basis of the harm of their crime and re-directing low risk offenders to constructive alternatives, substantially reduces repeat crime. Furthermore, the Howard League over the last six years has worked with police nationally to reduce children's and young people's arrests by 66 per cent. These approaches together mean less need to use the full weight of the courts and prison to solve the problems of social exclusion and offending. The better solutions are increasingly well known and proving no less satisfactory to victims of crime and to wider society's sense of justice. Movement on this is the legacy we want to leave behind.

We did not wish the Fellowship's efforts to be exclusive, so decided to work on the answer to a new question periodically. We are delighted that, as well as the core Fellowship members, other excellent experts and practitioners with whom we have worked have offered such rich and diverse answers to "What do those at risk of offending, prisoners and ex-offenders need to learn?" Future years' work and thinking together mean that we can look forward to a huge store of lively wisdom and expertise that will be a worthy legacy from Simon Sainsbury's aspiration for social renewal, especially for young people in trouble and prisoners.

The Monument Trust is very grateful to all those who have contributed to this conclusion of the first year of our Fellowship, its core members and particularly to Gerard Lemos and Paul Crane who have animated our attention to the question and produced this magnificent book.

Editor's note and Acknowledgements

PAUL CRANE
Partner, Lemos&Crane

The essays, poems and pictures in the collection are broadly organised into three parts: diverting people arrested from criminal prosecution and custody together with the special position of young people; the experiences of those convicted and sentenced to imprisonment; and the last part contains essays about returning to the community after release. There are contributions, as you will see in the contents pages, about work in male and female establishments, including high security prisons, institutions for young offenders, the needs of those struggling with addictions, to name but a few. With more than 50 essays, together with poems and artworks, we hope the collection represents a substantial body of diverse knowledge, practice, insight and lived experience that may inspire, encourage and challenge readers from many different backgrounds and with a variety of interests.

The contributors to this book come from a very wide range of circumstances, as you will see from the short biographies that follow this note. As well as currently serving and ex-offenders, contributors include people who work in prisons, probation officers, health workers, former police officers, chaplains, academics and researchers, people who work in museums and galleries, or for charities, a horticulturalist, the theatre director Phyllida Lloyd, musicians like Sir Richard Stilgoe and the sculptor Sir Antony Gormley. We are pleased and proud to have received so many responses to the question posed by the Monument Fellowship, representing such a range and depth of experience and wisdom. We extend our deepest gratitude to them for their commitment and enthusiasm for the project.

We are also grateful to the Trustees of The Monument Trust, and also in particular to Mark Woodruff of The Monument Trust for the support and encouragement they have given to the eight organisations that constitute the Monument Fellowship.

Contributors

Anonymous

Residents at the following institutions have contributed prose, poetry and artworks to this collection: H.M.P. Berwyn, H.M.P. Channings Wood, H.M.P. Downview, H.M.P./Y.O.I. Drake Hall, H.M.P. Dumfries, Fromeside Clinic, H.M.P. Grendon, Katherine Price Hughes House, H.M.P. Leyhill, H.M.P. Low Moss, H.M.P. Parc, H.M.P. Peterborough, H.M.P. Styal, H.M.P. Wymott.

Julian Adler

Julian Adler is the director of research-practice strategies at the Center for Court Innovation, spanning the agency's three primary areas of work: social science research, national technical assistance and local operating programmes in New York and New Jersey, U.S.A. He is a New York State licensed clinical social worker and attorney.

Norman Anderson

From childhood unti! now, in this order: Norman has been a runaway, a drug addict, a criminal, and a prisoner. He is now an artist, an M.F.A. student in fine art at Sheffield Hallam University. Norman is a Quaker and is exploring a new way of being.

Greg Berman

Greg Berman is the director of the Center for Court Innovation. As part of the founding team responsible for creating the Center, he has helped guide the organisation from start-up to an annual budget of more than $40 million. He is the author/co-author of *Reducing Crime; Reducing Incarceration: essays on criminal justice innovation; Trial and Error in Criminal Justice Reform: learning from failure; and Good Courts: the case for problem-solving justice.*

Phil Bowen

As director of the Centre for Justice Innovation, Phil Bowen sets and leads the work and overall strategy of the organisation. Prior to being director, Phil spent the majority of this career in the British civil service. He worked for the Home Office and the Ministry of Justice, before working at H.M. Treasury and the Cabinet Office as a delivery adviser to the Prime Minister on criminal justice reform.

Mary Brown

Mary Brown is a Quaker, aged 80 with four adult children and eight grandchildren. She is a retired teacher of adults (including in colleges, a prison and Open University tutoring); and a Prison Chaplain. She is the author of *Inside Art* (Waterside Press, 2002), *Confessions of a Prison Chaplain* (Waterside Press, 2014) and *The Undiscovered Country: conversations about death* (KCA Publishing, 2017).

Patrick Campbell

Patrick Campbell, born 10 October 1964. Served a life sentence, 2000 to 2015. Part of the Alumni Network of the Prison Education Trust. Offered a job as manager of a charity shop, just waiting to relocate.

Paul Crane

Paul Crane is a partner at Lemos&Crane responsible for publishing over a hundred books, reports and websites. He is the author of two law books.

As a lawyer he took part in the landmark case before the European Court of Human Rights that led to the decriminalisation of homosexuality in Northern Ireland.

Kate Davey

Kate Davey is the communications and engagement officer at the National Criminal Justice Arts Alliance. Kate has worked with the NCJAA since 2013, where she is responsible for communications and membership engagement. Her previous roles include project co-ordination and communications for arts charities working with marginalised people.

Peter Dawson

Peter Dawson took up post as director of the Prison Reform Trust in August 2016. His career before that included prisons policy in the Home Office during the 1990s, governing two prisons between 2004 and 2012, and a subsequent spell in the private sector with Sodexo.

Nathan Dick

As part of the senior management team Nathan supports Clinks to develop both strategically and operationally. He oversees the policy work of Clinks and provides leadership to the communications and membership team. In addition, he assists colleagues to interpret the emerging criminal justice environment and develop sustainable opportunities for Clinks and its members in the wider voluntary sector.

Liz Dixon

Liz Dixon is a Restorative Manager in London Community Rehabilitation Company. She has been a probation practitioner for over 30 years working in prisons and the community. During that time she has designed and delivered group work and one-to-one programmes with male and female offenders. She has also specialised in work with hate crime perpetrators and those who are driven by extremist ideologies. More recently she has been engaged in restorative justice and she is an accredited practitioner and is a Trustee of the Restorative Justice Board. She was a practitioner academic for ten years at Brunel and Hertfordshire University and has a number of publications to her name; she was also on the editorial board of the Probation Journal for many years.

Caroline Drummond

Caroline Drummond is a member of the policy and public affairs team at Nacro, working to influence and shape policy alongside colleagues in Nacro's education and criminal justice service delivery. She has worked in health, fundraising and wider voluntary sector policy roles in the U.K. and the U.S.A.

Philip Emery

Philip Emery has wide-ranging experience in the criminal justice sector as a charity and social enterprise director, having managed education in prisons after over 20 years' teaching experience. As a Fellow of the Royal Society of Arts he has worked on every R.S.A. prison project.

Gareth Evans

Gareth Evans is a freelance researcher and former prisoner. He is studying criminology at Anglia Ruskin University and has published work in two academic journals. He has won an Oxford-Brookes University award for social innovation and is awaiting the publication of research on how people serving death-row sentences experience time.

Phil Forder

Phil Forder is the Community Engagement Manager at H.M.P and Y.O.I Parc. He received The Butler Trust Commendation 2015-16 for his contribution to promoting a more inclusive LGBT environment at Parc and across the sector. Phil is the founder of Hay in the Parc, a collaboration of many years between the Hay Literary Festival and Parc prison.

Penelope Gibbs

In 2012 Penelope Gibbs set up Transform Justice, a charity that advocates a better justice system in England and Wales: a system which is fairer, more open, more humane and more effective. She has also volunteered in the justice system and has sat as a magistrate for three years and is currently deputy chair of the Standing Committee for Youth Justice.

Gordon

Gordon first started writing while at H.M.P. Guernsey, where he helped found the prison's first- ever magazine called *Banged Up*. Gordon went on to win a Bronze Award from the Koestler Trust in the Life Story category for his piece 'From Punk to Prison', and was later offered a place on the Koestler Trust's mentoring scheme when he left custody in 2015.

Sir Antony Gormley OBE

Antony Gormley is acclaimed for his sculptures, installations and public artworks that investigate the relationship of the human body to space. His work has been widely exhibited in the U.K. and internationally. In 2017 he curated the Koestler Trust's annual exhibition of art by offenders, secure patients and detainees held in the Southbank, London.

Dr Paul Hamilton

Paul Hamilton is senior lecturer in criminology at Nottingham Trent University. Paul's main research interests are in the fields of 'crime and prejudice' and desistance from crime, particularly with regard to transformative learning and the role of 'offender management' in promoting identity change. Paul has also researched and written about disability hate crime, prison-community transitions, probation mentoring and the impact of educational interventions in reducing knife crime.

John Harding OBE

John Harding is the former Chief Probation Officer for Inner London. He is currently Acting Chair of the Penoptical Trust.

JLBJ

JLBJ is an employee at Project Future, who has a varied role including consulting the project on how to best support the community and training other professionals in working with young people.

Andy Keen-Downs

Andy Keen-Downs has been Chief Executive of Pact (Prison Advice and Care Trust) since 2005 and Group C.E.O. of Pact Futures CIC since 2015. For much of his working life, Andy has worked in the voluntary sector and was previously deputy director of Gingerbread (One Parent Families). In 2015, he received the Longford Prize on behalf of Pact, and secured the support of Michael Palin for the charity's work for prisoners' families.

Dr Hannah King

Hannah King is Assistant Professor in Criminology at Durham University and Inside-Out facilitator with her co-authors. Hannah completed the Inside-Out instructor training in 2015 and established Inside-Out at postgraduate level in H.M.P. Low Newton in 2016, the first programme in a women's prison in Europe.

Elaine Knibbs

Elaine Knibbs started her career working in male prisons as prison officer, resettlement worker and programmes facilitator. In the last 15 years she has delivered a range of programmes and interventions for offenders as part of the probation service, before moving to RISE. Elaine currently leads the team delivering trauma-based interventions and other programmes in several prison estates.

Sheena Leaf

Sheena Leaf is a Fellow of the School for Social Entrepreneurs and the founder/director of The Entrepreneur Inside CIC, an 'in prison' entrepreneurship programme supported by the local business and academic community in the south-west of England.

Gerard Lemos CMG

Gerard Lemos was described by Community Care magazine as 'one of the U.K.'s leading thinkers on social policy'. His books include *The Good Prison: conscience, crime and punishment; The End of the Chinese*

Dream: Why Chinese people fear the future (published by Yale University Press) and *The Communities We Have Lost and Can Regain*, co-authored with the late Lord Michael Young. He has held many public appointments including as a non-executive director of the Crown Prosecution Service and chair of the council of the University of York.

Phyllida Lloyd CBE

Phyllida Lloyd is a theatre, film and opera director. Her recent work includes *Mary Stuart*, and the all-female Shakespeare trilogy for the Donmar Warehouse. Her opera work includes *Peter Grimes* and *Gloriana* for Opera North, *The Carmelites* and *The Handmaid's Tale* for ENO. Her work on film includes *Gloriana: A Film, Mamma Mia, The Iron Lady* and *Julius Caesar*.

Professor Fiona Measham

Fiona Measham is Professor of Criminology at Durham University, Director of the B.A. Criminology degree programme and Director of the Inside-Out prison exchange programme. Fiona was the first European to complete the U.S. Inside-Out instructor training and set up an Inside-Out prison education programme, at Durham University, along with her co-authors.

Jennie McCreight

Jennie McCreight is employed by Touchstone, a third-sector mental health organisation specialising in working with people from different cultural backgrounds. Jennie overseas Touchstone's employability projects, including WY-FI's ETE provision. She has worked with people with complex needs for over seven years in forensic and community settings. Jennie promotes adult learning as a mechanism for sustained recovery.

Ruth McFarlane

Ruth McFarlane is a learning and teaching development manager at the Open University, focusing on adult distance learning. With a background in prison education, her work has a strong student focus and a particular interest in support for students who have not previously engaged well in education.

David Romero Mcguire

In 2008 David Mcguire moved from Spain to establish the Diagrama Foundation UK, which now has around 300 employees delivering services supporting vulnerable people. He is a member of Diagrama's international innovation and improvement group, and also a member of the European Society of Criminology and the European Prison Education Association.

Tom Millest

Tom Millest was born is 1956 and educated at Winchester College and Oxford University (theology and philosophy). Between 1979 and 2009 he served with the Metropolitan Police. In 1994 he was a Harkness Fellow at the Harvard School of Government, and surveyed community orientated problem-solving policing initiatives. Tom was the Head of the Met's public order policy unit in 2000-2001 and then joined Sir Ian Blair's police reform team. He has been a member of the Parole Board since 2010.

Corin Morgan-Armstrong

Corin Morgan-Armstrong has pioneered the family interventions programme and Invisible Walls Wales project at G4S-managed H.M.P. and Y.O.I. Parc in Bridgend, south Wales for eight years and has worked in the prison service for 20 years. He is now seeking to share the benefits of family intervention with prisons in the U.K. and internationally.

Nick Moss

Nick Moss is a writer and poet. In 2016 he was awarded a Mary Turnbull Scholarship.

Peter Neyroud CBE, QPM

Peter Neyroud is lecturer in evidence-based policing at the Insitute of Criminology in the University of Cambridge. He is general editor of *Policing: a journal of policy and practice*; co-chair of Campbell Collaboration (Crime and Justice); and editor of *European Police Science and Research Bulletin*.

John Noble

John Noble is the prison co-ordinator for Garden Organic's Master Gardener Programme. He currently runs the H.M.P. Rye Hill garden project. He has spent his career working with and advocating the use of horticultural therapies to help aid recovery and change within marginalised communities.

Dr Kate O'Brien

Kate O'Brien is Programme Director of the MSc in Criminology and Criminal Justice at Durham University and Inside-Out facilitator. Kate completed the Inside-Out instructor training in 2014 and went on to co-facilitate the first Inside-Out programme in Europe, at H.M.P. Durham, in the autumn of that year. Since 2016, Kate has convened and co-delivered a postgraduate level Inside-Out module (Prisons, Crime and Criminal Justice) at H.M.P. Low Newton.

Dr Anne O'Grady

Anne O'Grady is principal lecturer in academic studies of education at Nottingham Trent University. Her main research interests lie in the role of prison education as a mechanism for social justice; the voice of prisoners as they experience education across the life course; and the professional identity of prison educators. Anne has published two books: *Lifelong Learning in the U.K.: an introductory guide for education studies;* and a co-edited collection, *Exploring Education at Postgraduate Level: policy, theory and practice.*

Claire O'Sullivan

Claire O'Sullivan is a probation officer with 20 years' experience of working in prisons and the community. Currently based at H.M.P. Frankland, a high-security prison in the north-east of England, Claire recently completed an MSt at the University of Cambridge.

Dr Greg Parston

Greg Parston is chairman of Dartington Hall Trust and executive adviser to the director of the Institute of Global Health Innovation at Imperial

College, London. He was deputy director of the King's Fund College, co-founded and led the Office for Public Management and directed Accenture's Global Institute for Public Service Value. Greg was the chair of the Barrow Cadbury Commission on Young Adults and the Criminal Justice System, which published its report in 2005.

Tom Pauk

Tom Pauk is a retired solicitor and is involved with a number of charities in the areas of criminal justice (as an Official Prison Visitor and mentor for young offenders), dementia care, animal welfare and mental health.

Anna Peaston

Anna Peaston is bid co-ordinator for Pact (Prison Advice and Care Trust), a national charity that provides support to prisoners, people with criminal convictions, and their families through a range of services.

Hilary Peters

Hilary Peters was brought up rich, gave away her money, became a gardener, started a city farm, lived on a boat, then in a van. "Cracking out of an imprisoning situation may be something I can pass on? I hope so."

Dr Anne Pike

Anne Pike is a researcher at the Open University's Institute of Educational Technology and an independent consultant in prison education. Her award-winning doctoral study investigated transformative learning for prisoners through the gate. She is a lecturer in mathematics, a visiting lecturer in criminology, and works with the University of Southern Queensland.

Mgr Roger Reader

Monsignor Roger Reader was born in north London and educated at Highgate School and Exeter University. He started working in prison in 1986 at H.M.P. Pentonville. Since then he has been the Catholic chaplain at H.M.P. Whitemoor and H.M.Y.O.I. Feltham. He is currently the Catholic Bishops' Prisons Adviser.

Ricky

Ricky is a volunteer at Project Future and undertakes a diverse set of responsibilities including catering for the project and presenting at conferences.

Lisa Rowles

Lisa Rowles is programme design and development director for Khulisa (an award-winning national charity, focused on supporting improved well-being, emotional resilience and reduced offending in young people). She has been working in the social justice sector since 2009 and is responsible for developing and researching Khulisa's innovative programme offer in the U.K.

Mark Sillery

Mark Sillery is director of support and mentoring at The Clink Charity, which he joined in 2013 after working in the homelessness sector for six years. Prior to that he was a chef for over 20 years in hotels and restaurants around the U.K. So when the opportunity arose to combine both careers he felt it made perfect sense. Mark manages a national team of support workers and is responsible for the development of the support and mentoring programme which is the crucial element of The Clink programme.

Jane Slater

Jane A. Slater works in prison education teaching business and self-employment to adult men convicted or charged with a sexual offence. She is a part-time Ph.D student in the psychology department of Nottingham Trent University and holds a masters degree in criminology and criminal psychology.

Gary Stephenson

Gary Stephenson has been working with Restorative Solutions, which is a community interest company committed to developing and progressing innovative restorative approaches and services in the public sector and communities for the last ten years. He has managed a number of national programmes aimed at implementing restorative practice in a diverse range of sectors.

Jess Stubbs

Jess Stubbs is a researcher at the Centre for Mental Health based in London, who has been evaluating the impact of Project Future alongside young people. Jess has a degree in social policy with a focus on criminology from the London School of Economics and has a Master's degree from Oxford in evidence-based social intervention.

Sir Richard Stilgoe OBE, DL

After more than 50 years as a performer, song-writer, lyricist (*Cats, Starlight Express, Phantom of the Opera*) and broadcaster, the last few years have seen Richard working with disadvantaged young people to get them actively involved in music and performance. In 1998 he founded the Orpheus Centre, where young disabled people train for independent living and gain self-esteem through song-writing and performance. Orpheus students take their skills into prisons and young offender institutions, as well as performing at venues as diverse as Glastonbury and Buckingham Palace.

Kirstine Szifris

Kirstine Szifris's thesis, *Philosophy in Prisons: an exploration of personal development*, was supervised by Professor Alison Liebling at the University of Cambridge. It explores the interaction of the individual in the context of a prison environment through engaging prisoners in philosophical dialogue. She is currently working as a Research Associate at the Policy Evaluation and Research Unit, Manchester Metropolitan University.

Shirl Tanner

Shirl Tanner is the operations director of Sussex Pathways. She joined in 2009 as part of her social work Master's Degree, found her niche in working with offenders and has stayed ever since. Sussex Pathways, a small charitable organisation with four paid members of staff and over 50 volunteers, has worked in H.M.P. Lewes for about nine years.

Trevor Urch

Trevor Urch is recovery and service user involvement manager for Birmingham and Solihull Mental Health Foundation Trust at H.M.P. Birmingham. He has extensive experience of working across a broad range of secure and non-secure mental health services over the last 20 years. He is especially proud of peer-led involvement with prisoners in H.M.P. Birmingham since 2010.

Kara Wescome Blackman FRSA

Kara Wescombe Blackman is responsible for learning and public programmes for Watts Gallery Trust. She previously curated programmes for the Courtauld Institute of Art Gallery, the Somerset House Trust and the V&A. She has worked in museums and galleries for 20 years, with over 100 exhibitions and on five major building projects.

Ella Whittlestone

Ella Whittlestone is an artist and art teacher, specialising in drawing. After graduating from Lancaster University in 2014 with a B.A. Hons in fine art, she completed her secondary P.G.C.E in art at Cambridge University. Ella spent the last year teaching art on the female education wing of H.M.P. Peterborough.

Molly Wright

Molly Wright studied psychology at the University of Southampton and gained an MSc in forensic psychology at the University of Kent. She began volunteering as a resettlement case worker before gaining full-time employment as a facilitator in H.M.P. Thameside. Currently working for RISE, Molly is part of the prison team.

Introduction
what do those at risk of offending, prisoners and ex-offenders need to learn? why this question?

GERARD LEMOS CMG
Partner, Lemos&Crane

The organisations working together in the Monument Fellowship – Centre for Justice Innovation, Clinks, Diagrama Foundation UK, Koestler Trust, Khulisa UK, Lemos&Crane, National Criminal Justice Arts Alliance and Restorative Solutions – came together in autumn 2016 to work together to improve criminal justice. As well as our group we hope to involve a wide range of people in our thinking and debate. We are keen to involve experts, academics and commentators, but we want to particularly emphasise and encourage practitioners – the do-ers - and, indeed, to hear and respond to the voices of offenders and ex-offenders themselves.

We hope also to reach beyond the boundaries of much contemporary debate about criminal justice, which can be crudely characterised between two poles: 'prison is necessary and it works' on the one hand, 'prison fails to reform people and is harmful' on the other. Whether either set of views are right or wrong is not our concern here. We also do not want to re-state familiar arguments about prison numbers and length of sentences, not because these aren't important, but because they receive plenty of attention elsewhere. Instead we seek to throw open a wider conversation about what is being done and what might be done about the issue at the heart of criminal justice: how should we respond to those that break society's rules? That led us to a question from which we hope everyone, at whichever stage and in whatever part of the criminal justice system they operate, can devise many formal and informal responses: what do those at risk of offending, offenders and ex-offenders need to learn?

The question was posed on public platforms, online and by email, as well as in meetings, seminars and conferences, and disseminated widely by the organisations in the Fellowship. The range and number of responses and the great diversity of thought and practice they reflected has exceeded our greatest expectations. This collection of responses to the question has been deliberately brought together without a governing 'theory of change'. Instead it is a large collection of voices and views from action on the ground. The contributions are also not ordered thematically because our intention is to stress range, diversity and originality, rather than a rigid framework of pre-formed ideas.

Nevertheless across the entire collection some important themes emerge and recur. The single largest proportion of contributors focus in different ways on the need for personal development for offenders - to strengthen their non-criminal identities and enhance their self-confidence with the help of others as someone who can take their place in the world outside criminal justice and live a full, individual and good life. The second theme is the many original and insightful ways of learning, both pedagogically and in terms of content. There is a considerable range of possibilities between learning philosophy and learning how to make spectacles (both represented in the collection) – but they are all important ways of learning practical things – the 'how' as well as the 'what'. The importance of creative insight and expression through making and appreciating art is a rich vein of rehabilitative activity for offenders; this is the third large theme. Last but not least, the fourth theme is the importance of maintaining and building family life and other strong emotional ties despite the limitations of prison life. If it is not too simplistic, there is an emphasis throughout on learning about yourself as well as learning about 'things'. Although we make no theoretical claims for the collection, for readers familiar with the growing academic literature on desistance these themes will come as no surprise – a gratifying harmony between theory and practice.

But what does the collection actually tell us? Above all else, taken together, they reinforce the need to be respectful and grateful for the good work that goes on in criminal justice at a time when some would say that there is nothing good going on at all. False optimism can be misleading, but false pessimism is disastrous. A reasonably close reading of the collection draws attention not just to the range of ideas and practice, many of them original, inspiring and surprising, but there are also some fascinating differences in the paradigms on which practitioners at all stages of the criminal justice system choose to operate: their assumptions or 'received wisdom' about what they do and why they do it are many and varied.

Some contributors focus on the need to be less judgmental, eschewing wherever possible stigmatising labels. Those of us who are interested in improving criminal justice should, it is argued, recognise the many extenuating circumstances which may lead people into crime. Furthermore many of the responses by the criminal justice system, particularly imprisonment, achieve only intolerance and exclusion in the short and the long term. People arguing this perspective propose instead the need to listen more to offenders and judge them less. Others, by contrast, argue that a considerable failing in the current system is that offenders are given too few opportunities to discuss, recognise, come to terms with and make amends for what they have done. True desistance from crime requires acknowledgement of the damage done as well as self-awareness, along with compassion and forgiveness. That is the essential proposition of those who support a substantial expansion of restorative approaches in sentencing. Some would go on to say that a failure to recognise the seriousness of a crime committed, its impact on victims and the absence of a clear and open willingness to judge your own offence to some extent as society judges the crime considerably reduces the chance of being released on licence or parole. That could mean that offenders simply end up serving even longer sentences – something nobody in this collection at least argues in favour of, though others might. Longer sentences are not, to be clear, only a cause espoused by those with a more coercive view of criminal justice. Even people who may in general terms argue for shorter sentences have not opposed longer sentences for hate crimes or child sexual abuse, for example.

Another conundrum arises from those who argue for the benefits of peer support and mentoring among offenders and ex-offenders. The contrary view is that too much time spent with peers, particularly in prison, simply reinforces assumptions and patterns of criminogenic influence. Both views are represented in this collection. In another paradox, some would argue that serious offenders need to be removed from society for a long time; that deters them from further crime as well as being exemplary to others. But a strong case is made in this collection for offenders in prisons to have their ties with the community, and in particular with their families, strongly and proactively maintained. The case for that is partly humanity but also that such contact and relationships may have a beneficial impact on offenders' mental welfare while in prison as well as improving their prospects for resettlement and not reoffending on release. They will hopefully, to put it simply, have someone to meet them and somewhere to go when they get out.

It is tempting to argue - and almost indisputable - that the many good ideas contained in this collection – ranging from teaching prisoners philosophy, being inspired by objects from museum collections, beekeeping and learning how to become a chef, to mention only a few – should be expanded and replicated, but the wider implication of the range of opinions and activities represented here is the need for many different ways of working and even more new ideas. Nothing in this collection suggests that even if money was no object the simple expansion and replication of the ideas suggested here or elsewhere would solve all the problems of criminal behaviour in British society. The case for continued and determined innovation is strongly made by this collection.

But by far the strongest conclusion that emerges from these reflective and sometimes disarmingly honest, vivid and personal contributions, with the many paradoxes and conundrums they reflect and pose, is the need to recognise the whole human being, the 3D human as described in one contribution, not just the offence that makes someone an offender, nor even just the person that will need a job and somewhere to live when they get out if they are to have any chance. The wider sense of individuality and diversity of offenders, in their lifestyles and experiences, but also in what they think, feel and do that comes through this collection makes the strongest case for a much greater openness to all aspects of people's experience and character which can limit or enable their capacity for change. That capacity for change for the better with the help and belief of others is the sense of hope that can be inferred from every contribution in this collection. If, however, there is a warning given by this collection, it is a warning against generalities and shallow simplification.

PART ONE
DIVERSION AND YOUNG PEOPLE

Pre-court diversion of offenders:
lessons from the past, present and for the future

PETER NEYROUD CBE, QPM
Lecturer, Institute of Criminology, University of Cambridge

Pre-court disposals, led by the police, offer promising potential rewards: faster, more effective, cost-saving disposals that offer the opportunity to increase perceptions of police legitimacy, raise the satisfaction of victims, and hold more offenders to account. They also pose risks. They could backfire on reoffending and victim satisfaction, be inconsistent, incoherent, and unenforceable. New research, Operation Turning Point in Birmingham, has demonstrated that all the benefits are achievable where careful attention is paid to implementation and has opened up a new interest in diversion.

Out of court disposals: lessons from the past

Since the nineteenth century, the police have used diversion through cautions for offences such as drunkenness and prostitution. In the 1960s they became an established part of a welfare-based approach to dealing with young offenders; adding rehabilitative conditions such as counselling or cognitive behavioural therapy to a caution also has a long history.

In the mid-1960s Rose and Hamilton (1970) tested a 'cautioning-plus' scheme in which one group of offenders was offered a caution with additional support from a Youth Liaison team. In the 2000s conditional cautions – attaching an agreed set of conditions to a formal caution with the threat of prosecution for non-compliance – were added to a growing list of pre-court disposals available to the police.

There are compelling reasons to divert offenders. The prosecution of offenders, particularly young offenders, is often both costly and ineffective. A Campbell Systematic Review in the U.S.A. of the 'formal system processing of juveniles' (prosecution) found that it 'appears to not have a crime control effect, and across all measures appears to increase delinquency' (Petrosino *et al*, 2010:6); findings that almost certainly extend to young adults (Britton, 2014). While almost all the studies that Petrosino *et al* reviewed were U.S. based, U.K. studies have also emphasised the value of police exercising their discretion not to prosecute (Steer, 1970) and the benefits of a quick process rather than delayed decision-making (Jones, 1982). Yet they also raised concerns that an expansion of diversion through the 1970s and 1980s created an unhelpful diversity of practice and impacted on the fairness and justice of the system (Campbell, 1997).

Conditional cautioning, which can include restorative conditions, is the most recent pre-court development in the U.K. Early implementation (Blakeborough and Pierpont, 2007) produced considerable variation between and within the six forces studied. Most conditional cautions were for damage and the most frequent condition was payment to the victim. The paucity of rehabilitative or restorative conditions suggested that there might be some serious challenges in implementation, partly because of the availability of appropriate programmes and partly because of the logistics of organising restorative conferences.

Two further studies examined the introduction of specific conditions for women (Easton *et al*, 2010) and community payback conditions (Rice, 2010). They found problems in the custody suite with custody officers finding the conditions complex and the task of matching suitable cases to the conditions one that they were unprepared for by training or guidance.

The lessons from the past are clear. Firstly, formally processing offenders – particularly young offenders – can cause more harm than good, while diversion appears to be promising. However, 50 years of studies repeatedly reaffirms that the consistent exercise of discretion is a really tough issue for the police. Those studies that have looked at the police involvement in the setting of conditions show that the police are not well prepared for this task, particularly if it involves rehabilitative or restorative conditions. The right ingredients all need to be put into an approach that is perceived by both victims and offenders to be fair, certain (consistent follow-through on breaches of conditions), swift (a rapid process from arrest to final disposal) and with evidence-based interventions. Too much emphasis on severity of punishment and formal processing will probably cause adverse consequences rather than a reduction of reoffending. Moreover, with the exception of the restorative justice studies, too little attention has been paid to the victim's involvement, motives and confidence in the outcomes.

Operation Turning Point: lessons from the present

The experiment focused on offenders whom the police had decided that it was in the public interest to prosecute (informal warning and cautions having already been discarded) and where there was sufficient evidence to do so. Eligible offenders, both juveniles and adults, were identified by a screening tool. This excluded offenders with multiple convictions, a high likelihood of prison and a serious offence. They were then randomly assigned to prosecution or the Turning Point diversion.

Offenders given the Turning Point diversion were asked to attend a meeting within forty-eight hours with a police offender manager or a member of the Youth Offending Service. Turning Point offenders were warned at each stage that non-compliance with this attendance requirement, reoffending or failure to meet the terms of the Turning Point contract would result in immediate prosecution.

Participants were required to agree a contract after a structured conversation at their meeting. The contract was voluntary, but was backed up by the threat of prosecution. The contract contained two standard conditions – no reoffending within the four-month contract period and compliance with a few agreed conditions, which could be deterrent (such as curfews or community payback), reparative (apology or compensation), restorative or rehabilitative. The choice of conditions was determined by the pathways to crime disclosed in the discussion with the police officer. A major aim of the conversation was to allow the officer to encourage the offender to identify the reasons for their offending and to learn how to support their own desistance from crime by undertaking the agreed programme of conditions. The ultimate incentive was that successful completion of the contract would result in no further action.

The experiment was rolled out in careful stages, starting with two local policing areas and then expanded to the whole of Birmingham. In the final stage, from 2013-2014, more than 400 offenders were randomly assigned to Turning Point and prosecution, with a high degree of treatment integrity. The subsequent evaluation (full results of which are in preparation at the time of writing) has shown very promising outcomes from the Turning Point condition when compared to prosecution: reduced harm; lower cost; increased victim satisfaction. Given the history of pre-court diversions, it was equally important that the experiment was able to develop and test a more effective implementation model for pre-court diversion. First and foremost, there was tight and repeated cyle of training, tracking outcomes and providing feedback (Slothower, 2015). On top of this, the offender management teams and researchers built a 'prescibing tool' to enable officers to provide specific and tailored treatment conditions to each offender.

Lessons for the future of pre-court diversion

While the Turning Point experiment was running, the Ministry of Justice launched a consultation on reform of pre-court disposals. The model that was then piloted in three police forces during 2014 was intended to be a 'simplified' approach with only two potential disposals: (a) the conditional caution plus (CC+) based on the existing conditional caution; and (b) the community resolution plus (CR+) for lower level offences.

The Ministry of Justice consultation paper specified that the conditions which officers were required to deploy must be either rehabilitative (attendance on a treatment course, which include anger management or other forms of cognitive behavioural therapy) and/or reparative (giving an apology to the victim and/or compensation for damage or loss from the crime) and/or punitive (a financial penalty).

The evaluation report of the pilot has yet to be published and the future model for pre-court diversion is very much in debate. However, Turning Point and two further field experiments – Operation CARA in Hampshire and Operation Checkpoint in Durham – suggest that, as the options for future reform are considered, there are opportunities to use the experimental evidence to build a robust and effective regime of police-led pre-court diversion. Moreover, it is clear, from Turning Point that pre-court diversion can be used effectively as a genuine alternative to prosecution rather than just a way of resulting minor damage cases. Operation CARA suggests that pre-court interventions can also be successfully applied to low-risk domestic violence cases. Finally, Operation Checkpoint has been testing a risk triage tool to assess eligibility for pre-court diversion or prosecution, which should ensure a better match between the risk presented by an offender and the treatments proposed.

For policy-makers and practitioners seeking an evidence-based approach to the future use of police led pre-court diversions, there is a growing body of evidence showing not only 'what works' but also how to ensure that it works consistently in the field. The 'science' can drive improvements by continuing the programme of field tests that The Monument Trust has funded (Weisburd and Neyroud, 2011). Effective pre-court diversion can offer an opportunity for a citizen, young or older, to learn how to stop offending before they become identified and labelled as an offender with all the consequences for their future life and prospects.

DESISTANCE AND COURT REFORM:
change comes from within

PHIL BOWEN
Director, Centre for Justice Innovation

A Zen master goes up to a hot dog vendor and says, "Make me one with everything." The hot dog vendor fixes a hot dog and hands it to the Zen master, who pays with a £20 note. The vendor puts the note in the till and closes it. "Excuse me, but where's my change?" asks the Zen master. The vendor responds, "Ah, change comes from within."

This old joke about the Buddhist and the hot dog seller came to me when I was sat in a criminal court, watching a court case involving a young man called Andy. Andy was close to finishing his community sentence. He had been a persistent and repeat offender. His speciality had been domestic burglary. Or, more accurately, his speciality had been being caught for domestic burglary. Having undergone a long programme of drug treatment, support and monitoring by a judge, he was about to fully regain his liberty. Asked by the judge what had changed, Andy mumbled with a heart-warming whisper, "I just want to stop all that stuff I used to do... I want to do more with my life." For anyone who sits in court regularly it feels like this type of transformation is rare indeed.

Our criminal justice system can be a dismal place - the same cases and, many times, the same faces. In the face of new reforms, new policies, new initiatives, the grey reality of the revolving door of offending clatters away unabated. But seeing the case made me think anew about why it is that some people like Andy do turn away from crime. Understanding that seems, to me, to be the key to answering the question of not only what offenders need to learn but what we need to learn to help people like Andy leave offending behind.

The relatively recent study of the processes that lead people out of a pattern of offending has been given the fancy name of 'desistance' by criminologists. But in many ways its lessons are as old as the hills. For example, desistance research is confirming what has long been an empirical truism in criminology— that growing older is the most significant factor in predicting desistance from offending. Most young offenders are essentially law-abiding children who are temporarily drawn into adolescent delinquency. They quickly grow out of it as developmental maturity proceeds and self-control improves. Learning this has huge implications for youth court practice and policy. First, it means that running through the panoply of prosecution, court and disposal for most early stage young people is likely to be a waste of time. Second, it means we should be careful about shackling people from a young age with the label and consequences of criminality, such as the practical effects of a criminal record on their future employment.

Unfortunately, there are many people for whom this simple process of growing older does not lead to desistance in offending. These people have criminal careers which start earlier than the average person, escalate quicker and continue for longer. And this group, while small as a percentage of the population of people who commit crime at any one time in their life, makes a large proportion of the people who come back around again and again.

Luckily, desistance research has identified the mechanisms by which these more prolific offenders can change. What we know now is that desistance tends to involve an initial openness to change and exposure to routes that offer a positive way out. We know this is often because of little things— an excellent probation officer, a newly discovered passion for art, a significant relationship or a new found responsibility. Following that, making a decision to change often accentuates a new conception of themselves. Old behaviours are no longer seen as desirable— the person who sees himself as foremost a father or an entrepreneur, rather than an ex-drug dealer.

In short, what this means is that even for prolific offenders change is possible. And there are crucial moments when that change can be accelerated and acted upon in our courts, my special area of interest. It's what happened for Andy. He was being supervised in what is known as a 'problem-solving court.' What distinguishes problem-solving courts from a traditional court process is how a case is regularly overseen by a judge, whose role is to encourage behaviour change, through regular monitoring and engagement with the offender. As one U.S. problem-solving court judge told me, her job is to, "understand the story behind the behaviour... the story behind the story they tell themselves about why they are stuck."

Desistance theory permeates problem-solving court practice. It recognises the need for individualised and bespoke sentencing, following one of the key findings from desistance that the criminal justice system needs to be responsive to the personal and social needs, attributes and assets of each individual. It recognises the need to be realistic about the almost inevitable false starts. For people who have been involved in persistent offending, desistance from offending is a difficult and complex process, and one that is likely to involve relapses. By regularly bringing people back to court to check on how they are doing, a process known as judicial monitoring, problem-solving courts place the judge right at the heart of sensitively managing setbacks.

Problem-solving practice does not just concentrate on the negative but seeks actively to encourage the positive. For people who have perhaps never had anyone in authority praise them, having a judge congratulate them on finishing a programme of drug treatment can be just the trigger that helps people decide to turn around their lives. And there is strong evidence that much of what explains why problem-solving courts work is this relationship between the judge and the offenders. By establishing a regular and consistent relationship, the judge plays a key role in supporting desistance in raising their self-esteem and sense of achievement when they succeed.

This judicial role in problem-solving is not just an unbiased mechanism, not just a clever device, neutral of values. No, it emphasises something not often found in our criminal justice system: belief in other people's capacity to change. For at the heart of successful work with offenders, whether that be in a problem-solving court or in a successful prison arts programme or giving bored young kids something better to do, is a sense of hope that offenders' have it in themselves to turn away from crime. And so, at the end, perhaps the most important thing that prisoners and offenders need to learn is that it is ultimately within them to change. Despite all the paraphernalia of the criminal justice system, the police, the wigs and gowns, the treatment services and the like, Andy's decision to change had come from within. The system cannot change people, but it can play a crucial role in helping them at the right time and in the right place.

Maybe it is a lesson that requires not so much teaching to, as believing in. In a world whose horizons can seem constrained by the poverty of management speak and sound-bite tested nonsense masquerading as policy, talk of hope and change can sometimes seem naïve (and, sin of all sins, costly). But rediscovering that naïve belief in change, or redemption if you have religious bent, is vital - for it is there to be stirred in the heart of everyone. And belief in change is the bedrock of any aspirational vision of a better justice system and the good life.

LESSONS FROM INNOVATIVE APPROACHES IN THE U.S.A.

love is (almost) all you need

GREG BERMAN and JULIAN ADLER
Center for Court Innovation, New York City, U.S.A.

The Beatles got it right: love is all you need. Well, it may not be all that a person needs, but it likely explains why some individuals are better able to alter their life trajectories and avoid further contact with the criminal justice system than others. In our experience, the best way to change the behaviour of defendants is by creating caring relationships with social workers, judges, mentors, clergy, family members, employers, and others. Almost no one transforms their life without positive connections with their fellow human beings.

In short, what offenders, prisoners, and ex-offenders need to learn is that someone cares about them.

Don't get us wrong: evidence-based, cognitive-behavioural therapies are important. We can and should be working to spread these kinds of interventions. But a highly-calibrated treatment protocol rarely succeeds without a caring relationship to support it. The best programmes attempt to bring, for lack of a better expression, a dose of love into the lives of defendants. The effectiveness of this approach is strongly supported by neuroscience. "The human brain is a 'social organ of adaptation' stimulated to grow through positive and negative interactions with others." writes Pepperdine University Professor of Psychology Louis Cozolino. "The quality and nature of our relationships become encoded within the neural infrastructure of our brains."

We believe in the human capacity for change, particularly if people are given the proper supports and encouragement. Over the past year, we have been working on a book about how to reduce incarceration, to be published in 2018. As part of our research, we have documented numerous success stories, addicts getting clean, delinquent young people re-engaging in school, and gang members becoming advocates for non-violent conflict resolution.

The common denominator in many of these stories is the presence of a caring professional who is willing to take the time to listen – and to articulate high expectations. Sometimes, this person is a social worker who takes pains to make sure that a defendant actually makes it into a residential drug treatment programme. Sometimes it is a probation official going above and beyond the call of duty to find a programme particularly tailored to the needs of a troubled young person. And sometimes, the caring professional is a judge. We have watched Victoria Pratt at Newark Community Solutions in New Jersey and Alex Calabrese of the Red Hook Community Justice Center in Brooklyn, New York engage directly with defendants, encouraging law-abiding behaviour through respectful treatment and praise for progress in treatment. As Judge Pratt said, her job is to explain to defendants that, "they are better than the last worst thing they did."

How do we encourage all justice professionals to act in a similar fashion? We think any reform agenda should be simultaneously small-bore and big-picture. We need culture change if we are to move away from a factory model in which cases are processed as quickly as possible with little attention to the basic humanity of defendants or the complicated histories (of trauma and addiction and unemployment) that they bring with them.

This kind of transformation won't happen overnight. And it won't happen without the active participation of the people who actually run the criminal justice system – the police, prosecutors, probation officials, judges, and correctional officers who work with defendants on a daily basis.

We can begin by helping justice professionals make micro-adjustments. The details matter. Does a police officer make eye contact during a traffic stop? Can a defendant understand what is happening during a court appearance? Is a probation office easy to find and well-maintained? Recognizing and rewarding these kinds of behaviours are important steps toward establishing a criminal justice system that embodies the values of dignity and respect; and that genuinely cares about those in its charge. We should aspire to a world in which this is the minimum expectation of our justice system rather than a platonic ideal.

As hard as it will be to inspire an ethic of care and concern among justice professionals, it may prove just as difficult to encourage defendants to be receptive. Many defendants, particularly people of colour, have had negative experiences with the justice system. In many places, the justice system has historically caused great harm. And so along with love, we will need another virtue: patience. It took us years to get into this mess, and we should expect that it will take us years to get out of it.

TRANSITION TO ADULTHOOD IN YOUNG OFFENDERS
become the subject, not the object

Dr GREG PARSTON
Chairman, The Dartington Hall Trust, former Chairman, The Barrow
Cadbury Commission on Young Adults and the Criminal Justice System

The Barrow Cadbury Commission on Young Adults and the Criminal Justice System argued, over 10 years ago, that the division between youth and criminal justice systems in the U.K. (delineated by an offender being under or over the age of 18) was "unwise and prevents sensible approaches for dealing with well-understood problems of young adult offenders."[1] Instead, the Commission advocated a "life-course" approach to dealing with all offenders, a unified system that would enable the best application of resources to assist offenders based on individual assessments of need, rather than on age.

The Commission, which I was honoured to chair, acknowledged that an integrated criminal justice system could only be a long-term aspiration, given the political, economic and organizational self-interests of existing ways of doing things. As an interim and more immediate measure, therefore, the Commission further recommended the establishment of Transition to Adulthood (T2A) teams. The Commission envisaged these as local bodies with obligations to help ensure co-ordinated provision of public services for young offenders, not only from criminal justice agencies but also from local health, education, housing and social services as well.

Over the next few years, implementation of this proposal took the form of pilots and demonstration projects across the country, coordinated by the T2A Alliance,[2] with support from Barrow Cadbury and the collaboration of nearly 20 charitable organisations. T2A teams were intended to be expedient alternatives in the absence of "life-course" approaches to criminal justice, whether for young offenders or adult offenders. The objective was to co-ordinate public service provision tailored to the individual needs of each young offender.

Independent evaluation of the initial T2A pilots, which ran between 2009 and 2013 and which engaged over 1,000 young adults at various stages within the criminal justice system, showed remarkable results: only nine per cent of young people involved were reconvicted in this time period; only nine per cent breached the terms of their community order or licence; employment rates trebled; and levels of those not in education, employment or training (NEET) halved.[3]

Why did this work? Because T2As actually orchestrated delivery of services from various and often unconnected, not to say disjointed, public and charitable sector agencies to affect more meaningful, bespoke help for each young offender. They did not provide new services in and of themselves; instead, they orchestrated what was already there (from services that were and remain largely unco-ordinated and untargeted) for the young persons in transition.

Unconnected service delivery

The absence of harmonisation between public service providers is not an issue only for young offenders or even for all offenders. It is a major issue facing all users of all public and charitable services almost all of the time. This debilitating lack of connection between programmes of public service providers has been long recognised as a real problem in attempts to affect improved social outcomes. The result of 'silo-ed' delivery can be frustration and even damage.

The lack of co-ordination between public services and with common-cause charitable organisations was a key concern in the public service reform agenda of the 1997 New Labour government, which advocated 'joined-up solutions' to 'wicked problems'. Perversely, although probably not intentionally, the same government exacerbated the lack of connection by encouraging greater diversity of service provision, including from the private sector, which fuelled the lack of co-ordination. Even then, though, there were significant attempts to find more effective ways of joining up the delivery – and more important, the impacts – of diverse providers.[4] 'Joined-up management' became an aspiration, though unfulfilled.

The struggle to co-ordinate and harmonise public and social service provision around personal and community needs continues today, two decades later, in the face of what the Institute for Government identifies as a failure to "translate into system-wide change". The enduring obstacles are short-term policy and funding cycles; misaligned geographies and the patchwork of commissioning, funding and regulatory processes; cultural differences (and battles) between professions; barriers to data sharing; and limited sharing of 'what works'.[5]

Now, the "life-course" approach advocated for those in the criminal justice by the Commission for Young Adults involves psychological, sociological and developmental assessments that provide crucial information in determining effective interventions and assistance to support offenders in their return to civil society.[6] The "life course" approach is largely directed at assisting the supply-side of the supportive interaction between service provider and the offender-user, ignoring for the moment the inability of those services systems to integrate their disparate, though well-intended, interventions.

Creating co-producers

So, in the face of all that, how does one respond to the important question,

"What do people at risk of offending, prisoners and ex-offenders need to learn?" Reflecting on the experience of T2As, extrapolating to the offender population more widely and acknowledging the disarray of public service provision has brought me to the conclusion that treating ex-offenders as the objects of public service delivery – the people for whom or to whom things are done – may not be enough. Today, we know more about how to support the demand side of public services and, rather than focusing on supply, perhaps that is where an answer may lie.

There has been considerable work done since 2005 to explore the potential of more proactive roles on the part of all citizens in producing value from public services – not just in receiving it. Citizens are more widely regarded today as potential 'collaborators' and 'co-producers'[7] in service design and in the creation of value, as can be produced through healthy behaviours to minimise clinical interventions, neighbourhood watch to reduce threats of crime, homework clubs to increase the value of formal education. As co-producers, citizens are key actors in public service delivery rather than people who have things done for them or to them.

Perhaps we underestimated that collaborative and demanding role of service users in the work of the Commission. With greater understanding of its potential today, productive and potentially beneficial answer to, *"What to learn?"* is to make it possible for offenders to learn to how make the connections between public services and themselves, how to maximise the contribution of public services by facilitating their interplay, how to use one service to help leverage the support of others.

Citizens, whether offenders or not, are too often treated as objects of policy making and of service delivery decisions, rather than as active participants in the service changes that will directly affects their lives. The consequence can be apathy, disillusionment and even anger – with 50 per cent of citizens polled in recent research saying that they are hardly ever or never involved in decisions about services and two-thirds saying they have neither the time nor the interest in working with public services to improve the quality of their lives.[8]

At the same time that politicians and the media personalities argue about the proper role of government in health, education and public safety, the public is noticeably absent or ignored in those debates. Indeed, citizens' knowledge and access to detailed information about public policy and service issues are often intentionally restricted, sometime distorted and almost always over-simplified. This disempowers citizens; and the culprits are short-sighted politicians, self-serving professional interests, a lazy media and service providers themselves. Within this field of ignorance and ignoring is the purported network of support available for ex-offenders (perhaps more in need of public services than many others) as they leave prison. What ex-offenders need to learn before they leave prison is how to stand up for themselves in this quagmire, express their demands forcefully and make the best use of the services that are meant to serve them. Waiting for someone else or some other agency (whether a T2A or another) isn't good enough. Yet, while programmes do exist to inform prisoners of services and employment opportunities that can be available after their release, the House of Commons Work and Pensions Committee report last year noted, "All too often prisoners face a cliff edge in support once they reach the prison gate."[9]

Learning to manoeuvre

Among the principal factors that the Commission on Young Adults noted contribute to reducing reoffending is employment. Jobcenter Plus is the government's principal employment service agency, one toward which many offenders naturally gravitate on their release from prison. Yet the House of Commons Committee goes on to note the inadequacy and inconsistency of the agency in relation to ex-offenders, identifying the tendency to dismiss offenders as "hard cases" too difficult to help.

So ex-offenders are likely to have to fend for themselves, and this may be in circuitous ways. They need to learn how to do that. For example, ex-offenders' access to health care is not just about how and where to sign up with a general practitioner, but also about introductions to one of the country's largest employer, which is dedicated to non-discriminatory employment of ex-offenders. The best way to find that opportunity might not be through the NHS application process itself but through organisations like the St. Giles's Trust, which specifically assists ex-offenders in the search for work.[10]

Similarly, seeking housing is not simply about putting one's name on a local council's waiting list, but actively seeking help from groups like Shelter, which offers specific advice to offenders and counsellors both in and out of prison.[11] Learning new skills might be about enrolling in formal education programmes; but it might also be more accessible and relevant through programmes such as Goldsmiths' Open Book, which offers non-traditional learning activities that encourage students to value and reflect on their own life experiences including offending.[12]

How to find one's way through the contradictory, non-conventional and often confusing array of organisations that are out there but are often unresponsive to ex-offenders needs is a key challenge, but one in which offenders can be taught to manoeuvre intelligently. Asking the right questions, seeking out relevant agencies, using new sources of information, expressing one's needs confidently: these are all skills that can be taught.

The key challenge to those seeking to equip offenders for the search for support, stabilisation and well-being is to help build their confidence, knowledge and capacity to become active citizens in relation to the public services which are meant to serve them. The answer isn't to provide more T2As or agencies like them that aim to help ex-offenders 'move their lives forward'. The answer is to instruct and equip offenders to become co-producers, to use the services and agencies that are already out there more confidently and more effectively, to create value from them for themselves and their fellows. The answer is to help offenders learn how to be the subjects, not the objects, of the services that are there to assist them.

Essential elements for providing education and skills to young people involved with the criminal justice system

CAROLINE DRUMMOND
Policy Officer, Nacro

The focus of this article is specifically on young people, given Nacro's extensive experience of delivering education provision to this group. Our experiences in delivery, research and policy have highlighted three cross-cutting themes across education delivery in both custodial and community settings, which are explored below. While a core curriculum including English and maths provides a critical foundation, personal development needs to sit alongside this to ensure progression throughout the young person's life. Having a sense of a positive pathway is absolutely key for the young person to feel they are moving forward. Through Nacro's experience working with young people who have been in contact with the criminal justice system, both in community and secure settings, such as Medway Secure Training Centre, it is clear how fundamental education is to rehabilitation. Through our Beyond Youth Custody (BYC) programme, has demonstrated that successful resettlement is reinforced by education and the individualised support that is provided around it. BYC is a Big Lottery Funded learning and awareness-raising project, designed to challenge, advance and promote better thinking in policy and practice for the effective resettlement of young people.

The findings of a review of the youth justice system led by the chair of the Youth Justice Board, Charlie Taylor, were published in December 2016. Recognising the inadequacies of the current system, the government pledged to, "put education and health at the heart of youth custody", signalling a step change in direction to address the educational needs of young people in custody. Having support in place is essential before a young person in contact with the criminal justice system can start to engage and progress in education. Many will have experienced significant gaps in their previous education, had periods of disengagement and experienced significant trauma preventing them from learning effectively. Alongside education delivery, ensuring to help ensure young people can gain both the skills and confidence they need to progress into further education, training or employment are considered as follows.

High quality relationships

Positive, stable and long-term relationships between young people and the staff working with them play a crucial role in helping young people to engage with services that are there to support them. Having someone believe in the young person and not give up on them can be a powerful catalyst for change. Highly trained and skilled education practitioners, with experience in areas such as mental health would ensure that education had a therapeutic element, moving away from the traditional classroom model that so often fails to address many of the underlying causes of disengagement. Research suggests that young people are more likely to form effective relationships with staff that possess certain qualities, including a non-judgmental attitude and demonstrable empathy. In turn, this enhances engagement with services such as education. Nacro's research from Beyond Youth Custody has highlighted the fact that positive relationships between staff and service users are predicated on mutual respect and these are key to successful engagement, enhancing confidence and trust to enable the young person to build a positive future narrative, which is a critical element of desistance from crime.

Development of communication skills

Alongside the core curriculum, developing communication skills is vital to ensuring the young person has the tools to progress into further training or employment. Many young people in contact with the criminal justice system have been excluded from school or have had poor or disjointed experiences of the school system, and therefore replication of similar environments is often not appropriate to develop these skills and can perpetuate negative associations around learning. It is critical that practitioners have the resources to create an environment that facilitates maximum engagement and communication. In custodial settings, bringing in external facilitators can be extremely effective in developing communication. For example, in Medway Secure Training Centre (S.T.C.) young people have taken part in artistic activities with staff outside the institution; the use of temporary release can facilitate the development of communication skills, giving young people the ability to connect with the wider community and help with the transition from custody when they are released. Participatory approaches which involve the learner can help to build trust and confidence and in turn, improve engagement and communication skills; for example, Nacro's horticulture work at Medway S.T.C. where young people are involved in designing and creating vegetable gardens using the produce for catering classes.

A therapeutic approach

The prevalence of health inequalities among adults in the criminal justice system is well documented and this is mirrored in the youth estate. The presence of mental health issues in childhood can have a long-term, negative impact on educational outcomes.[1] Addressing and tracking mental health issues, therefore, needs to be at the centre of a young person's personalised plan. Progress in terms of both educational outcomes and personal development outcomes should be tracked to ensure continuous support. Adopting a tailored approach to the young person's mental health needs is critical and should be embedded in both a general approach and a practical sense, for example, ensuring that any outpatient appointments do not conflict with education sessions through managing this outside of core teaching hours. It is crucial that sub-threshold levels of mental health are also addressed to prevent problems developing further. Young people in contact with the criminal justice system have experienced a disproportionate amount of trauma in their childhood and/or adolescence.[2] Trauma often manifests itself in a number of ways including violence, anxiety and depression, having a direct impact upon a young persons' engagement and ability to learn. It is therefore critical that the prevalence of trauma is recognised and acted upon by practitioners; failure to understand the impact can be a significant barrier to a young persons' educational progress. Recognising and responding to the often highly complex health needs of young people in contact with the criminal justice system is vital to ensure all aspects of successful rehabilitation, including education, are effective and sustainable.

Placing high quality education and training at the heart of the youth justice system provides an opportunity to tackle the destructive cycle of offending that some young people get caught up in and struggle to get out of. By enhancing educational progression through supportive relationships, development of communication skills and being complemented by a therapeutic approach, we can help many more young people in the future to move on from offending, achieve their aspirations and flourish in our communities.

Responses from
young people:
what we want learn

LISA ROWLES
Programme Design and Development Director, Khulisa UK

To answer The Monument Fellowship question, Khulisa (as a provider of programmes building emotional resilience for those caught in the cycle of crime and/or violence) decided that the best people to answer this were our participants. In giving them a voice, we hope to help the reader to gain a valuable insight into the lives of some of those in (or at risk of being) in our criminal justice system. We surveyed a cross section from our programmes in all three pathways: *young people at risk* (those we aim to prevent pursuing a life of crime); *offenders in prison* (those we aim to rehabilitate, to desist from a life of crime) and *ex-offenders* (those we aim to reintegrate to a crime-free life, within their community)

Our survey is a snapshot, a small sample. It offers an honest and indicative representation of the stories and experiences we hear daily in the course of our work. We focus on helping individuals to reveal their authentic selves, the person inside, behind the violent and risky behaviour - yet still possessing the potential to live a crime-free life. The responses are concurrently uplifting, saddening and unsurprising to us; but we are eternal optimists. We believe that working together alongside partners that share our values, we can help release that potential for those brave enough to share their story; to allow us access behind their mask of violence, shame, trauma and low self-worth. The survey focused on *boys and girls in school* (Year 9/ 13 to 14 years) (during a one-day awareness building session); males in prison (18 to 35 years) both before and after involvement in our programme (Silence the Violence, behaviour change programme); and *male and female ex-offenders* (18 to 35 years), recently released into the community and accessing our Milestones mentoring project. We received a wide range of responses that we were able to distil into key themes that are identified below. All of the comments in italics are taken from actual participants' comments.

The responses from **young people at risk** focused on three core learning themes. (1) Learning how to deal with peer pressure: *"Watch who your friends are." "Don't follow the crowd."* (2) Learning from respected others: *"Organisations like Khulisa." "The law ... know the definition of assault." "Hear the experience of young offenders." "Encourage ...not to commit crime." "Businessmen to help with goals...keep focused."* (3) Learning to be self-aware: *"Take up some hobbies and interests." "A full timetable ... less likely to become involved in crime." "Mindful of music... certain music can have a negative influence on behaviour." "Victim impact ... the impact on family and wider community."*

The capacity and insight of these young people, compared to their elders, tells us that they are aware of the dangers. They get the 'what', it's the 'how' that eludes them. They need support (not sanction) in learning how to behave and to access the positive belonging and role models they seek.

When asked the same questions, **teachers** (Year 9 and 11 Heads) responded similarly. (1) Learn about the impact of crime: *"Remember what it is really like in prison... effect on physical/ mental health/family, prospects afterwards."* (2) Learn to be aware of self and others: *"How and why attracted to a negative influence." "Dealing with disappointment." "Alternative ways of getting excitement." "Importance of belonging to positive group." "Experience success and failure." "Respect is earned."* (3) Learn about peer pressure: *"'family' inside or on the street... false loyalty."*

With those **in prison pre-programmes,** our responses fell into four core categories of 'learning': (1) Learn how not to get caught; (2) Learn new skills; (3) Learn how to change their ways; (3) Learn how to respect self and others. As we would anticipate, the same individuals **in prison post-programmes,** gave responses that relay a deeper awareness of self and of the impact of their behaviour on others. As a result of the opportunity and space to think more widely and examine their behaviour and its consequences, in a safe environment our participants were able to focus more clearly on their 'learning': (1) Learn how to think for myself and communicate my needs: *"Speaking properly." "Asking for every-day daily things." "See there are different ways of handling problems."* (2) Learn life skills and people skills: *"Education on violence." "Mental health provision." "Education about NPS." "How to think for ourselves."* (3) Learn that only we can change our lives: *"How to think before acting." "How to walk a different life."* (4) Learn how to see things from other people's perspectives: *"See problems with different perspectives." "Be more open-minded."*

This provides a clear indication of the power of providing space to help individuals to understand the 'how' as well as the 'what'. It also indicates what happens when trust is built and people feel able to share their true hopes and fears. This is where learning truly begins.

With those **ex-offenders** recently released into our mentoring programme, responses are much starker, seemingly much more survival based and were also split by nature of offence. In the first category, the respondents had been convicted of assault and domestic violence offences and felt that they had been wronged, that their actions were justified; they had no other choice. The remaining responses were given by those who had been convicted of acquisitive crimes. (1) I don't need to learn anything: *"I behaved as everyone would behave in this situation."* This type of response was given by those with assault and domestic violence convictions. (2) Learn how to access the system: *"Social living, benefits, employment, education,"* (3) Learn what you're supposed to do: *"How to play the game ... you're expected to know."* (4) Learn how to survive: *"How to support myself." "How to avoid being homeless." "How to get work."*

There's a brutal anxiety we hear about missing out on a vital piece of education, on how to live safely in society. Reading their words, the sense of panic and survival mechanisms fuelling their thought processes is clear. They are duty-bound to respond with their most basic instincts. Their intellectual capacity has been bypassed by their emotional reptilian brain (biologically, adrenalin, cortisone and other 'fight/flight' chemicals hijack brain and body). In essence, they can't think straight and their usual patterns of behaviour are bound to prevail (violence, substance abuse, crime and so on).

Learning to learn: reality and perception

We're hoping that, by reading this, you're mostly inspired at the insight offered to us by those who might otherwise purely be labelled as 'marginalised', 'criminal' or 'at risk'. We're hoping that you can see potential, and in the bulk of the responses, a thirst for learning and knowledge.

What you might also read is that so many of these individuals have a need to 'learn how to learn' at the most basic level. They 'don't know what they don't know' so they've made it up as they went along. In most cases, this has led them to violence, crime and substance misuse; as they ignorantly navigate both their own thoughts, feelings and responses amidst the complex nature of both their own survival responses and the U.K. social support systems. Systems that let them or their family down early in life and (by now) they lack motivation and capacity to navigate.

So often the perception is that those caught up in the criminal justice system somehow know what they're doing, how they got there and how to behave differently. Our experience is that they don't. The reality is vastly different to this perception. They often lack the most basic of skills to think, feel and communicate; or are consistently so 'triggered' by circumstance that their reactions pull a violent mask over the capability they do have to think clearly.

What we have learnt (which re-affirms our mission and our work) is that all those touched by violence and crime have significant reasons for their behaviour. Early childhood trauma, a lack of emotional resilience or good coping skills and the role models to create them, all of these things have the potential to leave some individuals no choice but to use the only strategy they have, violence and crime, to survive.

What this tells us is that our unwieldy criminal justice system could benefit from a significant shift in focus. It tells us that an investment in emotional resilience, neuropsychology and greater investment in mental health provision within education and local communities might herald a reduction for those entering the criminal justice system. It also reminds us that our prisons are unwittingly reinforcing many of the habits that we seek for them to change and reduce.

If we can help those in our care to think and feel more effectively, to express themselves clearly and communicate their needs, hopes and fears; listen and support their growth – we would see a far greater return on investment in education, criminal justice and the various employment and training schemes in place for prisoners and ex-offenders.

Young offenders in custody:
lessons from Spain for the U.K.

DAVID ROMERO McGUIRE
Chief Executive, Diagrama Foundation UK

"By February this year [2017] we had reached the conclusion that there was not a single establishment that we inspected in England and Wales in which it was safe to hold children and young people." This was the shocking conclusion reached by H.M. Inspector of Prisons, Peter Clarke. His Annual Report for 2016-17 talks of a system of custody in need of urgent change – caught in a cycle of violence, with rates of assaults and self-harm rising and children unable to access education, training and programmes to help them re-engage with society.

Over 25 years ago, Spain set out on a journey to change its failing system of custody for children and young people. Diagrama has been at the heart of this from the beginning and over time has developed a model of care that supports children and young people in custody and reintegrates them with their families and communities. Diagrama now runs around 70 per cent of children and young people's custodial centres in Spain.

The centres (for between 50 and 80 children and young people) are mostly staffed by professionally trained educators responsible for day-to-day care and support. All residents are engaged in a full programme of learning and enrichment activities, delivered by qualified teachers and educators working together. They also take part in specific learning programmes to address offending behaviour and address other needs, overseen and delivered by psychologists and other specialists.

A 'technical team' formed of on-site professionals including a psychologist, social worker, social educator, teacher, lawyer and a doctor leads case management for each young person. The team is led by the centre's deputy director, who is the nominated case manager with a personal interest in every young person. The technical team is the key to applying the model of care consistently to every resident and throughout the whole centre.

A crucial part of the model is that each young person is given responsibility for their own progression while in the centre. In this they are supported by the technical team, who they meet with regularly so that they can discuss progress and any issues together, and day-to-day by educators and other staff. Families are engaged in this process as far as possible too.

Levels of violence and restraints are very low (an average of five per year per centre) and the staff team is supported by a small number of security staff. While they are available to manage any incidents, should these happen, the main role of the security staff is to keep the centre secure, for example, stopping prohibited items getting in so that the residents and staff can focus on rehabilitation.

In Spain, children's criminal records are wiped out when they become 18. However, a study in 2015 that had tracked 209 children released from one of Diagrama's centres in the Murcia region for between four and five years found that only 28 per cent received a subsequent criminal conviction. Youth Justice statistics for 2015-17 show that 68.7 per cent of children released from custody in England and Wales reoffend within one year.

More important than all of that, though, is that Diagrama's model is based on genuine affection, respect and care by every single member of staff who are parenting the children and young people in our centres. They call it 'love' in Spain: sometimes we are more reserved in our language here in Britain but we don't feel it any less for that. The model lets children become children again. It lets them learn clear boundaries from adults who act as role models and helps them understand that hard work, effort and co-operation is rewarded by freedoms, including temporary release for school and work opportunities and responsibility for themselves. It lets them try, sometimes fail, and ultimately succeed in a setting that will support them, champion and care about them.

What have we learned from that experience? Diagrama has over 25 years' experience of running custodial settings in Spain and France and employs more than 3,500 staff, the majority of whom are working with over 2,800 children and young people in custody every year. We came to the U.K. in 2008. Since then we've talked to government and partners at all levels to share our experience and help them to understand how the challenges to changing the system in England and Wales can be overcome. Through our work in the youth justice field in 21 countries we've seen that they *can* be overcome. In the last nine years we've answered just about every question you could think of about whether our model would work in the U.K.

No, our centres are not holiday camps, and neither are they boot camps. Yes, we set clear boundaries for children and No, that's not incompatible with genuine trust and affection and that's not a 'cultural difference' between Spain and the U.K. Would you really expect your own children to grow up without love? Yes, you can value, recruit and train qualified staff who want to work with children and young people here in the U.K. Again, why would you think that professionals here are different to those in every other country in that regard? We have had discussions with a university to develop a social educator degree. No, running our model doesn't cost the earth and you can deliver centres at the same or lower cost than Secure Training Centres. And as a not-for-profit organisation we put all the funds back into the service for children and young people.

Yes, there are differences between the Spanish justice system's approach to children and ours in England and Wales, some of which we would love to see here. The perception of the purpose in custody has shifted in Spain and has become more receptive to the importance of rehabilitation and education, and recognises the need for a highly-skilled workforce. Only public sector or not-for-profit service providers are allowed and there has been a move away from a risk-averse culture to one that supports innovation, quality and outcomes. Responsibility for children in custody has been regionalised, which has enabled children to be placed close to home, making family involvement easier. There is a united, multi-disciplinary, approach with the judiciary, professionals from government departments, including the health service and education working alongside providers, supported by a more flexible system of sentencing and case management. However, our staff's experience of working in custodial settings in the U.K. also shows us that our model can be implemented now, without any legislative change.

We know from personal experience that it takes phenomenal amounts of hard work and patience to bring in a new model of custody, particularly at the beginning, working with children and young people who often know as much about prisons as do the staff who work with them. Changing their expectations is just as challenging as changing those of the staff and partners. It takes careful planning and constant commitment and leadership from all staff and managers. Any change can be seen as a risk, but we owe it to children in custody now and in the future to take those first steps. It's taken a quarter of a century for the system in Spain to develop as far as it has, to build trust between centres and their communities so that rather than replicating children's chaotic lives in custody, our centres become the safe foundation for their learning to develop positive futures and their reintegration back into society. It's time to start here.

PART TWO
ADULTS IN PRISON

Poetry in prison

All poems produced by writers in custody are reproduced courtesy of the Koestler Trust.

Sonnet for a Cretan Tree
Anonymous H.M.P. Wymott
Koestler Trust Gold Award

Outside my window there's a foreign tree,
Each morning it's the first thing that I see.
I often wonder how it came to stand
Upon this very piece of no-man's land.
Those who planned the prison let it grow,
And built this place around it years ago.
The R.H.S. have blessed it with a plaque.

But does it ever dream of going back,
Across the years, the miles, across the sea?
Does it long for friends and family?
Although its leaves dance on this English air,
Does it yearn to blossom over there?

It has no choice. It is a refugee.
My fellow prisoner, the migrant tree.

Father behind the glass

Anonymous, H.M.P. Dumfries
Koestler Trust Silver Award

As I stand looking out the dirty glass I take in the morning fresh air
And admire the blue sky and the green grass
Thinking one day I'll be free at last
Back being a father
A father to my wee lass
Looking around there isn't much to see
Oh

Here comes g4s with another three
Standing here looking out the dirty glass
Knowing soon my time here is done at last
Soon I'll be free
Floating like an oyster catcher I often see
Standing here looking out the dirty glass
Always remembering this life isn't for me
I've changed my ways as I can't spend anymore of my
precious days looking out this dirty glass
Knowing I should have been a father to my wee lass

Sour Grapes

Anonymous, Fromside Clinic
Koestler Trust Silver Award

As the long train home thunders away I think of yesterday.
So what did I achieve from this time in prison?
I learnt how to make wine from grapes,
In fact I got really good at it, the best
In the whole jail, so some say.
Not much of an achievement I know.
I was just the best of a bad bunch.

If

Anonymous, H.M.P./Y.O.I. Drake Hall
Koestler Trust Silver Award

If you can sleep in bed while tannoys beckon
A long and seemingly endless list of names
Keep a strong, tight hold on your possessions
Whilst others try to win them with mind games…
If you can stay out of other people's business
And ensure others stay out of your own
Think: "It could be worse, in some ways we are lucky"
Whilst everyone around you wants to moan…
If you can cope with having no say in decisions,
Nod and smile, although you don't agree
In your room, display your chapel calendar
And not mark off the days until you're free…
If you can put up with clothing going missing,
And wearing the same shoes daily on your feet,
Gulp down heaps of potatoes, rice and pasta
Feel blessed to find a single chunk of meat.
If you can watch friends leave and not be saddened,
Knowing that it will be your time soon,
Return to your room and dance around wildly,
To the latest over-played pop-tune…
If you can keep your head held high through all your times of hardship
And leave, a stronger person in the end…
Then this is your cell and everything that's in it,
And what's more you can do prison, my friend.

Little Did I Know

Anonymous, H.M.P. Low Moss
Koestler Trust Commended Entry

Little did I know that Education
Was the gateway to imagination.
When I was young it made no sense,
Is it too late for recompense?
For all the rules that I did bend
I'm paying attention to make amends,
For the slacking off in school I did,
I long to go back to be a kid,
To do the sums I've never done
But out of the classroom I would run,
To play football in the park
Staying out till it grew dark,
The smell of grass, glow of streetlights,
Long school days, delinquent nights,
The thud of the ball bouncing off the wall
The only sound I'd hear till my mother's call.
To stop me from scribbling on my desk
My teacher towered, statuesque
She knew my name, said I was a pest,
Separated me from all the rest.
She could have taken me by the hand,
Across the playing fields to distant lands,
Over the seas and through the glens
My map – my paper, my compass – my pen,
Past autumn trees to meet exotic strangers,
To sweet escape and dark dangers,
To desert islands my mind could have wandered,
These are the stories I' should have pondered,

To all the verses I never wrote
My time I now pledge to devote.
Little did I know that Education
Was the gateway to imagination.

Little did I know

A Prison Boy

Anonymous, H.M.P. Berwyn
Koestler Trust First-time Entrant Award

A prison boy came home one day,
To find his true love had gone away.
When he asked the reason why?
He true love did then reply,
"If you choose to live, a normal life,
Then today I'd be your loyal wife.
But if you choose a life of crime,
Then prison boy go do your time!"
So to prison he did go.
And in his cell, he cried like hell
And in the morning they found him dead.
In his hand a letter read
Dig my grave and dig it deep,
And lie white lilies at my feet.
Upon my chest a snow white dove,
To show the world I died for love!
So all you girls bare in my mind,
That a prison boy is hard to find.
So if you find one, love him true,
Coz a prison boy would die for you.

When you find where I live..."

Anonymous, H.M.P. Parc
Koestler Trust Platinum Award

"When you find where I live
will you love me enough?"
he asked.

Years passed without a visitor,
no polite conversation,
tea time chat.

Where I live shifted;
Love shifts, I know that.

Inside

Anonymous, H.M.P. Grendon
Koestler Trust Bronze Award

I came into prison very broken, with such a rotten core,
Now I need to get the root of it, I need to find out more
There's something deep within me, a feeling ever so strong
A need to try and correct, everything I've done wrong
To get inside my head, and this damaged soul of mine
To become a better person whilst inside doing my time
A deep burning desire, so deep down, deep within,
To seek out salvation and redemption, be forgiven for my sins,
To look really hard inside and seek that inner belief
To find hope and inspiration, turn over a brand new leaf,
You may think I sit here rotting, inside my concrete box
Blunting my thirst for knowledge with the turning of your locks
Yes I deserve to be in prison because it was me who broke the law
But my insatiable quest for answers will break down your flimsy door
To exercise all my demons in my mind, finally to set free,
To look at myself in the mirror and be at peace with who I see,
I owe it to my victims, and my family, I owe it to myself,
To enrich my voyage of discovery, to gain an inner wealth,

I want to stand one day, ever so tall and proud,
To stand out like a shining beacon stand out amongst the crowd,
Like a pebble hitting the water, causing ripples I want to make,
To open that door fully, the door inside my mind,
To move always forward spiritually, and never look behind,
It's all in my hands, to redefine my destiny and redefine my fate,
To consign to history all this bitterness, and all this hate.
I will be a better person, become a better man,
To flourish inside with humanity, and be all that I can,
To seek guidance and support, slowly building a future I can see,
I'm standing at the beginning, finally concentrate on me
It's never too late to change everything is in my hands
So that one day I can walk in peace through …
… green and pleasant lands.

Therapy

Anonymous, H.M.P. Grendon
Koestler Trust Gold Award

Iced lakes and withered branches
Chilled feet and numb ears
Are signs of summer's end.

Men walk backwards through time
In search of yesterday,
Yet, to no avail, find
Yesterday has fallen
Like the leaves of autumn.

Truth is on the stove
To warm bitter bones
That are as cold
As primeval thrones.

Tears defrost and fall,
Burning through masks
That are icy sharp,
As therapy thaws
Arctic hearts.

A PRISONER'S LEARNING JOURNEY:
to love yourself

PATRICK CAMPBELL
Prisoners' Education Trust Alumni Network Member

M y school days are tainted with memories of underperforming and fighting, the fighting came out of a mixture of not understanding the subjects being taught and living in a household that bred violence. I became a product of my environment and used this for many years to justify my own behaviour. At the age of 13, I could not spell 'cat' or 'dog', this led to me being bullied daily by other pupils and expressing myself with the only method that I knew how: violence. Taking qualifications was never mentioned to me in my school life. Me and the academic world parted with little given and even less taken. At 15, I started the journey that would last the next 35 years, I became a recidivist.

I completed many prison sentences and I have spent countless years being incarcerated in the U.K. prison system, many of those sentences were spent in exactly the same way, I lived my life on the inside as I lived on the outside, high on drugs and in a state of ignorant bliss, or so I thought. In being ignorant I only had myself to think about and lacking in, even the basic self-respect, life felt uncomplicated. I steam rolled through life in a violent aggressive manner.

Then in 2000 I started a life sentence, now this could have been the moment I gave up but the opposite actually occurred. I participated in a six-month drug rehabilitation course and it was a nightmare. I was a category A prisoner with at least 12 years ahead of me. There were some professional drug users in the group, they would pop and smoke any drug available having no preference more than what they could obtain on any given day.

This gave me time in an environment I had no good memories of, the dreaded classroom. My mind was full of negative images of being bullied, feeling stupid, an emotion I was well too familiar with, and struggling with my anger issues. So not a situation I expected to find myself in or felt confident with, this was for 'those' people, who had brains and used big words, authority figures I guess I meant. So I started my academic walk, with my back to the wall, no eye contact and few communication skills.

To my surprise I found I enjoyed this time, I felt relaxed being released out of the prison regime. Once the course was completed and I was placed back into the chaotic life of the wings, I found I had a choice, carry on taking drugs or improve myself. I went to education full of fear, thoughts of other students laughing at me and everyone seeing what I already knew, that I was and actually looked forward to these sessions.

Of course life never turns out like we expect or imagine. I got the shock of my life to see that I could hold my own in conversations. I was still in the 'bottom' class, a place that used to fit me like a glove, the students here were the kind of people that I knew, broken family backgrounds, lack of positive role models and negative outlooks in life, the world owed us a favour and we were happy to share this with anyone who showed an interest.

Excellent teachers then broke down my walls, first they treated me like a person and not just a number. They called me by my first name. This act is not to be under-estimated in building a person up and breeds respect. Ross, Jean, Karen, Vilma, Cathy and Nicky to name a few. With support from a fantastic offender manager, they knew how to inspire me and shut that demon I had carried for years down. I was learning and I was loving it.

There were many hours spent in books, taking on each role of the characters in these pages opened up a whole new exciting world to me. One day I could be the heroic knight in shining armour or become lost on an island, it did not matter, I was greedy to learn and gain knowledge and consumed a myriad of genres. Education changed my world; it is as serious as that. The books that stand out for different reasons, either recommended or part of my studies are Thomas Hardy's *Jude the Obscure*, John Steinbeck's *Of Mice and Men*, Shakespeare's *Othello*, and *The Ragged Trousered Philanthropists* by Robert Tressell. These books made a huge impact on me and how I seen the world. This impacted then, in how I dealt with other people, those I would have seen as victims in the past became real, I came out of my disillusioned thinking. I realised in *Othello* that there were more manipulative and back-stabbing people than me. In other books I gained insight into empathy and how we all by our actions make an impact on society.

The skills I gained with my new knowledge gave me a wider perspective. I became aware that I may be a professional prisoner but I also had a sensitive, caring side and instead of this making me feel vulnerable it made me feel stronger. I learnt about the Suffragette movement, Aung san Suu Kyi, Isambard Kingdom Brunel and each subject took me further away from that recidivist and brought new life into me, giving me a fresh hope for a life away from crime.

At this stage a teacher suggested I make a commitment to her class. I succeeded in completing a GCSE in English, me? I felt on top of the world. I went on to complete a 9295 City and Guilds tutoring course and the 'stupid' kid became a tutor on the education block: what an achievement!

A big gap in my learning over the years has been technology. The prison is so far behind in the use of computers that my first few months free were hampered by this missing skill, I found myself continuously frustrated in a society that had become to rely on this advancement while prisoners were left behind.

Without education how can a person take part in offending behaviour courses? How can a person understand any patterns of offending in their lives or even begin to change? In my case, criminal behaviour was who I had become. I needed a whole personality transplant but if you take some part of a person it requires an offering to fill the recess. I had found my offence-free future, a future I had never even contemplated before I met George and Lenny or Desdemona.

I went on to study with the OU and was funded by the Prisoners Education Trust. I am a very proud member of the Alumni for PET, a role that enhances my life enormously. So what did I learn through education? It is quite simple really: to love myself... *carpe diem.*

REFLECTIONS ON 30 YEARS WORKING IN PROBATION AND CRIMINAL JUSTICE:
towards making amends

LIZ DIXON
Restorative Justice Manager and Senior Probation Officer, London C.R.C.

Despite 30 odd years working as a probation officer I feel as daunted in responding to the question, What do those at risk of offending, prisoners and ex-offenders need to learn?, as I did at the outset of my probation career. It remains a very challenging question and I hope to share some reflections rather than 'answer the question'. I was lucky to enter a profession where the emphasis was on self-awareness, reflection and continuous professional development. It was clear at the outset that as a practitioner I needed to become self-aware and to keep learning about myself so that I could respond effectively to the challenges I would meet in my work. I entered the profession when the legislation instructed me to 'assist, guide and befriend' the client group. Probation officers were tasked to ensure they balanced 'care and control' while supervising court order and prison licences. In the 1980s my assessors were looking to see if I could 'use my authority' as an officer of the court and also work with the client to change offending behaviours. My colleagues and I were encouraged to stay alert in the work and were highly motivated to learn more to help us better understand our professional encounters with offenders. Key objectives of 'offender management' are more explicit in 2017, as the task suggests. Probation practitioners are tasked 'to reduce the risk of reoffending and protect the public; enforcement and compliance are central to the work. The theories, research and knowledge base that staff draw on to do their work has changed over the decades but some have remained relevant throughout my career as I hope to show in this essay.

The pathways into offending and the pathways 'out' are unique to each individual. It seems that many of us can desist from damaging behaviours on our own and most offenders do not need to see 'someone' to help them change. The offenders I have met in my career have often experienced some kind of deprivation or had abusive or difficult life histories and have developed patterns of offending, or have committed serious offences and so come under statutory supervision. In this piece I hope to reflect on my own how my own learning about 'what works' with offenders and how that has changed over the decades. I will draw on case material to highlight how emerging issues like identity, empowerment and restoration have helped expand my professional thinking.

In the early 1980s I worked in a female probation hostel in Liverpool as an unqualified assistant warden or residential worker and used relationship building and my own instincts in my work with the women. Most needed to develop more life skills, such as sustaining positive relationships in their lives. I recall developing 'workshops on basic good health and self-management' and I encouraged the women to pursue work and education opportunities. As a residential unit what we offered was companionship guidance and support, which often involved listening to their desperate or harrowing life stories and then support their attempts to make different life choices. I did not have any aspirations to teach them how not to offend. I felt my job was to enable them to make better choices: it was clear that offending had negative consequences and they did not want to reoffend.

My probation training and post-graduate studies helped me realise that I could be more ambitious going forward. I valued my excellent training course and placements where I was exposed to skilled and experienced colleagues and challenging clients from different disciplines. I had invaluable placements at the Maudsley Hospital and on a summer play scheme with children we then called 'latch-key kids'. I realised I had to prove my own legitimacy in order to bring influence to bear on the 'client'. If the client could not trust or relate to me then there was little hope that I could help them deal with their issues or learn new behaviours. I decided to be an eclectic worker and to learn from all the theories and ideas at hand. I drew on my professional value base, which was as important as my knowledge and skills. On reflection I learnt most by working on the job. I continue to learn a great deal from the offenders with whom I work: the relationships we develop are intimate and privileged.

I initially drew on person-focused intervention models such as Rogerian humanistic psychology and was taken with notions of self-development as they resonated with my probation experiences. The 'people-centred' approach, which was eventually developed into desistance theory, has proved of most value to assist me carry out my responsibilities as a probation officer. I was drawn to change theories, rather than 'deficit models' captured in the cognitive behavioural theories, which I would describe as a sort of medical model. The latter seemed too rigid to me and did not fit easily into the working relationships I was forming. However, I learnt to value cognitive behavioural theory when I started to better appreciate how such theories helped persistent and prolific offenders change.

In the early 1990s I worked in an intensive treatment day centre for 16 to 21 year-olds called Sherbourne House, based in Bermondsey, south-east London. We ran offending behaviour groups in the mornings and used offending manuals, such as Priestly and McGuire's *Skills and Stratagems for Going Straight*, and designed our own exercises. We ran a variety of workshops and activities in the afternoon that focused on self-development to improve employment life skills and education. The research showed that employment and reclamation of family links were important to reduce the risk of reoffending, but practitioners could see that offenders needed to unlearn offending habits and learn how to resist negative peer pressure. We 'role played' scenarios to help the young people practice 'resistance': it often took several takes before they managed to resist. It was clear that the young people struggled with peer pressure and were often anxious about *not* 'taking the opportunities' offending behaviour offered in face of other offenders.

We drew on many ideas and theories. One that stood out for me was the practical application of Paulo Freire's theory of 'praxis', a theory of the oppressed. In essence it helped those experiencing similar problems see the structural issues influencing their behaviours, which proved insightful and empowering. We used theatre workshops to help the young people reflect on their common life experiences and reactions to them. They predominantly came from poor backgrounds with limited role models and basic education and a criminal record. Through participation in drama workshops they learnt that they did have choices that they had 'forgotten' when subject to group think or negative cultures. They learnt to reframe their lives and consider themselves as 'good' people with positive futures. We 'taught' them to develop their thinking skills so that they could make good decisions and rein in impulsive negative reactions to conflict. They developed good habits and routines and self-discipline as a result of compulsory attendance and group participation. They learnt how to secure and maintain employment and appreciate the benefits of routine and self-discipline. This helped them manage challenge and instruction: they told us they would often walk out when reprimanded by an employer for being late or rude. Their time in Sherbourne House helped them take more responsibility for themselves and their behaviour. As a staff group we were non-judgmental but we imposed boundaries that were enforced and this led to the creation of a respectful environment. It was so rewarding and encouraging to watch persistent and often high-risk offenders transform, learn and grow. The young people learnt to develop confidence in their better selves while working on their offending selves. The relationship we built with them as workers and change agents was key to the success of the project; our role as witnesses to their change was significant. I remember Gary became very attached to the centre where he learnt how to be assertive and hold his own. Gary subsequently disclosed a history of sexual abuse and resolved to report the perpetrator. I took him to the Old Bailey in preparation for the ensuing criminal court case and was able to ensure that my colleagues arranged support for him during his testimony. Dealing with such a grave underlying issue improved his confidence and self-esteem and looking back I feel that he matured and evolved.

My colleagues and I subsequently designed and delivered group work programmed in H.M.P. Holloway. The women needed to learn to value themselves, recognise their patterns of offending and confront their issues. We ran big groups for 18 to 21 year-old young female offenders, thirty young women at a time, called 'Choice and Change' which were popular with the women and all the other agencies. The young women came to the conclusion that they too needed to deal with their offending habits and the obstacles that stopped them taking work opportunities. We worked on their offending but also invited speakers from a range of organisations including the Prince's Trust, Women's Education and Building (WEB) drug and alcohol agencies and Women's Aid. The women realised they needed to stay away from negative peer groups and walk away from violent relationships. Many recognised the violence they had internalised and signed up for the anger management programmes that we also ran in the prison.

We designed foreign national groups for women who had been convicted of drug importation. They did not get any services or attention in the prison as they were compliant and not deemed a risk. They worked 12-hour days in the kitchen where they could earn the maximum wage to send home to their children. They were predominantly the 'foot soldiers' or 'mules' rather than the drug barons, who were rarely caught. These women needed to learn survival skills as their sentences were excessive. I learnt about the role of resilience; these women had it and could draw on it. The groups played a huge part in creating solidarity and support for these women who developed coping strategies together. I remember one woman who had not spoken since her arrest and was of huge concern to the medics. She was facing the prospect of a 14-year sentence. She was bought to the group and over a period of time was able to start speaking again. We worked with the women and used the group forum to raise issues about the specific needs of these mostly African, Caribbean and South American women, which ranged from the lack of health and toiletry provision to the blatant discrimination in sentencing to a lack of diverse provision in the prison estate in the early 1990s. At the women's request we invited prison governors, medical representatives and finally a representative of the judiciary to the group to learn about the women's experiences. I remember a judge attending from Snaresbrook Crown Court. One of the women asked him why her sentence was so much longer than the white women she encountered who had carried less drugs than her. The judge was disarmed by the dignity of the women and opened up. He said, "I think it is because it is easier to sentence someone who is not one of your own: it does not hurt as much." He was somewhat appalled by this reflection and said having met the group he was now educated as he could see the individuals and he assured the women he would share his experience with his fellow judges and seek training on anti-racism and xenophobia. The women thanked him for coming and for his openness! The women learnt how to cope and survive the prison experience by engaging with each other and specialised voluntary agencies we connected with who helped them with their families back home. These women did not have histories of offending and it would have been crass to engage in offending behaviour exercises. On reflection I think we were using Freire praxis theory which was better suited to this work. The women worked together and recognised their common issues and decided to find solutions together.

The research confirms that group participation is more empowering and effective. Groups can help offenders consider alternative non-offending lives as constructive dialogue with each other in the groups supports the desistance script that many offenders are aspiring to. They can rehearse the new strategies and thinking behaviours with other participants. Group work facilitation is a skilled activity, staff need to be knowledgeable, reflective and assertive and need to know about group dynamics so that they can create safe environments with good boundaries.

The 1990s saw the arrival of the 'what works' era or evidenced-based practice. Extensive research into the outcomes of group work programme threw doubt into the efficacy of some groups especially those based on psychodynamic theories. New offending behaviour groups for anger management, domestic violence and sexual offending perpetrators developed and were seen to be more effective, as they taught offenders lasting strategies. The evidence suggested that men and woman who offend have deficits in their thinking and behaviours and they needed to learn new skills from accredited programmes. Cognitive behavioural theories were in the ascendancy and the emerging offending groups, such as 'think first', aggression replacement treatment and drug rehabilitation treatment programmes were soon prescriptive. Former groups were delegated to the status of legacy groups and discontinued. The What Works agenda became the only show in town; it decreed that offenders had deficits and needed to learn to think differently and then develop new behaviours to help them refrain from abusive and deviant behaviours. Pro-social modelling was recommended and the use of relationship and group interaction was less valued. The groups are monitored and evaluated and have proved effective in reducing reoffending with serious offenders, but access to the groups are restricted as they are expensive. There has been a loosening of the prescriptive and very expensive accredited programme model in the wake of the government's Transforming Rehabilitation programme introduced in 2015. The new private community rehabilitation companies have been encouraged to develop innovative interventions to reduce reoffending; they are financially incentivised by the payment by results regime with the notion that this should motivate workers to design more accessible and sustainable interventions.

The racist murder of Stephen Lawrence in 1993 and the subsequent Lawrence Inquiry in 1999 heralded a new challenge: what did those with prejudices and even ideology need to learn to avoid reoffending? The similarities with domestic violence were significant. Men had to acknowledge how their own coercive and controlling behaviour stemmed from poor models of masculinity and then change and evolve so that they were better men. 'Identity' was an evolving concept in the 'hate crime perpetrator programmes' and in work with those charged under the Terrorism Acts. Perpetrators whose offending was informed by hate crime had to learn develop more awareness about their own racial identity and prejudice and then they were able to better understand the harm they caused to the victim group. The London Diversity and Prejudice pack/ toolkit (DAPP) was designed to show perpetrators how the threat of 'the other' informed and aggravated deviant behaviour and their aggressive responses to conflict. We were able to work with them to develop awareness about racial identity so they could see how they dehumanised the victim, and then worked with them to adopt strategies to manage their aggression and their prejudices, as the following case study illustrates.

Ian Smith carried out a racially aggravated assault on a young man along with three other offenders. Ian assaulted the young victim Ahmed, who was trying to protect himself from the group of perpetrators, following a period of persistent racial harassment on two Indian families on the estate. The teenagers stood up to the bullies and told the perpetrators to leave their parent's house alone. One of the perpetrators, Carol, called her dad Ian and told him she had been physically threatened by the victims and was afraid. Ian arrived and assaulted Ahmed with an iron rod. Although Ian had a history of offending he had managed to stay crime free, was off drugs and in employment at the time of the offence; he had been a heroin addict so this was a significant achievement. Ian had been sentenced to four years when I met him in prison. He was angry that he had reacted so impulsively and was now back in prison, but he was not motivated to engage. He did not feel he needed to do any work on his behaviour and 'did not need to learn anything'; he already knew he had messed up. On his release he was more receptive and I worked with him to help him with his rehabilitation. In this instance he wanted to see how he could learn to manage his thinking and control his impulses and aggression. He engaged with the DAPP programme and what emerged was a man who had the capacity and ability to reflect on his abusive behaviour and seek out strategies to manage them. His strong relationship with his probation officer paved the way for a good relationship where we could explore his racial identity so that we could start to see how prejudice had informed his offending.

I remember he was very affected by Finkelhor's theory of abuse which we use in the intervention. This in essence shows how an offender gives themselves permission to offend by clearing the four 'hurdles' that keep most of us in check. A perpetrator has (1) *strong motivation* (Ian wanted to 'protect his daughter'); (2) You *overcome your internal inhibitors* (these were the thoughts that told him he was justified in hitting out); (3) He then *overcame the external inhibitors* (by surrounding himself with those who would not challenge him); and (4) *dehumanise the victim* (Ian failed to respond to the victim's plea to stop assaulting him and chose to ignore his suffering). As Ian gained insight into his aggression he was able to see that Ahmed's ethnicity had played a role in why he was so ferocious and Ian admitted that he would have been less violent with a white person. In time he developed insight into his behaviours, empathised with the victims who had experienced persistent racial harassment. He demonstrated remorse and sought out a way to make reparation by mentoring young offenders. He was deemed low risk by the time his licence ended.

I worked with Peter, one of the co-defendants who had been drawn into the offence under the influence of Ian. Peter was afraid of Ian so joined in without much thought about the fear and terror he instilled in the victims. Peter had a history of offending and his risk was increasing. Peter was horrified when the victims' statements were read out at court and wanted to work on his behaviour and attitudes. We managed to progress to an enhanced location where he worked and enrolled on a series of offending programmes including working with the diversity and prejudice pack. As part of the programme Peter wrote to the victims and the letter showed that he had matured and developed victim empathy and worked on his attitudes and behaviours. We did not send the letter and the police officer who arrested the offenders told us that this could cause more harm to the young man who we learnt was profoundly injured by the attack. Peter found this sobering and strengthened his resolve to desist. He disclosed that had he not gone to prison he could have ended up serving a life sentence as he feels he was out of control and caught up in the racism and violence of his peer group on the estate.

An emerging literature, termed desistance theory, emerged at the same time (2001) and this informs current policy and practice and is popular with probation practitioners as it chimes with their experience. It is based on seminal research of an offending cohort in Liverpool by Shadd Maruna. He tracked the offenders for 18 months and compared those who stopped offending and those who continued and published his findings in *Making Good: how ex-convicts reform and rebuild their lives*. One of the key messages was that 'desisters' developed a redemptive script while persisters persevered with condemned scripts. The 'desisters' reframed their live experiences. They re-discovered their non-offending younger selves and decided to desist from their offending lifestyles so that they 'could be good again'. Their narrative helped them with their offending self, which ultimately helped them carry what Shadd Maruna called 'the burden of shame'.

Following the racist murder of Zahid Mubarek by his cell mate in 2001, Feltham young offenders institution decided to pilot offending behaviour programmes with men who were sentenced under the new legislation or who were put on report following racist incidents. I received a disproportionate number of referrals from young Irish travellers and decided to try group work rather than one-to-one work drawing on both Freire's praxis theory and the desistance literature. The young men experienced racism regularly and retaliated; their language was often more offensive than the taunts they had suffered so they were causing harm. The young men found incarceration intolerable and felt disempowered. The chaplaincy ran Irish traveller groups and I worked with the facilitators to look at their own cultural identity and offending attitudes and behaviours. They enjoyed the work which helped them find a voice and they came to accept they had choices. Together they made positive choices such as attending education and dealing with their deviant behaviours. The work would not have been possible without Fr. Roger Reader and Yvonne McNamara, who helped them with their families and problems. I was surprised to learn that they attended Mass every Sunday. This gave them a very valuable space to reflect and value their culture and religion and on reflection to cope with the burden of shame.

The probation service also worked on identity issues when dealing with those who had been sentenced under the Terrorism Acts and had active ideologies. We came to see that 'extremists' had developed what could be called a dominant identity mindset and were in effect 'mission offenders'. They felt called to act on their responsibility as a defender of the faith or culture. Prison and probation practitioners worked with mentors and designed programmes that worked to help them to reclaim or develop 'healthy identities'. We helped them reflect on how and why they had fixated on the dominant identity at the expense of other identities. We helped them develop other less harmful ways of dealing with legitimate grievances they held and helped them to reflect on the fact that they were neglecting other critical identities which would keep them and their families and the community safe. Specific religious or community mentors are often better placed to do this work. The motivation to do this work arose from a concern that once in prison Terrorism Act offenders may radicalise other offenders. These offenders, like other serious offenders, are subject to rigorous MAPPa (multi-agency and public protection arrangements) supervision.

I will conclude with my current thoughts about what offenders need to learn. Throughout my career I feel have under-estimated the challenge that those who offend have in carrying what Shadd Maruna calls 'the burden of shame'. I have learnt that offenders may not exhibit any shame for their acts but are often struggling with private shame, which trigger unbearable feelings that are frequently overwhelming so are better ignored and managed away. Erwin James, who wrote a book called *A Life Inside* to reflect on his journey out of crime, once told a packed audience at the annual meeting of the Forgiveness Project that the walls of most prisons 'are dripping in shame'. This has fuelled my desire to promote restorative justice in the probation service, using re-integrative shaming as a way to help offenders manage the shame while also offering something to victims. I am currently piloting a group work initiative called Making Amends which draws on restorative practices and principles and I feel that this is a good way for perpetrators and harmers to learn from their past behaviours and seek to repair the damage they have caused by attending to their obligations and making amends where possible.

AN EDUCATOR'S REFLECTIONS:
the most important subject prisoners need to learn about

PHILIP EMERY
Director, Pictora and Insider Access

Maybe the best starting point is to establish what my response does not attempt to address. What follows is not a review of the Offender Learning and Skills Service in all its forms and contracts, neither is it a critique of the 'curriculum' in prisons or, indeed, an attempt to write another one. This brief article is based on experience gained in education as an educational practitioner with over 35 years in the public, private and voluntary sectors as a teacher and Deputy Head Teacher, prison educator, Head of Learning and Skills and charity leader taking the arts into prisons. The focus will be predominantly on what prisoners need to learn rather than concentrating on those at risk of offending or the learning needs of ex-offenders.

For the purposes of this piece it is accepted that, of course, prisoners need to have the opportunity to learn basic skills such as numeracy and literacy to address previously missed opportunities. However, the learning journey is a much more complex one than simply taking prisoners to a prison classroom and providing lessons in reading and mathematics. In fact, what happens before, during, after and, perhaps, instead of that classroom experience is likely to be the more important 'what' in the question, 'What do prisoners need to learn?'

Far too often the 'what' is determined by the 'how' in prisons, such that outcomes in the form of a positive experience of learning suffer. For many prisoners school was not a good experience and not the easiest of places for learning. All too often the environment for learning in a prison is a repeat of that experience for prisoners, bringing back just the kind of negative feelings to discourage learning: a long, dark corridor of classrooms in which an over-didactic 'chalk-and-talk' diet is provided to ensure 'quick wins' in numeracy and literacy. This may, indeed, provide some 'quick wins' but cannot be seen as a way to encourage learning in the longer term, which is likely to be essential for the future for many prisoners on release to lay the foundations for successful resettlement underpinned by employment.

Surely, the better option, although not necessarily one determined by the demands of the provider contracts in their many forms, is that the 'what' is determined by the needs of the prisoner learner and, just as important, the strengths as well as the weaknesses of that learner. When someone comes into prison, especially someone entering prison for the first time, everything is done 'to' them, including a multitude of assessments, which also include education. In this 'quick and dirty' baseline assessment it is much easier to find out (or think one has found out) what a prisoner cannot do and decide what they need to learn to address that deficit. There is little scope (or resource) for 'strengths finding'. On entering prison for the first time a fragile, confused and vulnerable individual is quickly reminded of what they cannot do (or think they cannot do) and so, very quickly, the negative learning experience is re-started, this time in prison. This can be negative in more than just the resulting attitude and motivation towards learning, but literally a backward step in learning. It is an oft-repeated mantra from prisoners who are returning to prison that they are presented with the same as or worse than they have previously been offered in terms of prison education. What they are offered is the 'same old, same old' basic skills menu, although the items on the menu are far from nourishing and, to continue the analogy, more than likely to be out of their sell by date. But it satisfies a resource-strapped prison education offer, served by 'race-to-the-bottom' contracts instead of being the biggest chance to engage a learner in meaningful education for the first time in years or, perhaps, decades and make a real difference to that person's view of education, themselves and their future.

By this time in their lives, prisoners have actually leant to be very good at something, in fact, they are often experts in the subject: failure. In a formal education setting they are likely to have been told that they are failing time and time again, as well as in other aspects of their lives, too. It only takes a short time to realise that it is much easier to live up to expectations and fail over and over again until such a cumulative approach to life ends in the failure that leads to the increasing risk of offending behaviour and the increasing risk of getting caught before a custodial sentence is the outcome.

The flaws in this cycle of failure are many. The first is that failure is seen as exclusively negative. The quick-fix education approach which begins with school league tables (a culture and system where it is very easy to get rid of a problem or failing learner so that the risk of harm to league table status is minimised is one in which the future prisoner is likely to suffer most, although this is the subject for a different review of education). Good education relies on failure. One of the key differences between good and bad education is how failure is used, how it is viewed and how response to failure is communicated. A positive education cycle based on failure is essential. The steam engine was not perfected first time around. Good failure leads to good learning managed by good teachers who encourage innovation, experiment, risk-taking, more failure, more success and more learning.

It is, perhaps, the nature of prison to view failure as a 'bad thing', not least in what prisoners learn. A different approach to what prisoners learn should not be afraid of failure but provide prisoners with a proper chance to understand and use both their successes and failures. Risk management expert, Dr David Hillson has identified ten characteristics of failure, with a range of negative and positive aspects:

- failure is natural
- failure is universal
- failure is inevitable
- failure is pain
- failure is opportunity
- failure is learning
- failure is information
- failure is directional
- failure is stimulation
- failure is fun[1]

Dr Hillson is keen to point out that not all of these characteristics are evident in every instance of failure, but is keen to emphasize the positive aspects, whilst recognising the negatives. Nobody likes to fail, and sometimes fear of failure is the dominant emotion ruling out the opportunities of failure to teach good lessons. In Hillson's list he points out that failure is the opportunity to draw a line under the past, and that it teaches us where further effort would be wasted, that it encourages competition and innovation and when used positively can be the most creative stimulant to learning.

Instead of identifying an instant deficit, and providing more opportunities for negative failure in, say, numeracy, the 'quick win' may actually be more easily found in starting from strengths and encouraging success to begin a positive cycle of success, failure, innovation and creativity: learning to learn well and learning to value learning and the impact it can have on an individual. For example, many prisoners find that the arts provide just the route into learning that is all too often avoided or deemed not appropriate or not available as it may be perceived to be a poor use of resources. Whether it be through painting or music or poetry, there is no substitute for the early experience of success for a prisoner learner. The value of the arts within criminal justice is summed up well in a 2011 study headed by Professor Fergus McNeill of the University of Glasgow:

"Although involvement in the arts is sometimes presented within the criminal justice context simply as a way for prisoners to pass the time, the reality is that the artistic process is often a challenging one, and one that requires dedication, patience and the learning of new skills (The Arts Alliance, 2010). Our literature review explored the literature across a range of art forms (including singing, instrumental music, creative writing and storytelling, theatre, visual arts and dance), but here we rehearse only the general themes that emerged across the different art forms. The review provided evidence that arts projects often support the development of better relationships between prisoners (Goddard, 2005; Silber, 2010), between prisoners and prison staff (Menning, 2010), and between prisoners and their families (Boswell et al, 2004; Palidofsky, 2010). It also suggested that arts interventions play an important role in improving self-esteem and self-confidence (Cohen, 2009; Cox & Gelsthorpe, 2008; Digard et al, 2007; Silber, 2005), in developing communication and social skills (Cohen, 2009; Miles & Strauss, 2008) and in enabling people to work as part of a group (Moller, 2003; Palidofsky, 2010)."[2]

This points to what many prisoners need to learn above all else: self-esteem, confidence, trust and self-respect. So many employers constantly say that it is not a specific skill that they require of an ex-offender employee (they are happy to teach them that) but work readiness, which is so reliant on qualities like confidence to achieve sustainable employment on release from those enlightened employers willing to take on an ex-offender. Prisoners are, clearly, natural risk-takers. They are also, clearly, not necessarily experts in risk management. However, what prisoners need to learn is that because of this they are creative, entrepreneurial and innovative human beings. What employer would turn down someone able to offer such qualities? Often, when given the right opportunities and asked the right questions, prisoners know what they need to learn and can so articulately express what has real impact. The following comment is part of a response of a participant in a programme run by Music in Prisons:

"So much of what is done in prison whether education or the courses we have to do is all evaluated and we are expected to progress in certain ways. To have something outside of that without any kind of ulterior motive,

something about the sheer joy of being able to create some music was incredibly validating in the sense that it's so easy to become lost and alone in the system and not have anything that promotes any sense of self-value. Even though we do lots of work on self-esteem, talking about what it is and how to get it, it's just not the same as having it. To have a project like this with no motive other than making music was an incredibly enriching experience. Regardless of whatever else happens or whatever else has an effect on me whilst I'm in prison this is something that has enriched me and in a completely different way that the therapy courses you do, quite genuinely helped me re-evaluate a lot of things about me."

Maybe, the next question to address is not so much what prisoners need to learn but what prison needs to learn about prisoner learners.

We need to learn about prisoner learners and we also need the best prisoner teachers. We all remember our favourite teacher and what we learnt from them. This will have been based on their professional expertise and subject knowledge, and, probably most of all on the relationship built and nurtured between teacher and learner. When we realise what prisoners need to learn there should also be a realisation that to be successful it is necessary to invest in education staff and their training so they are increasingly able and well-resourced enough to provide the teaching and build the relationships which will make lasting differences in prison education. What prisoners don't need to learn is enshrined in what the great educator, Sir Ken Robinson, said in a lecture in 2008, "The great problem with human society is not that we aim too high and fail, but that we aim too low and succeed." We can try to save money by reducing the contract price each time so whoever is available teaches what is deemed necessary for prisoners to learn or we can save much more money and change many more lives by providing an environment which doesn't offer a carbon copy of previous negative learning experiences but starts from strengths and not just failures. Yes, prisoners will learn to be more literate and numerate and, more importantly, they will learn about themselves and, perhaps, this is the most important subject about which prisoners need to learn.

A PERSONAL VIEW FROM
A PAROLE BOARD MEMBER
what do prisoners really need to learn before returning to the community?

TOM MILLEST
Member, Parole Board of England and Wales

I should say first that what follows is a personal view from an experienced member of the Parole Board and does not purport to be a statement of Parole Board policy, nor to represent the views of all members of the Parole Board. There are about 200 of us, we are independent-minded and mature individuals, and we rarely have the opportunity to discuss and agree such questions as a full group. However, I would be surprised if most of what I say would not be agreed by most members; though many might wish to add or subtract a few items or re-prioritise.

I have sat on parole oral hearing panels (of two or three members) since 2011, attending at prisons (or occasionally by video-link from Ministry of Justice offices) on about 100 days a year, hearing usually two cases a day (sometimes one, very occasionally three). So I have seen between 750 and 1,000 prisoners in that time, for between two and three hours each; of which at least an hour on average will be spent talking to and listening to the prisoner. These have been a mix of life-sentenced prisoners, those serving indeterminate sentences for public protection (I.P.P.), extended sentence and determinate sentenced prisoners with longer sentences. We rarely see prisoners with sentences of two years or less. Some of these are pre-tariff, some are periodic reviews, and some are reviews following recall to prison from a period of licence in the community.

I have also considered a similar number of cases 'on the papers', from home without meeting the offender. These are mostly of a particular type (determinate sentence recalls) where often there are clear and well-justified recommendations for or against re-release and the decision is relatively straightforward. Often there is less than a year remaining before sentence expiry and less is 'at stake'. When a lifer or I.P.P. case is referred to me for a 'paper panel' the outcome is almost always that I refer it for an oral hearing, having made what I consider appropriate (quasi-judicial) directions for witnesses to attend, new reports or other documents to be added to the dossier, and about the logistics of the day: the number of panel members required, whether a specialist member is needed (such as a forensic psychologist), an estimate of how many hours to allow, and whether it is suitable for a video-link hearing. In a paper panel, clearly I learn less about the offender and their risks and needs.

It is an important and probably well-understood principle that the Parole Board's first duty, in assessing a prisoner's current level of risk of reoffending and causing serious harm before making our decisions whether to direct a prisoner's release or recommend their progression to open prison, is to protect the public. This is interpreted as meaning protection from serious harm 'to life and limb' (i.e. not financial or material harm, but including psychological, emotional and sexual harm) which would be difficult or impossible to recover from fully. The interests and benefit of the prisoner may be important but are a secondary factor. This balance or dilemma often presents itself when, for example, a probation officer gives evidence to a hearing that they are not very confident that the prisoner will not reoffend and do harm if released now - but that it is in Probation's view better for the long term that they be released now, to be supervised by Probation on licence for a period, rather than to be kept in custody and released only at sentence expiry date, with no probation supervision.

The Parole Board panel is obliged to take the narrower view, considering only whether the risk is manageable/acceptable/no more than minimal, during the period before sentence expiry, if released on licence now.

In terms of what prisoners need to learn there is some difference (in degree, not absolute) between life or indeterminate sentenced prisoners, and determinate sentenced prisoners particularly those with sentences of between two and three years or less. When an offender is in custody post-sentence for anything less than 18 months or so, they will not be given priority for some of the key interventions that may reduce their risks. They may make useful progress in areas such as detoxification from drug and alcohol abuse, and learning simple strategies for abstinence; and they may benefit from education, training and communication skills to improve their employability. But they are unlikely to be considered for accredited programmes that will improve for example their anger-management skills, choice of violence or intimidation to 'solve problems', their attitudes to sex and relationships, or their anti-social and pro-crime attitudes, thinking habits, aspirations, long-term goals and choice of associates. Nor are they likely to receive structured psychological assessment and effective counselling or therapeutic input addressing the root causes of their offending in their childhood and environment. In terms of the function or purposes of imprisonment, protecting the public by incarceration, punishment and deterrence may be met as aims, but long-lasting rehabilitation is less likely to be met (in shorter-term determinate prisoners).

So what I am about to say is of relevance mainly to life sentence, I.P.P. and long (say, six years or more) determinate sentence prisoners. Much of the following seems obvious, but it is not part of the mind-set of many serious offenders. A prisoner needs to learn and believe:

1. Life is better if you don't keep coming back to prison.

2. Most of the staff in the criminal justice system (prison staff, Probation, NOMS psychologists, even police officers) have their best interests at heart and want them to improve, rehabilitate and lead a pro-social

life. Their role is to help prisoners be successful, to identify problems and find solutions; not to 'trip up' or 'catch out' prisoners. A prisoner will do much better if he/she can learn to believe this and to trust staff. It is fair to say that this is not a universal truth; there are unhelpful staff but it is true most of the time and to a reasonable degree.

3. That they themselves have, or can acquire, the life-skills, problem-solving skills and temperament or habits that will enable them to lead a life that brings a reasonable standard of life (both material and emotional) without committing crime or using violence

4. That during their sentence and during their future life on licence or beyond it, things can get worse without being irretrievable; especially if they share the problem with the right people at an early stage

5. That many (maybe most) other prisoners do *not* have their best interests at heart; and that those prisoners' values, opinions, and interpretation of their own and others' experiences, both inside and outside prison, are often unhelpful and misleading. Again there are many exceptions to this, and prisoners can benefit hugely from the support of other prisoners who are given official roles as mentors, listeners and supporters.

6. How to resolve conflicts and solve problems without using intimidation, physical force, or emotional manipulation – in other words, to have empathy with and respect for others.

7. How to manage their own feelings (whether anger, grief, sense of inadequacy, frustration, disappointment etc.) without using harmful mind-altering substances like alcohol to excess, or drugs.

8. That it is worth (particularly on an I.P.P. or life sentence) spending a bit longer than you might want in prison getting yourself right and ready; rather than being released at the earliest possible opportunity having perhaps concealed ways in which you still need to develop in order to keep yourself safe in the community.

9. That you won't be of greatest use to your partner / children / parents 'outside' if you haven't changed your thinking, attitudes, associates and lifestyle aspirations; because you are then likely to reoffend and perhaps return to prison for a longer time.

10. That when you are released into the community, it is worth staying put in one place even if things get tough; so that you can establish connections and support, and qualify for state benefits if necessary, which there should be no shame in claiming.

I suppose in a nutshell that what a Parole Board panel is hoping to see is someone who has gained insight into why they have offended (usually repeatedly, persistently and habitually); has made some sort of personal commitment to think and behave differently; can evidence this from how their conduct in custody (and where relevant on leave in the community whether for work or home visits); has changed over the course of their sentence; and who has a realistic plan for how to manage themselves after release, including who to turn to for support. This plan needs to cover and be balanced between several areas: accommodation; work and other constructive activity; social life with family and friends; as well as continuing rehabilitation work with Probation and other support agencies, which must also have been discussed and agreed with Probation.

LEARNING HOW LEARNING FEELS

PETER DAWSON
Director, Prison Reform Trust

'Wind your neck in'. 'Keep your head down'. 'Stay off your bell'. 'No shorts on the landing'. 'Accept that the system always wins'. Whatever prisoners might need to learn, prisons spend a lot of time teaching them what suits prisons. And the very first thing, as it has been for as long as anyone can remember, is how to be a prisoner. 'Learn how to go into neutral when the boredom is overwhelming'. 'Learn which staff care about which rules'. 'Learn the words which signify contrition, and those which you need to forget, that signify risk or recalcitrance'. 'Learn whose gaze you must always avoid, whose offer of help you must refuse, whose cell you should never enter'. 'Learn a brave face for visits'. With all of that to absorb, do we seriously think there is space to learn much else?

Personally, I struggle with the underlying premise of the question, What do those at risk of offending, prisoners and ex-offenders need to learn? It implies that if only these people would learn the error of their ways, the whole issue would go away. As so much of the language of reducing offending does, it suggests that the core task is to identify and address deficits. Yet there is good evidence that the path to desistance is paved with discovered strengths and defined by a vision of its destination. We all need a reason to rise to a challenge. And the bigger the challenge, the better the reason needs to be.

The best test, always, of what life in prison should be like is what we would wish for a life spent anywhere else. It is also the law. In the case of *Raymond v Honey*, as long ago as 1981, the House of Lords held that "under English law, a convicted prisoner, in spite of his imprisonment, retains all civil rights which are not taken away expressly or by necessary implication." There is no statute in English law that an adult must learn anything, and no necessary implication of being sent to prison to justify such an approach. If we think prisoners should be learning, we need to explain why.

The standard answer to that question is that learning new skills will equip prisoners to hold down reasonably paid jobs on release. Of course that will be true for some, and for many the opportunity to acquire those skills in childhood has been missed. But the system surely speaks with forked tongue when so many obstacles to secure employment remain, regardless of what skills a prisoner has acquired. So if we want the motivation of earning a decent salary on release to serve as a reason to learn, we need root and branch reform of the Rehabilitation of Offenders Act, of the regulations that prevent ex-offenders from getting insurance, or credit, even a bank account into which that salary might be paid. Professions which would positively benefit from the experience of ex-offenders – and that includes the prison and probation services – need to move from isolated examples of good practice to a policy of welcoming applications from people who have turned their lives around. In short, we need to learn to stop giving a catastrophically mixed message.

Why else does anyone bother to learn? Perhaps because learning in itself gives a sense of purpose. For the incarcerated, it can give time inside a personal significance that transcends the meanings the system imposes – whether punishment or rehabilitation. Thirty years ago, a handful of visionaries in the Samaritans and the prison service conceived the idea of training prisoners to be Listeners. Thousands of prisoners have since learned the detailed and sophisticated rules of engagement that save lives week after week in the hardest of circumstances. To its great credit, the prison service has since allowed other organisations to adopt a similar model: the Shannon Trust Toe by Toe reading scheme (now the Turning Pages reading plan), the pioneering work of the St Giles Trust in training prisoners in advice and guidance work, the work of inspirational prison instructors in helping prisoners first to gain qualifications and then to become teachers and assessors themselves. We learn to help others and we like the way that makes us feel.

There is so much more that could be done through this active citizenship in prisons, and it has never been more necessary to harness the motivation of prisoners to help build prison communities that are both safe and purposeful. What we need to learn is to trust the decades of experience we have of making this work, to be brave.

And sometimes people learn simply for the joy of it. Joy is a curious word in the prison context, but I have seen it many times in the realisation of individual potential. Discovering what we are capable of, that we have talents and strengths beyond our imagining – these are reasons to learn. No-one is ever just a prisoner, any more than they are just an accountant, or just a mother, or just a prison officer. We all need to learn what we can be, and sometimes we learn that best by doing it together. In less straitened times, when I was governing a prison, we set up a week's song-writing workshop in the prison. The twist was that it involved six young men with a wide range of disabilities coming in to the prison to work alongside six prisoners, all facilitated by the brilliance of the Orpheus centre in Surrey. The visitors overcame their fear of prison and prisoners – the prisoners overcame their discomfort with disability and their fear of performance. Together they produced songs that still make me laugh out loud and weep in equal measure. The prison officer who oiled the wheels of the whole week thanked me for the best five days of his life. If learning is defined at least in part by the depth and permanence of its impact on a person's outlook, it would be hard to set a higher standard for what can be achieved.

So perhaps what prisoners and offenders should have the opportunity to learn is simply what learning feels like. Given the opportunities of a digital age, every individual can then make their own mind up about what they need.

THE RIGHT TO EXPRESS YOURSELF

NICK MOSS
Writer and poet; Mary Turnbull Scholarship 2016 award winner

I should make clear that I personally didn't find jail time hard. I started out at Belmarsh prison and had good cellmates. In such circumstances, being three'd up isn't always as bad as it sounds. Three middle-aged crims happy to talk shit and swap war stories? Soaps, afternoon quizzes, and plenty of sport on the tv. Mostly we were perfectly happy; it was like being back at school but without being allowed home at day's end. There's comfort in the routine: you see your mates every day and you can, for the most part, keep each other laughing - although having a semi-open toilet at the end of your bed doesn't help the atmosphere. You're guaranteed a game of pool at unlock. Some days there will be sponge and custard. After you've watched the soaps, bantered and played cards, you settle down on your blue plastic mattress. That's when you get to hear the cries of the poor desperate bastards who can't cope with being locked up; the suicidal, the schizophrenic, the lonely, the twitching skaghead. The majority of the prison population. The ones who can't deal with life outside and sink when they're inside. Screaming, shouting and raving and banging on their doors for hours into the night. Because jails aren't full of contented villains living life like Mr Bridger in *The Italian Job*. Those of us who were in there because we had, through unruffled volition, chosen to commit an act outside the law were an exiguous group within the jail population.

Most prisoners end up in jail for the same reason they end up in police cells in the first place. Poverty, addiction, mental illness throw them from disaster to catastrophe to jail. On repeat. This being the case, the reality is that most prisoners are treated as badly inside as they were outside. Thus, as things stand, jails are just one more institution which fails the vulnerable. Containment, rather than rehabilitation, is the clear intent.

The stability of Belmarsh prison, the lack of financial responsibility, the three-meals-a-day and a roof over your head seduction of jail made me grasp how easy it would be to slip into a burned-out institutionalisation. Leaning by the fence one day I was joined by a kid of about 22 with a mad Afro and darting, frightened eyes. This kid, who was remanded for a series of street robberies, was typical of so many who washed up in jail. He belonged in a hospital but either there was no bed available for him, or he wasn't sectionable. He wasn't sure why he was there. He didn't grasp the charges, or their consequences. He was just rotting in Belmarsh, waiting for the various institutions within which he was ensnared (court, jail, probation) to decide what course his life would follow for the next few years. What was particularly sad was that, had the accidents of birth and class turned out differently, he could have made good on the promise he showed. He was a born storyteller. He loved Tolkien and had created a detailed fantasy universe which he would sketch out for me in our chats in the yard. It was vivid, coherent, and showed a real grasp of the intricacies of genre. All of this he'd mapped out in his head, as literacy wasn't his greatest strength. One day he was taken to court, and never came back. Whether he went to another jail, to hospital, or was released, I never found out. What I think is clear is that the creative potential he displayed would never be realised. He will only ever be seen as a 'problem'.

The poet Lemn Sissay has said of his experience in the care system, "I was in care for 18 years. The care system should be a place where 18 years is a gift because you've got all the resources, the best education, the best psychotherapeutic work, and actually it was 18 years of betrayal, secrets, lies, beatings, incarceration." The same can be said of jails. If they were designed to rehabilitate, they'd function differently. We wouldn't just be pointing to the good works of an exhausted few, struggling to keep going in the face of institutions that keep on failing those detained within them, with predictable results. Deborah Coles, co-director of INQUEST, comments on the ever-growing death toll within the prison estate, "The prison service must be held accountable for failures to implement recommendations and this litany of failures. They have clearly ignored warnings about the risks to health and safety of prisoners and the necessary sanctions should be enacted against those responsible." For most prisoners, in such conditions, if lives are changed at all by jail, they are most likely to have been made worse.

It's easy enough to see what would actually be required to help most of the people doing jail time turn their lives around. Decent jobs, decent housing, decent rehab facilities. That they are not available is a product of coherent design, not unhappy accident. Our jails are full because the most vulnerable have been left as flotsam on the tide that's carried the rich to new highs. All that the proposed 'reforms' offer is greater numbers banged up, with a McJob as a measure of their rehabilitation. Our starting point should therefore not be what prisoners and ex-offenders need to learn, but how we struggle to preserve such gains as have been made in prisoner education despite the funding restrictions already imposed.

And yet I know people who went into jails barely able to read and came out with doctorates in psychology. I know people who went into jails barely able to read and can now read stories to their kids at night. So should our starting point be what did the jails do right, or what did our education system do so badly? Part of the problem is that so much of the debate is framed such that prisoners are presented as if education and access to the arts ought to be a privilege. A BBC Panorama programme about H.M.P. Northumberland drew attention to a prisoner arts class where prisoners were colouring Peppa Pig pictures. This was dismissed with a sneer. The prisoners were probably making cards or storybooks for their kids and this was a key means of maintaining or rebuilding family contact. Even the prison paper 'Converse' in February 2015 condemned prison art classes for a high profile prisoner, with a rehashed *Sun* editorial,

'Killer Paints Mural on Prison Wall'. If those who purport to speak for prisoners refuse to take a position on our side, then the first lesson we need to learn is that we need to speak for ourselves; that demanding access to arts and writing materials is a coherent step towards this, and that we should aim to have prisoner-produced magazines in each jail, as part of finding our own voice.

For those involved in art education within the prisons estate, the key, at a time when endless vocational courses are likely to be the focus for years to come, has to be to argue for art in prison as an end in itself. The writer Norman Mailer was widely condemned for his support for the life sentenced prisoner-writer and activist Jack Henry Abbot. Mailer, impressed by Abbott's writings, helped the essay collection *In the Belly of the Beast* find a publisher and advocated that Abbott be paroled. Abbott was released on licence in 1981, and lasted six weeks before he was charged and subsequently convicted of manslaughter following a stabbing. Mailer, though, made clear that his support for Abbott was for "surviving and for having learned to write as well as he does." As such, whether Abbott demonstrated his rehabilitation or not was irrelevant to his right to artistic self-expression – that when "we do not speak of improving the prisons... but only of fortifying law and order" it becomes the duty of the writer to defend the right to a voice *per se* of his fellow, whose presence in jail is irrelevant to his ability or his right to expression. Mailer and Abbott corresponded initially when Mailer was working on his book on Gary Gilmore, *The Executioner's Song*. Of Gilmore, Mailer says that he sought, "Not preferred treatment, just fair and decent - that was all he ever asked for." We need to remember that asking for fair and decent treatment means demanding as *prisoners* all that we are entitled to, in order to live fully as human beings. If we fail to argue for these while inside, we will not raise the demand for them outside either. For those working on prisoners' behalf, the same is true. As Abbott wrote, "We have no legal rights as prisoners, only as citizens. The only 'rights' we have are those left to their 'discretion'. So we assert our rights the only way we can. It is a compromise, and in the end I greatly fear we as prisoners will lose - but the loss will be society's loss. We are only a few steps removed from society. After us, comes you." If we lose sight of the fact that prisoners are citizens who happen to be in jail, then we allow the notion of who or what is human to be defined solely by the state. Human rights are, essentially, rights to those things which define us as human.

If we need to package arts as rehabilitation in order to secure it within prison education, then we might reflect on the fact that seeing a prisoner as someone with something to express, and the right to express it, is fundamentally rehabilitative. The chances are, he/she will never have been seen through that lens before.

Relationships, survival outside, feeding the soul

ANDY KEEN-DOWNS and ANNA PEASTON
Prison Advice and Care Trust (Pact)

Each person in prison is a unique individual. Every offence has its own unique set of circumstances. Individuals all have different roads to recovery, reform and rehabilitation. Therefore, a person-centred approach to prisoners and offenders' learning is essential, and needs to be built on effective, professional relationships developed with trusted individuals in custody.

Looking at social characteristics of the prison population, however, the evidence on what works to reduce reoffending and based on Pact's own experience, we do believe there are some key priorities. The importance of factors such as engagement with families, engagement with communities, and building a sense of hope with and for prisoners and ex-offenders in their rehabilitation is well documented in desistance research. Therefore, in addition to literacy and numeracy, prisoners and offenders needs to learn about healthy relationships; how to survive outside; and how to feed the soul.

About Healthy Relationships

To live in satisfying, intentional, committed relationships

Learning how to develop and maintain mutually satisfying, supportive, committed relationships is a key skill for prisoners and ex-offenders to learn. This is important not only for their well-being and happiness, but also for the contribution which we know positive relationships make to reducing reoffending. The Ministry of Justice has stated that family contact reduces reoffending by 39 per cent. A joint thematic review by H.M. Inspectorate of Prisons, H.M. Inspectorate of Probation and Ofsted in September 2014 found, "...overwhelmingly this inspection confirmed... that an offender's family are the most effective resettlement agency..."

Learning to live in positive relationships includes a variety of skills such as listening and communication skills, empathy and learning to co-operate and co-parent with a partner. These can be developed through specific interventions such as relationship courses as well as through casework. Within Pact's own services we have found our one-to-one support has significantly improved family relationships, a study by the University of Roehampton found that Integrated Family Support Work improved family relationships by 74 per cent

Equally, prisoners and ex-offenders need to learn to be mindful of negative or destructive relationships and networks, which may impact negatively on them and on their chances of successful resettlement.

To parent positively

To have fulfilling relationships with their children and give their children the best support they can, prisoners and ex-offenders need to learn how to parent positively. We would consider that positive parenting includes understanding the impact of parental behaviour, both positive and negative, on children; being a role model for a child; engaging a child's education from a young age and being a child's first educator; how to parent children of different ages and getting a sense of satisfaction and reward from having a positive identity as a parent.

"This here, it's given me a new look on aspect of life – that it's not all about money and that life – trying to give them everything. As long as you're there for them, that's more important .... have time for them really."
(Dwain)

To understand the impact of offending on loved ones

Alongside victim empathy, it is vital that prisoners and offenders can learn to understand the impact of offending behaviour on loved ones. This can be a strong motivational factor leading to behavioural change for some offenders, and particularly effective for those who display a lack of empathy for victims who are unknown to them. Developing this understanding of the impact which offending has on loved ones is also an essential element of someone in prison preparing for release, especially if they are to be returning to live with their family.

How to Survive Outside

Preparing for release

Prisoners and ex-offenders need to learn to prepare for their release, including independent living skills and/or inter-dependent living skills, depending on the family dynamic. This can include:

- Returning to family life, where appropriate. This involves looking at the expectations and challenges which returning to family life might bring, and thinking proactively about how the offender and their family can make this work. This very much requires a whole family approach and engagement from the family to make it work.

- Leaving prison to live on your own, and the challenges this may bring.

Living crime free, on a low income

People need to be prepared for life on a low income in the community, how to work within their budget, find accommodation, cook and eat cheap and healthy meals, how to access support, navigate the various agencies they are likely to have to deal with, how to keep busy, build new social networks and avoid temptation. The reality for so many ex-prisoners is life on the breadline, which makes the temptation of quick cash too tempting.

Becoming employable

A key factor in reducing reoffending this, as all areas in which prisoners need to learn, is very much variable depending on the individual. For some this is about getting and maintain a job, and they might appreciate support around jobs advice, job searching, how to apply, interview skills, CV writing and similar skills. For others, this is a much longer journey, starting with personal presentation, forming new habits, core skills of inter-personal communication, problem solving, personal time management and dealing with underlying barriers to employment. These people might benefit from support with personal development planning, or getting a volunteer placement.

To be healthy on a budget

Basic nutritional information, healthy eating on a budget, food preparation and cooking are all very important skills. Eating a healthy diet also has important benefits in terms of mood, health, financial management, family life and relationships and self-efficacy.

To live in the digital age

For longer-term prisoners, or those who need it for any other reason, we need to prepare people for living in the digital age and recognise that technology may have changed significantly since the start of someone's sentence.

To Feed the Soul

For some prisoners and ex-offenders, their faith can provide a sense of hope and encouragement to cope in custody. It can play an important part of people's journey towards desistance, as detailed for example in *Belief and Belonging: The spiritual and pastoral role of Catholic chaplains for Catholic prisoners* (Lemos&Crane, 2016). And for all prisoners and ex-offenders, prison education should not be purely functional. Any education which lights a spark should be given space - be that through art, music, spirituality, literature, drama, sport, or physical and practical activities. This is important. For far too long, the model of the human being that has driven so much of the practice in justice systems around the world has been a kind of 'cognitive' one. The thinking seems to go that we humans are basically thinking (or sometimes unthinking) machines on legs. And people offend because they are not thinking, or not thinking right. The sense of so many 'interventions' has therefore been that if only people could think properly, they would be good. It is, of course, a kind of fake anthropology, which ignores the depths of human relational, emotional, artistic, creative and spiritual life that shapes us and drives so much of our behaviour, good and bad. Whatever one's belief system, and whether one believes in such a thing as a soul, we must all recognise that 'thinking' or 'cognition' is only one part of who we are as human beings? One doesn't need to look to the priests, artists, musicians or authors to tell us this. We can look at the structure of the human brain. What prisoners need to learn is how both to think, and also, how to feel. How to feel remorse, and how to feel forgiven and forgiveness. How to feel empathy, and connected. How to feel safe, attached, calm, and in control. How to feel love, and hope.

Understanding themselves

Some prisoners and ex-offenders could benefit from techniques such as mindfulness or yoga and guided meditation to stabilise emotions, develop self-awareness, and understand their triggers. This helps with understanding that impulsive behaviours have led to bad results in the past, and learning to deal with these in a more productive manner.

Some prisoners and ex-offenders also need to learn that small positive steps towards a greater goal and small developments are just as significant and valuable as more obvious achievements. Setbacks can and will happen but they do not mean failure. They can be learnt from, and it isn't wrong to seek help or guidance along the way.

Giving back

People who have offended against their communities should be given the opportunity to give back, to do something to restore their rightful place in the community. Learning to do this, and gaining a sense of having done something towards healing the hurt, such as a restorative approach, could be helpful to some prisoners and ex-offenders. This should not be restricted to people on probation or community orders but should be applied to prisoners too. We could ask, 'what would you like to do to say sorry?'

Through this, ex-offenders can learn that their dues have been paid. We could celebrate prisoners' achievements, and those who have shown good signs of personal reform should be able to graduate from prison with a sense of being welcomed back into society.

'PARENTING IS NOT FOR COWARDS'

(Rob Parsons, *The Sixty Second Father*)

CORIN MORGAN-ARMSTRONG
Head of Family Interventions H.M.P. and Y.O.I. Parc

2017 is my twentieth year working with prisoners, the last ten of which have increasingly been about working with those who become isolated, stigmatised, and socially disadvantaged: the children and families of prisoners. Much of my career has been about rehabilitation programmes; and after delivering and managing all kinds of accredited and organic interventions, it struck me that men were most engaged and motivated when the conversation was about their children and families. Even if they had destroyed those relationships through their criminal choices, there remained something raw, intrinsic, and indefatigable, a hope, or desire to repair damage, to try and somehow make things better. For me, this motivation for change above all other practical motivations (accommodation, employment, education etc.) is the most powerful, and critically the most sustainable. None of us ever reach the goal of being the perfect family man or woman (that is unattainable) but was matters, what makes it more sustainable than other motivations for change which are tangible, is the desire to strive towards that unreachable goal, while knowing it is unreachable, and knowing we will make stupid and regrettable mistakes along the way, but striving nonetheless, because it matters fundamentally more than anything else in life.

This of course will not be the case for all people in custody, but it will resonate with the majority to a lesser or greater degree. As such, all prisons possess a simple and accessible mechanism for change and cultural reform, that of harnessing and then amplifying opportunities for positive family engagement. I have witnessed this in prisons I have visited in the U.S., Europe, Africa, Singapore, Australia and elsewhere while they all have a distinct cultural identity, all prisons share similar challenges with managing prisoners, security, delivering real rehabilitation and reform, and derailing the depressing pre-determined outcomes for children and families of prisoners. The challenges are essentially the same everywhere, so too, in my opinion, are the solutions.

Family intervention work in the custodial environment is an extremely fragile construct. Even when everything is going to plan, you walk a constant tightrope between on the one hand, creating what is recognised by the Ministry of Justice as a causal factor in reducing reoffending and intergenerational transmission of crime,[1] and on the other hand, creating a vulnerable weak spot in the security armour of the prison, that can be exploited by a minority intent on the smuggling of contraband into the establishment. Thus understandably, prisons have remained risk adverse when it comes to family interventions. However, the emergence of credible research that supports the promotion and delivery of family intervention work in prisons, demands that we take some bold and ambitious steps, if we are to capitalise on what is clearly an effective approach to desistance and prison reform.[2]

So how can a prison maximise its ability to deliver positive family engagement opportunities and interventions, and thereby amplify the now well-evidenced causal impact this has on reducing reoffending and intergenerational offending? Our starting point for achieving this outcome was a Barnardo's organised visit to Governor Austin Treacy in Northern Ireland around ten years ago. It was said he had managed to incorporate the importance of positive family engagement within a category A establishment with arguably the most challenging cultural and community divisions in the U.K. I personally learnt a lot from Austin then and over the following years, but the message that was most clear (and which I have maintained as a key ingredient to our model at Parc) is to slowly but surely make all departments and aspects of the prison recognise the benefits of supporting and becoming involved in family intervention work. Crucially, the offender management process, sentence planning targets, and offender supervisors need to understand the correlation between relationships and parenting deficits and offending behaviour. Where appropriate to do so, 'repairing and maintaining positive family contact' should be a staple target for most prisoners. Encouraging (again subject to child/adult protection approvals) family visits, child contact, and participation in parenting/relationship interventions, even letter writing, emailing, drawing pictures, anything that makes a difference in the lives of the children left behind, which will in turn have a residual impact on the prisoner.

Similarly, other departments around the prison can become enthused and creative about family interventions, if only given the opportunity. Learning and skills is an obvious one, with many prisons now delivering regular homework clubs with qualification outcomes, father/mother and baby sessions, Scouts, Duke of Edinburgh Award Scheme, St John's Ambulance Cadets, Fire Fighter For A Day (with Fire & Rescue Services) shared reading schemes, story writing, etc. most of which is delivered within the visiting facility alongside regular visits, or during the not inconsiderable down time where no visits are running. The gym department is another valuable friend to get involved in family activity; this can include not only the physical but the dietary aspects, healthy living, cookery, and well-being and mindfulness. The more departments and individuals you can involve in family interventions, the more creativity, energy and shared resource will be generated, and the better the outputs and outcomes will be.

Perhaps the most critical department to become aligned and allied with is security. Family interventions and security are often viewed and indeed experienced as North and South poles, but to progress and establish a working strategy for family interventions, these two disparate bodies must work closely together. I have encountered many staff in different prisons working with the family remit who view security as the enemy, who go out of their way to block interventions and events, who deliberately sabotage the positive work they are trying to deliver. I have also met many security staff in many prisons who view the family teams and families themselves with deep suspicion, as people who do little, and understand less of what prison is about. The irony of this is that if these two bodies can come together, security can be improved by tapping into a rich source of intelligence that they do not normally access on this scale: the families. And at the same time family teams become upskilled in their own security awareness and knowledge of what is appropriate, safe, and what is likely to get approved. This way the work of both becomes leaner, more effective, and without the historical baggage of stereotypes, true innovation can flourish.

At Parc we have worked hard to align ourselves with and become part of the remit for all departments over the years, and this has without question paid off. Family teams often exist in isolation within a prison, whether directly employed or part of an external organisation/charity, therefore lacking real clout or credibility, and little inside social capital to get things done. Identifying the common ground and shared targets can change this dramatically. What I have found to work at Parc (but also with other prisons in the U.K. and internationally where we have shared our experience, over 70 prisons in the last four years) is a simple model based on three core components. Moving from a security-led prison visits system, to one based on positive family engagement. Identifying a residential area for more intense family focused work, ideally a small unit; our Family Intervention Unit has 64 beds and opened in 2010. Lastly, seeking out and embracing external partnerships with a range of different stakeholders in the local community.

Moving from a security-led visits delivery, means that the management and officers running visits come from a dedicated team, who are selected for their understanding and ability to work in this specific area. They obviously still need to fulfil all the necessary security functions, but this crucially needs to become more dynamic, smarter, and less obvious. An officer is perfectly capable of having a pleasant and genuine conversation with a family in the hall, while at the same time observing subtly what's on the table, any suspicious activity etc. Officers don't have to stand around a table with arms folded, a grim expression, and a propensity to leap into physical action at the slightest hint of rule breaking, and the visits team should not be a transient repository of officers who are uninterested, and disenfranchised from the rest of the prison. Visits should be seen as a specialist area, the front of house for the prison, working with prisoners, their children, families, and professional visitors takes a specific skill set. After a reboot of the visits team to a dedicated group of officers, we went from a weekly average of one hands-on removal from the visits hall a week, to three in seven years, simply by changing the approach of the officers, through awareness and support of their understanding. We still remove prisoners and visitors from the hall for the passing of contraband, but this is done quietly, humanely, and without others noticing. At the same time, drug dog indications on domestic visitors began to fall, families started to trust the staff, and talk to them, slowly but surely the culture in the visits hall started to shift.

While this was evolving we initiated a gradual process of adding colour to the walls. Our awareness of the impact that 'carceral geography' has on visitors from booking in, searching, escorting, visits and back out, quickly developed. Low cost tricks such as giving artistically gifted prisoners and/or community agents the chance to brighten up the visiting spaces, play areas, café (with profits going back into the children and families remit), etc., appealing to community partners for donations of good toys and sound furniture, (all risk assessed!) adding plants, all of these things make a difference, and families told us. But interestingly it also made a noticeable difference to the prisoners' behaviour in the hall, more respectful, less disruptive, and it also made for a safer, more satisfying environment for the staff to work in too.

I view a prison visiting hall as a shared space between the prison and the community. The only place inside can meet outside. As such it usually comes equipped with toilets, baby changing facilities, a café or vending, play area, and space. All of which you can use to fill the down time in the schedule to host community awareness events, parent-teacher sessions, school staff awareness training, the 'Hidden Sentence' programme for external professionals, mini conferences even. Inviting statutory, private, and voluntary sector agencies and individuals into the prison, creating partnerships, creating stakeholders. Creating resource opportunities and innovation.

Becoming outward facing in this manner will open up opportunities to bid for and draw down resources independently or in partnership. It is not uncommon to find that other external agencies and charities are able to access funding streams prisons have never even heard of, and they tend to possess impressive expertise in business development that again are often a struggle for prisons to field on their own. Increasingly prisons in the U.K. are utilising their local universities to create research opportunities that are of mutual benefit, and again the universities are well used to the ethics and N.R.C. approvals systems. This also generates student volunteers for help lines and other interventions. We have our volunteers fully vetted, which dispels any suspicions and opens up the remit of what they can do. Many of these volunteers have then gone onto compete for and secure full time employment in the prison, as officers, facilitators, and offender supervisors.

All of these approaches big and small help to achieve the tipping point necessary for an establishment to become family intervention focused, but it is important to remember that once the tipping point is reached, and the culture swings in favour of this agenda, it can also swing back. So the momentum must be maintained. No one prison can do any of this on their own; it absolutely necessitates partnership working, inside and outside of the wall.

The Ministry of Justice commissioned review into the impact on children, families, and prisoners of incarceration, headed by Lord Farmer, published its findings in August 2017 and made a series of very clear recommendations as well as a range of helpful suggestions about to how prisons can achieve a standard that is humane, effective and progressive[3].

I would like to see and hear the prison reform agenda to be inclusive of the impact on children and families. For if reform is solely focused on the current prison population, what we are doing with them while in custody and then on release, we are missing a huge opportunity to derail the next incarcerated generation. If we only try and deal with what's in front of us, we will be unable to do anything about what is coming next. Children of prisoners have a disproportionate pre-determined likelihood of becoming involved in criminality; this is internationally evidenced, and recognised by the British government. Therefore, reform should also be about ensuring prisons and schools are talking to one another, understanding one another, and working together to derail the shameful, inexorably, drift of children into pro-criminal lifestyles. Prison reform needs to be about custody and community, who is in prison now and crucially who is likely to be there next, this way we stand a decent chance of not only reducing our reoffending rates, but also reducing intergenerational offending too.

Experiences of learning and growth in a high security prison

CLAIRE O'SULLIVAN
Probation Officer, H.M.P. Frankland

Within the prison system, often portrayed as a dark and difficult place, there are men serving long custodial sentences who strive to achieve stability, to learn and to grow. What is it about these men and their prison environments that encourages and supports this learning and growth and why is this important? To answer these questions, I engaged with a small number of prisoners and completed a research thesis with the University of Cambridge, as part of the NOMS sponsored MSt Programme.

Serving a sentence in a high security prison is tough: these can be environments of fear and harm, of mistrust, trauma, powerlessness and violence . Hidden away from society, prisoners are often forgotten and feel 'worthless'.[1] That there are prisoners who manage to survive the 'pains of imprisonment', to engage eloquently, with thought and insight[2] is nothing short of miraculous. For Neil:

"There's people look at us in prison, especially society, who think we're worthless. We don't achieve nothing and we'll reoffend. Why give

them a chance? Why put money into them? But give them a chance to succeed. That will change their lives and their children's lives and their grandchildren's lives. [...] It can affect so many people's lives."

My research examined not only why prisoners should be 'given a chance', but also what this chance consists of, what it looks and feels like to prisoners, moving beyond 'survivability'[3] to how prisoners can flourish, how they can grow and learn in such an environment, achieving the 'glow'[4] of self-belief, relationships and enduring community.

How do prisoners learn and grow in prison?

At the commencement of this research it had been expected that participants would speak of learning and growth through examples of concrete, visible 'things' such as increased and diverse educational provision, or more access to the gym. However, prisoners talked about learning and growth as more than "what is done" but "how things are done". Prisoners spoke of developing the whole person, with learning being seen as individually transformative. Participants commented on learning from past 'mistakes', reflecting and trying to rebuild better and stronger lives following failures, reflecting the 'growth mindset'of Dweck.[5] Learning about oneself and past life choices was important, but this alone was not enough, participants said, to form a new identity. This was about being "who I can be, who I want to be" not just what "I need to be". Participants spoke of identities that "evolve as well as change". For prisoners, self-change (rather than imposed or enforced change) and the acknowledgement of this by others was important. Developing relationships within the prison environment, with prisoners, staff, and their families helps with this identity change, if it is to survive.

Conversation (two-way dialogue involving mutual appreciation and co-operation) supports learning and growth. When it happens conversation mirrors the 'attention + interest + conversation = joy' phenomenon described by Blyth.[6] Where interactions are limited to communications, requesting information, or issuing instructions, they do not contribute to learning and growth, though they might fulfil a need. To transform communication into conversation requires the creation of safe emotional and physical spaces. The support of staff and the 'basics' of looking at and listening to one another were highlighted in the research. This is more than just talking at one another, but talking to one another: 'the art of conversation'.

Alongside this relational context and the importance of conversation, participants noted that 'mirrors' and validation are important to learning and growth:

"The system needs mirrors, you need mirrors to see yourself honestly, to strip away all the lies that you tell, all the excuses that you make."

Mirrors were spoken of in terms of "seeing oneself clearly", "encouraging people to reflect", and "question themselves". This was described as a painful but necessary experience.

Where do prisoners learn and grow?

Participants spoke of learning and growth opportunities through formal and informal routes. While the social aspect of learning through dialogue with others was important, lone activities were also highlighted. Hobbies were described as a "godsend" and "an escape", a "form of freedom" with creativity seen as something representative of the self. Reading was seen as an "escape" and a chance for "time out of the prison world", more than a hobby to some but "a chance to survive here".

Barriers to learning and growth in prison

Perceptions of risk as a barrier to accessing learning opportunities were discussed at length. Participants voiced the view that the term 'risk' was itself misused to defend positions:

"So they say, it's a security issue, a risk issue, but what does that mean? Is it you don't trust me? Is it that you don't want to trust me, don't want to give me a chance? They never say. You can't challenge it. It's just how it is."

Risk (or the probability of an event happening based on evidence gathered) felt very different to participants to fear of an event happening. The impact of risk assessments on individuals, their sentence and progression was acutely felt. The perceived emphasis on past behaviours without a balance of current presentation was mentioned by a number of participants:

"Time, past, present, future. For a prisoner you are identified in the present by your past. The future is irrelevant, the only thing about your future is your future risk [...] I consider myself in terms of two things, my prospect of release and personal development ...which comes first?"

The perceived lack of trust, this fear, resulted in limited opportunities for prisoners to prove themselves; learning potential was subsumed or cauterised. Risk and fear can be managed in different ways. Participants stated that taking a chance, showing belief and trust and putting safeguards in place would mitigate risk. In the case of fear, this was about confronting the issues and trying to address fears through dialogue.

What does learning and growth in prison feel like?

Where opportunities for learning and growth did exist and were identified the question was asked of participants: what do these opportunities feel like? The term '3D human' was introduced, that is being seen as a whole person:

"You're a three dimensional human being. Two dimensional human beings are only seen as their offence. People are complex, not robots, programmed to behave in the same way all the time."

Asked why it was important to be seen as 3D people, participants spoke of this as being necessary for change. Engagement with the person as a whole is crucial for learning and growth to take place and is also important when thinking of the desistance journey; the necessity of validation and the support of others to move away from offending.

Certain areas within the prison were seen as supportive of the '3D human' and in turn of learning and growth, notably the library. This opportunity for normality in the often difficult and dangerous prison environment was spoken of by prisoners as a 'ray of light' in a dark place. This led to the introduction of the concept of "the glow". Prisoners spoke of feeling "great, happy, incredible," developing a sense of purpose, of fulfilment, when learning took place. This 'glow' increased when learning and subsequent growth was validated by others. As Neil commented:

"Well it just feels great. Before I came to prison I could hardly read and here I am with a degree. It started small, but then it just grew and grew, like a wildfire I suppose. I am different now, my family see this. I am not just that criminal. I am worth more."

Hope, defined as the expectation that things would get better, was seen as being of the utmost importance by participants, both the hope of making a life in the system and also for the future, on release.

What supports learning and growth in prison?

Safety (defined by participants as "not being attacked, psychologically, emotionally, not just physically") was seen as the bedrock for personal development. Positive, though not always present, *trust* was also necessary, but was seen as a fragile experience, taking a long time to build and could be destroyed in one second. *Humanity* was identified as interactions on a human level, recognition of their situation. *Dignity*, in terms of conditions, as well as staff-prisoner relationships, was also necessary for prisoners to flourish in prison. This dignity, treating a human being as a person and not a thing or an 'it' links to *respect*, a further condition identified by prisoners. This is respect between all present within the environment; prisoners and staff. Respect is denoted as being key to healthy relationships and good control. The role of *support* from peers, from staff and from family was identified as important and where experienced was memorable and generally linked to a specific person.

"I'll give you a recipe for a safe community. The key is mutual respect, enjoying your own space. Allow for personalities that don't intimidate or threaten, add a pinch of feeling safe and give stability for staff and prisoners."

Conclusions and implications

Prisoners defined their learning and growth as an individual journey of self-transformation, the building of self-esteem and the forming of a new identity. This identity develops through positive relationships, meaningful conversation, through 'mirrors' and validation. Prisoners described feelings of being a 'whole, 3D person,' experiencing the glow of learning and hope for the future when in safe physical and emotional spaces, where they can talk and interact and the identified barriers of risk and fear, the damages and deprivations of being in prison, are mitigated or overcome.

There was clear recognition that emotional and physical safety is 'hard to achieve' in the current climate and is 'fragile' but where individuals felt safe, trust and support could begin to flourish. Aspects of humanity and respect, likewise, could be fostered. These all led to the 'absolute' of hope. What was clear from the research was the drive of participants to positively influence their surroundings. Taking this research forward involves developing a community encompassing the identified conditions of safety, trust, humanity, respect, and support, promoting hope.

This was a profound research experience. To hear directly from serving prisoners of their hopes, dreams and aspirations for a safer future and their calls to improve life not only for themselves, but for others was a privilege. At times the research process was difficult and exasperating, at other times filled with laughter and hope. This in a small way reflects the challenges faced by prisoners and staff on a daily basis. That prisoners persist to pursue excellence in the most challenging of circumstances and that staff take their time to support this in ways that are seen and unseen is humbling and has been amazing to witness.

Things i'd wanted to say to the prisoner i visit, but didn't

TOM PAUK
Official Prison Visitor

*A*uthor's note: Names, places and other specific references have been *changed and 'Michael' is a composite of several prisoners the author has visited as an Official Prison Visitor.*

I'm an Official Prison Visitor (or O.P.V.) at a large men's prison where I've been visiting Michael for nearly two years. The O.P.V. scheme matches volunteer visitors such as myself with prisoners who don't ordinarily receive family visits. Michael is in his ninth year of a five-year sentence. He's an I.P.P. prisoner (indeterminate sentence for public protection), a category introduced in 2005 (then rightly scrapped in 2012), which unlike a life sentence imposes a tariff prior to which a prisoner may not be considered for a parole hearing.

As I walk from the carpark to the visitors' centre, I reflect, sadly, that our relationship is probably coming to an end. Michael's hearing is fast approaching and which depending on how it goes could see him transferred to a Cat. D facility (open prison) or even released. The O.P.V. scheme does not permit further contact once a prisoner has been moved or released. It's a selfish thought but I've come to enjoy our time together and will miss him a great deal.

Having checked in at the desk and left my valuables in a locker, I walk over to the main gate with the first groups of families: wives and girlfriends, over-excited toddlers, bored teenagers, resigned parents and grandparents, many of whom I've got to know over the last couple of years. I hope it's not a bad omen but the officer on duty this Sunday morning is invariably unpleasant; because O.P.Vs don't carry the usual V.O. (Visiting Order) paperwork like the families but use our own prison I.D., we're immediately conspicuous. In the eyes of some prison officers I've come across here (but by no means all), O.P.Vs probably have a screw or two loose. So this bloke's probably asking himself why a normal person would want to come and visit a total stranger, a dangerous criminal to boot. The officer studies my pass like a former East German border guard checking passports. When I remind him, all-smiles, that he and I know each other of old, he scowls and makes me wait behind the second group of families, delaying the start of my visit by another ten minutes. I do as I'm told. I always do here.

I pass silently through the metal detector, endure the fumbling full-body search of the new trainee officer (her supervisor makes her do it twice) and stroke Lucy the sniffer labrador. Her handler had taken me through my induction training two years back and we chat briefly. Once in the visits hall I hand over my pass to the female officer at the podium beneath a bank of ceiling-hung black and white monitors. She smiles at me quizzically, tells me it's table 18 today. I remind her to please keep my I.D. face-down on the front desk so my name isn't on display.

And there is Michael, seated, forlorn as always, on a moulded-plastic chair at table 18, arms clasped tightly together, head and torso curled foetus-like. And - this is definitely not a good sign - he's wearing his long-sleeved shirt, not the regulation short-sleeve. Then he spots me as I approach the table, rises as quickly as his huge bulk will permit, smiles a wide and generous toothy smile and hugs me tightly. It's going to be our longest hug, and by some margin as it turns out.

I'm immediately aware that Michael has not been looking after himself of late. His long, thinning hair is untidy and greasy and I doubt he's showered for at least a couple of days. His left trainer is unlaced and his tobacco-stained nails are bitten down to the quick. Like most prisoners Michael tends to take pride in his personal appearance for prison visits, to the point of vanity even - freshly ironed shirt, trimmed beard and neat sideburns, clean trainers, recently applied shower gel and toothpaste - but not today. Evidently something has happened since my last visit two weeks ago when he'd been on such good form, so excited, uncharacteristically positive even, about his forthcoming hearing. Mind you, we've been here plenty of times over the last two years; Michael's turbulent mental health, punctuated with bouts of prolonged and serious self-harm, have tempered my optimism about his prospects. Today is one such occasion.

"Lost my enhanced, started cutting again, didn't I."

"Oh…" I reply.

"On Basic, been moved to B Wing, which is shite."

Before I can ask, he continues: "Got a letter from Uncle Nick. Me Nan's ill again. Her cancer's back."

I tell Michael how sorry I am; I'm aware just how much his grandmother, his mum's mum, means to him as he's often spoken to me about her. She's his sole, meaningful link with family. When his parents died he and his younger brother were placed into foster care. He rolls up one sleeve gingerly, then the other, and shows me the cuts, shockingly new and pink, so deep they'll require plastic surgery when the stitches come out but neat and evenly spaced in parallel lines an inch or so apart. "Going back tomorrow, gobshite of a doctor said."

Despite his abrasive language, Michael is softly spoken. He has frightened, vulnerable eyes that roam the room frequently in case anyone might be listening to us. The truth is that his obesity makes him a frequent target of bullying on the wing, and I think all the extra staff resource and attention that his prolific self-harming demand probably breed more resentment still. With Michael I never see the banter and high-fiving that goes on among other prisoners as they enter the visits hall. What I do see is a lonely, frightened island of a man in a harsh, monochrome environment where, as is often remarked, there is no possibility of friendship.

"So how about some breakfast?" he asks anxiously, eyeing the café counter with its growing queue.

"The usual?"

"Yeh, but can you see if there's chicken nuggets."

"Michael, you know the nuggets are only in the afternoon, you know that" I reply, hearing the patronising tone in my voice and regretting it immediately.

"Yeh, I know but check anyway would you?"

I return with a small plastic tray on which I have crammed: two cups of instant coffee, ten sachets of low-cal sweetener (he says he's trying to lose weight), a Mars, a Twix, a Galaxy, a bacon butty drenched in brown sauce, three cans of diet coke and a bottle of still water (the water's for me). While he demolishes his breakfast, it all comes out: the letter he received a week ago in which his Uncle Pete writes of his Nan's cancer and how this time the doctors don't reckon she'll last long 'cos she's had everything they can give her. Michael is barely whispering now, voice broken, his face collapsing. "You know they wouldn't even let me go to Nicky's funeral" (Michael's brother Nick had died of a heroin overdose four or five years ago) "so they're not going to let me go to me Nan's either, are they? It's obvious innit."

Hence the cutting, hence the loss of his Enhanced status, hence the transfer to the more decrepit B Wing, and hence (I think though I do not say it) the likely postponement of that crucial parole hearing.

Over the next ninety minutes or so I listen but say very little. His toothache is back (do I have any idea how many weeks you have to wait to see a dentist in prison!); hear all about the antics of the oddball in the next door cell who keeps popping in for tobacco and won't take no for an answer; his nutritional analysis of prison food (spaghetti and boiled potatoes, burger with pizza, you get the picture); the disappearance of his Play Station in the move to B wing; and his witty, acerbic letter of complaint to the Governor. He's not actually going to write the hilarious diatribe he's dictating to me even now but he clearly revels in the idea of it.

You see Michael's not without humour, albeit of the driest, wickedest kind, often tinged with an irony so barely detectable I'm sometimes slightly nervous of responding. Like when he says, po-faced, "You can't trust anyone in here, bunch of effing criminals". Or "Even my brother never came to see me after I tried to kill his missus. Wonder why." A moment of tension before he guffaws, "I'm not being serious, it's a JOKE, you plonker!" Then we both laugh. In fact we laugh a lot during my visits. I like this man tremendously and I think he likes me too.

And I love listening to his endless philosophical tracts on crime and punishment that always begin "If I were in charge, I'd…" and end "it's basic psychology, innit!" In fact much of what he says is rather wise; after all Michael has been in prison for virtually all of his adult life and really knows his subject.

For my part (and yes, I do question myself from time to time) I don't think I'm being naïve; I know all about his lifelong addiction to alcohol and drugs, to violence as a means of accessing them, and in more recent times to the spice he buys by selling his anti-depressants and mood stabilisers. Nor am I rose-tinted about his prospects. But I've never judged him, and never will. A very long line of judges and juries has done that and will probably do so again. Friends and family often ask me why I do this, visiting men in prison, why do I bother? I usually respond, "because I enjoy it" and leave it at that. In fact it's one of the most important, meaningful and satisfying things I've ever done.

Of course I do have my views on criminal justice and the role of prison visiting in particular. Check out the recidivism stats: prisoners with no or tenuous family connections have the worst outcomes, it's as simple as that. And I believe that while both retribution and deterrence are significant factors, the imperative underpinning all criminal justice must surely always be rehabilitation, in practice not just in principle. There, mercifully, endeth the lesson.

"Times up!" screams an officer so ear-splittingly that the toddler two tables along starts to cry. It's the small bloke Michael tells me is a bit of a bully and who I smile at excessively whenever I see him. He's never smiled back. Across an expanse of tables that stretches from the café near the main door to the crèche at the rear, families now hurry to say their goodbyes, babies are lifted and handed back reluctantly to their mums, there is much kissing and eye-dabbing. Michael and I stand for our hug, now only a brief one before a second piercing reminder that visits this Sunday morning are well and truly over (in case we'd missed the first blast).

As we untangle ourselves Michael looks at me and says, "Thank you." Then, reddening and averting his eyes, "I mean it." There's no time to acknowledge the moment because a second officer is now nodding at me vigorously in an effort to hasten my departure. By now Michael has sat down, torso strangled by ruined arms, all shrunken back inside himself as if he was no longer there.

Separated from the prisoners, visitors are shepherded quickly out of the visits hall, past Lucy the labrador (dozing happily, her work for the morning done), through the metal detector and back to the main gate where our wristbands are cut off. And then we're free.

Walking back to my car via the visitors' centre, I reflect on today's visit, and, as I usually do when I leave Michael, worry. Worry about the man in the next cell, worry about his latest cuts and whether he'd go too far next time, worry about the parole hearing. As on previous visits there'd been so much I'd wanted to say but hadn't.

I'd intended to encourage him to sign up for CALM (Controlling Anger and Learning to Manage It), which is one of the many offender behaviour programmes on offer here but which he's been resisting ("'cos it's shite").

I'd wanted to 'rehearse' for his hearing, having been somewhat underwhelmed by his cunning plan to impress the parole board with a long list of suggested improvements to the prison regime.

I'd hoped to pluck up courage and raise the subject of his mysterious daughter whom he's mentioned just the once; does he actually have a daughter and is he still in contact with her? Previous efforts to extract information on this topic had been met with a stony-faced Don't Go There look. Ditto the mother of his daughter.

I'd been planning to talk openly about the cutting. Surely the one prison officer he always says is looking out for him isn't going to keep putting up with these midnight forays to Casualty. Moot point I suppose now he's been moved to B wing.

I'd wanted to try and manage his expectations about Uncle Pete's "fantastic" job offer of window cleaning when he does finally get out; we do need a Plan B. And if he really is so wonderful, this uncle, how come he's never bothered to visit his nephew in nearly nine years?

I'd wanted to encourage him to start using the gym. And to suggest, gently, that he stop selling his medication. And to let him know that I'm on holiday for the next fortnight so my next visit isn't for another three weeks.

In fact I've not said any of these things today.

On the following Wednesday morning I'm emailing the prison to book in my next visit; I've already written my postcard to Michael. He loves classic cars so he's going to love this one of an Aston Martin DB5 that I found on eBay. As I click Send I receive a new email. Coincidentally, it's from my O.P.V. supervisor, one of the chaplains at the prison, telling me that Michael B has been moved to another prison where it is felt that his needs may be more appropriately attended to, and asking whether I would like to visit Kenneth Y who has recently arrived and indicated that he would like a prison visitor.

Insights from the Clink Restaurants and Horticultual Projects:

an alternative way of seeing yourself

MARK SILLERY

Director of Support and Mentoring, The Clink Charity

What do prisoners and ex-offenders need to learn? Some would say they need to learn respect; the difference between right and wrong; how to behave; how to not commit crime and live a fulfilling life in society. Some would not. Personally, I think that's a very narrow-minded and typically 'old school' attitude to offenders. "They should know better! It's their own fault they end up here!" But should they? Is it? Who has been there for them to teach them a code for living in society, show them how to interact, learn, listen and navigate their way through an increasingly difficult journey into life? Is it their fault that the circumstances at home or in a peer group, area, school or college lends itself to a path well-trodden?

We often see that an offender's life and circumstances before custody are partially mapped out by the environment they find themselves in. They are in part powerless to change that until they are an adult. If they are growing up in a family that is inherently criminal, then of course there is a very high chance that they will follow. Drugs, alcohol, gang culture, peers and locality, among many others, are factors that can contribute to how a person learns in their early years including and up to their teens, and starts to encounter the attentions of the police and usually the first introduction to custody. And so it begins: another chapter of learning. Learning how to be a better criminal, honing their skills inside the walls, making connections, making contacts, doing deals. Or, so 'some' would have you believe. I beg to differ.

There is another way. Teach something worthwhile. Give someone a chance to see a different path, to realise their ambition or just to ignite a spark that shows people they don't have to live this way and with training and education they can become whatever they want. Of course this doesn't apply to everyone. I have met hundreds of offenders and one thing that links them all is poor decision making. Nothing more than that in terms of background, education, family, peers. As much as I have come across those from the aforementioned 'stereotypes' I have seen people highly educated, from wealthy upbringing and sound reasoning in prison for the same offences.

So what do they need to learn? Essentially, an alternative way of seeing themselves. A way to see a light at the end of the tunnel, proof that the cycle can be broken and that they can train, learn, achieve and lead a more fulfilling and productive life in society. The key is identifying what each person needs and what they want. There is an element of being too simple a concept but it works if you treat everyone with the circumstances and needs they present with and tailor their learning accordingly.

If someone has a good or even reasonable education and can read and write to a good standard then do they need to learn basic numeracy and literacy? The answer is no, probably not. We can educate them further of course but what about other skills? Life skills such as how to navigate forms, budgeting, cooking, time management, interview skills, CV and disclosure writing, employment searches, managing and sustaining a tenancy - the list is endless. If we teach a person what they need to learn as an individual instead of shoehorning them into workshops and programmes that aren't relevant to them or their circumstances and goals then they stand in far better stead of leaving prison and sustaining a job, a tenancy and rebuilding their life.

Give them work skills. There are a host of training programmes in prison for offenders to choose from. Everything from barbering to dry walling, baking to painting, carpentry to cooking. If someone can leave prison with a qualification, experience and support, they stand a chance of breaking their own cycle, changing their own as well as society's perception of them. If we have taught them to believe in themselves then we are winning.

For example, here at The Clink we take an offender for between six and 24 months at the end of their sentence in which time they will gain live working experience in a busy fine dining restaurant or horticultural project, a nationally recognised NVQ qualification and a dedicated support worker to see them through a minimum of the next 12 months after release. We will have identified that individual's learning needs and aspirations and will be actively, on a daily basis, helping them to achieve their goals. We treat each individual as an employee so for eight hours a day, they cease being just a prisoner.

They are chefs, waiters, hosts, cleaners and gardeners. They have made a conscious decision to better themselves and in recognition of that we are teaching them whatever they need to learn. Soft skills are developed by engaging with each other, becoming part of a team, taking ownership of their station or responsibilities, serving customers and engaging with the public. Our managers, chefs and trainers teach valuable industry skills and provide a realistic working environment in which to train. Life skills are developed and support plans honed to the individual's needs. Our support workers help with forms, managing appointments, budgeting, and interview techniques (all that were mentioned earlier). Whatever they need - teach them and they will learn. Don't tell them what they need to learn, ask. Watch, listen and empower.

I posed the same question to my team of support workers across the estate and have added some of their thoughts below. It is important to recognise, as so often isn't, that we are dealing with a complex group of individuals. We currently have four restaurants and one horticultural project as well as an external events company. We work with male and female offenders who each present with their own set of circumstances and needs. As each person is different so is the prison they are in and with that the offerings of further education and learning, whether educational or works programmes, there is no one size fits all. The key to our success is the recognition of the individual as reflected below.

Clink Restaurant at H.M.P. Styal (female)

- *"In relation to skills and education, offering a wider range of vocational courses that have the potential to turn into real jobs on release/relate to gaps in the job market, and that don't conform to stereotypes (women prisons do hairdressing and beauty and men do CSCS card/ fork lift truck courses). Purpose should be to raise aspirations, but currently options appear quite limited."*

- *"Access to learning about IT skills / being computer literate as many of my cases do not know how to send an email for example, which is crucial if looking for employment. One case who is a long term prisoner is obviously disadvantaged by her lack of understanding / experience of computer skills, which is yet another barrier to her accessing the job market either on ROTL or on release."*

- *"Prisoners need to learn how to do things for themselves, but the system is designed to make them reliant on others to do things for them, which when out in the community means that they have not necessarily learnt the skills to be self-reliant. Not sure how you get round this one!"*

- *"Properly identifying and then actually helping people address the issues they have – for example, in relation to depression / anxiety and any mental health issues they should have access to consistent, quality counselling rather than just medication – and ensuring this provision is joined up to the area they are returning to prior to release/ continuity of prescriptions (which doesn't always happen) and prior referrals to Community Mental Health Teams."*

Clink Restaurant and Gardens at H.M.P. High Down (male) and H.M.P. Send (female)

While in prison, life skills and practical things to learn include:

- *"Offenders need to learn skills that will enable them to try to change their offending lifestyle once released. This could be by gaining both practical skills and knowledge through education leading to qualifications. It is also vital that prisoners can learn read and write if unable to."*

- *"Learning about the consequences of their actions is also important as is learning the triggers that led to the offence and understanding and challenging these triggers. This ties with learning more about yourself and understanding about yourself."*

- *"Towards the end of their sentence, all prisoners should be informed about what to expect on release for example, what happens the day of release, how you will probably feel, what to expect from housing, benefits, banks for example and managing expectations re changes in relationships with family, friends, acquaintances and possible work colleagues, the area you are going back to and people's perception of you and how to deal with that. They need to learn what support they feel they will need on the outside and how they might access this support."*

After release, life skills and practical things to learn include:

- *"Life skills can range from basic skills such as cooking, setting up bank accounts, registering with the doctor, using public transport, driving, potentially getting to know a new area, to socialising with people who aren't prisoners or prison guards, communicating appropriately with people in different situations."*

- *"Although important to emphasize before release, it is also vital to continue to learn that adapting to life after release is difficult and reintegration takes time. People will have changed, you will have changed, lives around you will have changed so it's learning to understand this and preparing for setbacks."*

- *"How to apply for jobs, where to look, how to fill out application forms, how to prepare for and perform in interviews. How to accept a job, how to manage keeping a job down – managing payslips, contracts, for example."*
- *"IT skills (especially for those who have had longer sentences)."*
- *"General technology (especially new gadgets/systems e.g. contactless cards, oysters and smartphones)."*
- *"Navigating the benefit system – what they can apply for, how to apply, how long it will take."*

Clink Restaurant at H.M.P. Prescoed in Cardiff (male)

- *"You can educate prisoners with a lengthy and impressive list of qualifications to improve their chances of employment so they do not reoffend. Obvious skills are enhancing their confidence and social skills from those they have developed within the prison environment. It's the barriers that they come up against when they leave the gate."*
- *"After working with offenders and ex-offenders for over the last three years, I have come to notice the skills they mainly need to learn are those that we in better circumstances and backgrounds take for granted. Just because they present routine, stability and independence when in prison, once released others take for granted they are able to sustain this, even when they have been out working on stage two placements for long periods. Independence is a progressive skill. This is a primary lesson we can learn from them. These I have listed below:*
    - *Knowledge and understanding of the PAYE system, the pay slips, sickness procedures, maternity leave, holidays procedures*
    - *Budgeting, not just utility bills but everyday expenses, and managing their wages/benefits to last until the following pay day.*
    - *Understanding how to apply for benefits on the new and forever changing government benefits, essentially needing IT skills as all are now processed through computers, not on the telephone.*

- *Having the skills to deal with everyday challenges*
- *Time keeping, appearance, hygiene, house-keeping cleaning, and ability to compare providers of utilities, knowing the options of how to pay bills.*
- *Dealing with basic consumer rights when having to return items.*
- *Dealing with the instability of others, such as colleagues, customers and not taking things personal.*
- *Understanding procedures of their employers and how to approach a situation correctly as many are not confident to deal with arising issues themselves as they are anxious that they will be not be taken seriously.*
- *How to use a mobile phone.*
- *Essentially making sure they actually understand their licences. Every client I have had has never realised they have to seek authorisation to stay out just one night from the approved release address.*
- *One priority skill they need to have is believing in themselves and recognising they deserve to have the chance to change, love and be loved.*
- *Teaching them that praise is positive and an accomplishment.*
- *Confidence to break away from their old lifestyle and make new social circles and to be proud of who they are."*

Experience has shown us that if you teach a person something that they are interested in and can see a benefit of they will soak it up, they will enjoy it, become passionate about it and as with the majority of our clients they will manage to make a successful career of their choosing. Not one that we think is best for them or is the easiest option. Not by forcing them. They come to us....to be taught. If someone wants to learn how to become a painter and decorator, teach them that. If someone wants to develop numeracy and literacy then teach them how. Don't teach them something they can't use, something they haven't asked for or see the benefit in. It's a waste of time and resources.

Through training and support we can change people's lives. Offenders come into a programme uncertain of what awaits them but by giving them the beneficial skills we have people in multiple years of employment in the same place, having started at entry level progressed and been promoted on their own merit. Chefs, waiters, supervisors, assistant managers, business owners, trainers – they have all come through a programme tailored for their needs and what they needed to learn to get there.

So…what do prisoners and ex-offenders need to learn? Ask them: you might be surprised. Everyone is different and every time you ask the question I can almost guarantee a different answer. Listen to the answers and teach them what they need. It may be simple in concept but the reality is a very effective model, tried and tested. If you believe in them they will start to believe in themselves.

WE ARE ALL MEANT TO SHINE

MARY BROWN
Former Quaker Prison Chaplain

I believe that the most important thing that prisoners and ex-offenders need to learn is exactly the same as what the rest of us need to learn: the truth of the words spoken by Nelson Mandela, quoting Marianne Williamson's *A Return to Love*, "We are all meant to shine as children do. It's not just in some of us; it is in everyone. And as we let our own lights shine, we unconsciously give other people permission to do the same." This is not formal cognitive, classroom learning, it is emotional understanding that we all have the capacity to shine.

Many years ago, I taught what was then called, 'Basic Education' in an open prison. I used to ask men why they had opted for education, which was much worse paid than most jobs in a prison where all were expected to work. Most replied, 'because I'm thick, Miss.' I very quickly learned that almost all were far from 'thick,' but this is what they had learned in 11 years of compulsory education. Most, of course, had not spent much time in school, once they had learned that it had little to offer them, because they were 'thick'. At the end of the first term of full-time education in that prison, a small group of men wrote a poem as part of their (rejected) plea to be allowed to remain on education for more than one 10-week term. This ended: 'We may be the deviants / And we know we've been bad / But education's helped us / Get back what we had.' What was it we helped them get back? Perhaps their shining potential, possibly lost at school.

Much later, when I was a Quaker prison chaplain in a local prison, I told a man that, as a Quaker, I believed that he had 'that of God' or of good, or an 'Inner Light' within him, as has everyone. He told me that this was the first time in his life that anyone had told him that there might be something good about him. What a burden for anyone to have to carry through life. Were his parents, his teachers, his employers all blind to his shining potential?

Over the years I have heard of so many, diverse initiatives that lead to rehabilitation, or reduce reoffending: art, writing, music, religious faith, caring for animals, catering, horticulture, yoga and meditation, repairing old bicycles for use by third world health workers, and many, many more. All these myriad routes to rehabilitation have one thing in common: they help to uncover the shining potential that is in each one of us. Perhaps 'rehabilitation' is the wrong word, so many of those in prison seem never to have been 'habilitated' in the first place. Arbitrarily assigned to the lowest status in a society that punishes rather than helps the unfortunate, many of those in our prisons and ex-offenders seem to lack any sense of self-worth. They need to learn that they have worth, and those of us not in prison need to know and to value their worth. We all are meant to shine: our and their shining will help others to shine.

Winston Churchill, when home secretary, famously said, "The mood and temper of the public in regard to the treatment of crime and criminals is one of the most unfailing tests of the civilisation of any country." How does our civilisation fare on this test? Churchill went on to say, "There is a treasure, if only you can find it, in the heart of every person." To me, this treasure, which we all need to find within us, seems very similar to Williamson's shining, or to the Quaker 'that of God' within all.

One man whose shining I remember clearly from years ago, who used to be in my basic education class, was Charley. He was coming to the end of a life sentence for murder, and shone through his art. He told me of a troubled childhood, when he was always in what he called 'spots of bother'. Once, when sickening from whooping cough, he told his mother he did not feel well, she hit him with the poker. He started painting because of the cost of Christmas cards. The education officer in Kingston prison thought his work was good enough to be entered for the Koestler award. He won many prizes over the years, and shone. He was able to say, 'I'm an artist' instead of 'I'm a lifer'. This shining changed his life; and I am sure helped him eventually to get his release on licence.

A Quaker 'advice' says, "Remember that each one of us is unique, precious, a child of God." The 'us' here is everyone. Some of the more fortunate among us may like to castigate offenders: it helps us to deny our own failures and weaknesses as we point to others and declare them wicked, even evil. The media fans this with emotive headlines, which vilify people in prison, particularly sex offenders. The media has tremendous power to shape our views, and our legislation. They feed us stories of wickedness which make us feel comfortable, secure in the knowledge that we are not like them. In fact we are. All of us have within us, as well as Churchill's 'treasure', a propensity for evil. Solzhenitsyn wrote, "If only there were evil people somewhere insidiously committing evil deeds, and it were necessary only to separate them from the rest of us and destroy them. But the line dividing good and evil runs through the heart of every human being and who is willing to destroy a piece of his own heart?"

Linked to this treasure, this shining potential, and an important part of it, is the fact that we are not alone: all of us are part of the great web of life. We share a common humanity, and are linked at a very deep level. Jung called this the collective unconscious. I think this is also the Quakers' Inner Light, or that of God within. But one does not need to believe in a God, or even in Inner Light, to understand that we all have a place in this universal oneness: offenders, ex-offenders and all the rest of us. We are not essentially different. Desmond Tutu, in his book *No Future without Forgiveness*, writes of the African concept of *ubuntu*, which, he says, does not readily translate into English, "It speaks of the very essence of being human... We say, 'a person is a person through other people' ... 'I am human because I belong'... *Ubuntu* means that in a real sense even the supporters of apartheid were victims of the vicious system."

So we are all harmed by the harm done by our criminal justice system. Restorative justice attempts to limit this harm, but do we want to restore a system in which some people are perceived as having less value than others, to restore an unjust society? Rather than a society that punishes those who most need our help, we need is a society in which all recognise that all are born to shine. I believe we all have a responsibility to work for such a society. As the sixteenth century poet John Donne wrote, echoing Tutu's *ubuntu*, "No man is an island entire of itself....Any man's death diminishes me, because I am involved in mankind, and therefore never send to know for whom the bells tolls; it tolls for thee." (John Donne, *Meditation* No. XVII)

Optical training labs in prisons:
an experiment in second chance learning for offenders

JOHN HARDING CBE
Penoptical Trust Acting Chair; former Chief Probation Officer
for Inner London and the City of London

Tanjit Dosanjh is an optometrist. In 2003, his father commenced a long prison sentence for a serious criminal offence. He visited his father regularly and quickly observed the lack of decent vocational training available to offenders. Tanjit completed his optometric degree in 2008. He was encouraged by news of an optical programme in California prisons where one optical lab in 1989 had grown to five labs manufacturing over 400,000 spectacles for state health insurance companies. Several offenders have, since leaving prison, set up their own optical businesses and some have done further education to become qualified opticians.

Inspired, Tanjit set out to turn his vision into reality. In 2010, he approached the prison service to establish an optical lab in prison that could manufacture spectacles at below market rates and had the capacity to service the demands of the entire prison population. Frustratingly, even though supported by the prison service, he could not make any headway as commissioning arrangements for optical services were contracted out by other departments. Undaunted, Tanjit self-funded an optical lab in prison and gave up two days a week of his time to train a group of prisoners in optical skills. The pilot project became known as Liberty Needs Glasses. By the end of 2014, Tanjit could no longer continue without funding. Nonetheless, the pilot had proved that offenders could respond to training and gave him the confidence to apply to independent grant makers for full funding.

By 2015, Tanjit had secured start-up funding to finance an optical training lab in Maidstone. The grants totalling over £272,000 came from three charities: the Monument Trust, the Paul Hamlyn Foundation and the Triangle Trust. Simultaneously, he obtained charity commission approval to set up the Penoptical Trust with four trustees experienced in the world of optics and offender rehabilitation. Since then two further trustees have been appointed, one with job marketing skills, the other from a prison service background.

The charity has two main functions: setting up optical training laboratories to train offenders in optics and helping them secure employment and, secondly, delivering eye care/optical services to prisoners and providing their spectacles made in the Maidstone lab. To date, Tanjit has secured a contract with Care UK to provide optical services to 39 prisons in England and Wales. Prisoner eye tests are carried out by self-employed local optometrists. The contract will provide an annual income for the Trust making it no longer dependent on grant making agencies.

The first six trainees recruited on day release came from two local prisons in Kent - Standford Hill (men) and East Sutton Park (women). Each of the trainees will have been fully assessed by prison staff and interviewed by Tanjit. Most of the applicants for training will be coming towards the end of their sentence. As a Trust, we will have details about the presenting offence and conviction, and previous offences. The trainees are given a ten week training programme under the guidance of a qualified workshop manager. At the end of the period, the trainees sit an exam to obtain

NVQ level II in optical practice. The exam is set by the Association of Dispensing Opticians and the awarding body is the Worshipful Company of Spectacle Makers.

In broad terms, the training consists of ocular anatomy, understanding prescriptions, choosing spectacle lenses and frames, pre-screening and glazing. Importantly, the staff observe the trainees and assess whether they would make good employees who could be transferred on an outreach basis to the main Specsavers branch in Maidstone as paid staff, albeit still on day release from prison.

So how does a contributing prison view this initiative? Rosemary is a prison officer and a trustee:

"The opportunities offered by Tanjit are worth their weight in gold. The chance of training alone gives individuals self-confidence and esteem. Additionally, everyone is swept up with Tanjit's back story and enthusiasm. The right prisoners, who value a second chance will become hard-working and loyal employees."

Once training has been completed the majority of trainees are transferred as optical assistants to the local Specsavers branch. There, they receive a salary, part of which can be saved towards their release from prison and part to cover the costs of board and lodging and victim compensation. The director of the Maidstone branch, Sanjay Patel, was asked a series of questions as to the impact of trainees on his business:

"The trainees arrive motivated and keen to impress and ready to get a start into optics after their training. They have not appeared any different from other members of my team. It's not like that they have a badge stating where they spend their evenings and nobody would be able to tell. Many have natural customer service and people skills. Some have taken up positions in other Specsavers stores, or, if not, have gained valuable experience in work that will hold them in good stead in other roles. We

have already [employed some as long-term members of the team]. We would have taken all of the trainees so far, if it wasn't for the fact that they were relocating to their home areas."

Shauna is a trained, ex-prisoner, released and working for Sanjay:

"The Penoptical trust approach is different by stepping outside the box and by understanding we are not bad people, we are capable of holding down a job, learning new skills and improving who we are as individuals."

The Trust started training prisoners in September 2015. By the end of 2016, 21 prisoners had been trained in Maidstone. So far nine prisoners have set the level II NVQ exam. Out of that, three have gained the full qualification. If we look at a breakdown of how many units have been passed, then at the first set of exams in 2015 the trainees passed 21 units out of a total of 30; the second set of exams in June 2016, trainees passed 12 units out of 15. Fourteen prisoners have been placed with Specsavers prior to release. Thirteen prisoners have been released. Of the thirteen, we know nine are in employment in various fields including optics. Four are working in optics. A total of three trainees have been sent back to prison because they were not suitable for optics.

What of the future? The immediate challenge is to consolidate optometry services for prisoners in the 39 prisons. Beyond that, the Ministry of Justice have expressed an interest in the Trust establishing a prison-based workshop in another part of the country. The Trust also wishes to expand the number of optical employers willing to recruit ex-prisoners.

The Penoptical Trust is now part of a burgeoning initiative co-ordinated by the Traverse Trust to inspire and inform businesses to employ people with convictions. We already know that market leaders like B&Q, Timpson's and Marks & Spencer's have integrated offenders in their workforce. The Traverse Trust have set up a website (www.the exceptionals. org) which lists over twenty organisations many with catchy titles like Bounce Back, Switchback, Blue Sky, Bad Boy Bakery, who recruit, train and employ offenders, often from a prison background, into permanent jobs in catering, painting and decorating . Research carried out by the Traverse Trust shows that employment reduces an offender's chance of offending by 59 per cent. Additionally, 65 per cent of organisations providing an opportunity for ex-offenders, report a positive effect on their company's reputation.

Perhaps, the last word on Tanjit's enterprise and vision should rest with John, an ex-prisoner who says this about his experience:

"After prison, the optics training gave me self-worth and the strength to move on with my life. I got a job with a high street optical chain. I'm now starting a degree in optics with the company offering to pay my academic fees as they were so impressed by my level of commitment."

CONNECTING IS THE KEY

HILARY PETERS

I have known several prisoners who have changed their lives. They have all said that the very first step is recognising that there is someone who accepts them unconditionally.

Norman had his letter from his daughter... Lee started to talk about his crimes when he realised there was someone who knew what he had done and still did not reject him...Sally, found someone she could trust...

The first step is making contact with another person. It could be an animal, a course, a religion, but it is usually a person who gives the prisoner a different view of him/herself. Suddenly they feel worthwhile. Then it is worth making the effort to change.

That contact is like cracking a shell. The imprisoned person starts to grow.

Sometimes the prisoner has to make the first move, but connecting is always the key.

Lessons from a female prison education wing

ELLA WHITTLESTONE
Art tutor, H.M.P. Peterborough

Teaching art on the female education wing of a prison from 2016-17 provided me with a unique and privileged insight into the role that education plays within the context of rehabilitation. Being immersed in this locked-away community of people has taught me a lot about humanity, primarily that stereotypes serve very little purpose and are better off ignored. The diverse range of individuals I have crossed paths with during my time inside has reinforced my belief that 'criminal', 'prisoner', or 'offender' tells you very little about the person upon which this label is stuck. I have even on occasion felt compelled to challenge those who self-stigmatize with comments such as, "What do you expect? I'm a criminal", by responding that surely first and foremost and above all else, they are a person.

Stereotypes and stigma aside, teaching in a prison has allowed me to observe how different people present themselves to the world, while seeking out patterns and potential correlations. I have structured my response to the question (what do prisoners and ex-offenders need to learn?) around what I consider to be four key themes: acceptance; self-worth; conquering fear; and connection.

Acceptance

To be a person is hard: this is something that does not get acknowledged as much as it perhaps should. Throughout our lives we are faced with a near constant myriad of expectation, pressure and change outside of our control, all of which shape our sense of self and ability to create a meaningful existence.

As a general rule, resisting or fighting against something tends to lead only to further tension. A certain relief comes from the simple act of accepting things exactly as they are. In this chaotic world there is so much going on that is out of our hands, but the one things we can always change (or at least become more aware of) is how we *respond* to what is going on. Simply acknowledging when something has made you feel upset, angry, anxious etc. can be very helpful in both detaching from, and consequently dealing with, this feeling; the feeling is not you. It may sound simplistic, but understanding the difference between, for example, 'I *am* frustrated' and 'I *feel* frustrated' can help in letting go of something that need not define you. One of the female prison residents I worked with in the art class once wrote:

"Respect is a first requirement towards oneself, and respect towards the other is a logical consequence of the first."

I believe this applies similarly to acceptance, in that we are more likely to accept others if we first accept ourselves. Those who find fault in others are more than likely reflecting their own feelings of being at fault in some fundamental way, and in doing so attempting to lift or alleviate this pain. After all, why would you need to find fault in others if you were totally and completely content in yourself?

It is an experience we are probably all familiar with – someone else trying to bring you down in an attempt to raise themselves up. This can lead to a vicious circle, with both parties feeling worse about themselves, prompting yet more fault-finding and put-downs in further attempts to combat insecurity. Something has to break the cycle. I would suggest that in order to fully accept what is external to us (the situation we find ourselves in, the actions of those around us), we must first attempt to accept the messy internal world of ourselves.

Self-worth

I would argue that low self-worth is a significant contributing factor when it comes to crime. If you consider yourself to have little or no worth, this will be reflected in the choices you make – choices which as a result are more likely to cause harm.

Think about this within the context of monetary worth. Imagine you own two watches; one cost a fiver from a dodgy market stall, while the other is designer, priced at several hundred pounds. How does the way you treat these two watches differ? Which are you more likely to damage or lose?

As a general rule, the more you have invested in something, the better you will take care of it. Those who have not developed a strong sense of self-worth, often find themselves taking on the metaphorical role of the cheap market stall watch.

Though everyone ought to feel valued and worthy of existence, this is not something that comes easily. To complicate things further, in trying to feel okay about ourselves we will often look to others for reassurance. This is a problem because other people are insecure in their own unique ways, and likely to be immersed in a simultaneous struggle with their own sense of self-worth. Therefore, other people are generally not a reliable source of the validation we crave, often serving instead to further our sense of fault or unworthiness, through criticism or unkind behaviour.

The unfortunate truth would appear to be, that the less value you place on yourself, the less care you take when it comes to your well-being. I take the view that destructive behaviours and habits, such as abuse and addiction, arise from an emptiness where acceptance and self-worth ought to be. In attempts to fill this painful void, those that consider themselves to be cheap market stall watches seek to distract, impair or punish themselves in a number of ways, feeling on some level that they are worthy of no better. Self-harm in various forms, whether it be over-eating or injecting heroin into your eyeballs, serves to give yourself the message 'I am not worth looking after'. Even if there is a temporary sense of pleasure or release that accompanies such things, the reality and aftermath is rarely positive. Seeking help, taking steps towards recovery, choosing rehabilitation, all require the belief that you are a worn out or broken watch that is worthy of repair.

I therefore believe that one of the most important things for offenders and all people to learn is this: you have intrinsic value just as you are. This does not mean you cannot grow and improve yourself, but that in order to do so you must start from a place of self-acceptance, knowing that despite your imperfections and insecurities you are not intrinsically bad, nor wrong, nor unworthy of existence. Easier said than done, but perhaps deciding to unconditionally accept and value yourself as though an expensive designer watch is a leap of faith worth taking.

Conquering fear

Defence mechanisms seem to be a common trait of people who have been hurt or abused in some way. As a form of self-preservation, defences arise from a need to protect oneself from criticism, hostility, aggression; interesting then, that it is precisely these characteristics that are commonly expressed by those with such defence mechanisms.

Despite the seeming contradiction of this, those who shout the loudest are often the least confident in themselves; it takes a solid sense of self-worth to show vulnerability, to be confident enough to say that you really are not confident at all.

I once brought this up in class discussion, and one of the women referenced the analogy of a turtle's tough shell, designed to protect its soft and vulnerable insides. The sad thing is, defences intended to protect oneself from harm will often end up pushing people away, sacrificing the potential for positive connection out of fear that it could lead to further hurt, trauma or betrayal; like putting up a window to the weather, you may not suffer the storms so badly, but you also won't feel the full warmth of the sun.

Some would seem to have taken this to the extreme, moulding themselves into someone that others fear. This perhaps arises from a sense that becoming a source of fear will serve as protection, and allow for some autonomy. This is arguably just as relevant within the context of self-harm, which is particularly prevalent among prison residents. For those who have such low self-worth that they feel compelled to physically hurt themselves, at least it is something over which they have control.

I have come to recognise that the frequently stated 'I can't draw' is a form of defence mechanism. Many people would seemingly rather control and apply self-criticisms or negative labels than leave themselves open to receiving this from others. So what is the underlying cause of these defence mechanisms? I would argue fear; we defend ourselves when we are under threat and afraid.

One surprisingly common fear that I often come across in prison, is the fear of being wrong. The safety that comes with colouring inside the lines and thinking inside the box is predominantly favoured, as though drawing a line out of place would confirm a fear of being wrong in and of oneself. The art course I run has revolved largely around portraiture. Many of the women are hesitant to look in the mirror when it comes to drawing a self-portrait. They do not like what they see, and perhaps on some level even fear themselves.

By the way that I structure and deliver the course, I have sought to question and dismantle some of these fears, most notably the fear of difference. This seems to me to be a somewhat primitive fear that is likely to have once served us in terms of survival; trusting only what you know may well have saved you from many threats or predators back when we were hunter-gatherers. However, having now moved past the times of sticking to our tribe and distrust of 'imposters', fearing difference arguably no longer serves us so well. While you can see why concerned parents drill into their children that they must 'never trust strangers', I can't help but wonder if this mind-set is promoting unnecessarily high defences and distrust of others later on in life. Could it not be argued that instances of prejudice and discrimination arise from a deep-rooted fear of what is different?

In a similar vein, fear of the unknown is seemingly the fuel of inhibition when it comes to comfort zone expansion. We will often choose what is familiar over what is good for us, which would explain why so many people stay with abusive partners, or jobs that make them miserable, or return to lives of crime after release from prison. People often claim to regret *not* doing things or making changes, and it seems that fear is what gets in the way. Learning to trust in the unknown, to 'feel the fear and do it anyway' takes a great deal of courage, and is not something we can necessarily do on our own.

Connection

No one wants to be a puzzle piece that doesn't fit; I strongly believe that on some level we all want to belong and to be a part of something bigger than ourselves. Connecting with others and the environment around us gives life meaning in a way that arguably no substance can offer.

It is for this reason that I have taken the opportunity to initiate a collaborative community drawing project titled, 'Connect Draw'. I have invited school children, artists, university students, art teachers and trainees as well as prison residents and staff to offer their unique response to the same set of simple drawing instructions; those otherwise divided by labels and stereotypes are united in a shared artistic purpose, through the universally human act of drawing. The drawing outcomes will eventually be exhibited alongside one another, granted equal worth and status within a shared space. The project is intended to stand as a model of how an ideal society might be, at a time when there seems to be a greater emphasis on what divides as opposed to connects us.

Having offered my response to the question, what do prisoners and ex-offenders need to learn? I would now like to say that I consider the themes discussed to be of universal relevance. Acceptance of yourself and others in order to overcome fear and form meaningful connections is surely a lesson to be learnt by all of humanity, regardless of which side of the bars you happen to be on.

What i need to learn

ANONYMOUS
H.M.P. Downview

I need to be housed, not in a first stage hostel where numerous people are asking you for drugs or money. I need to learn more about 'why' I use and how to almost re-programme the way I think and my behaviour patterns. I need to learn new coping mechanisms and how to deal with triggers and paragraphs. I need regular help from 'mental health' to help me cope with the reasons I relapsed after two and half years' abstinence.

Myself and everyone in the prison system needs regular one-to-one contact with experienced professionals. Not only the day-to-day monotony of officers and prisoners! Such as prison O.M. workers, R.A.P.T., Mental Health and even just purely positive influences. We need to meet with encouraging, successful, helpful people. To help us feel like we are still part of the world and to feel assured that there is still a place for us to become a valued member of society.

Even in women's prisons, where the 'bang up' is a lot less and we don't have to choose between a shower or exercise, there is still not enough 'positive and meaningful' activity in the real sense of those words. Education and work is 'positive and meaningful' activity according to the powers that be! But within these activities where is the real inspiration for change? Not an adult sitting in a classroom when they don't want to be there! Taught this and taught that! This is all well and good if you wish to progress in an academic way. But for those who don't have that interest, where does their daily stimulation lie? Where is their slice of normality? Answer: it does not exist! Only officers screaming and shouting at them and a con talking about crime, drugs or violence? End result: no rehabilitation.

Prison education for prisoners convicted of a sexual offence

JANE SLATER
H.M.P. Nottingham, Phd researcher Nottingham Trent University
With **Dr Belinda Winder, Dr Anne O'Grady** and **Dr Phil Banyard** (NTU)

The particular issue that this article seeks to address is the nature of the learning opportunities available for those in custody who have been convicted of a sexual offence. In today's prison population, there is a growing number of incarcerated people who have been convicted of a sexual offence (Offender Management Statistics, 2016). Research from the Offender Management Statistics (2016) show that people who have been charged with a sexual offence has risen by nine per cent in the past twelve months, making a total of 12,771 sentenced individuals who have been convicted of a sexual offence representing 15 per cent of the total prison population (Offender Management Statistics, 2016). The rise in convicted sexual offenders provides opportunities for education providers to consider the range of learning opportunities that can be provided for this population, and the extent to which, if any, they should be differentiated. The most common offence that is found throughout the prison population is violence against the person, with one in every four offenders being sentenced for this criminal offence, equating to around 27 per cent of all offences (Allen and Dempsey, 2016). Sexual offences, theft and drug offences each account for around 15 per cent of the reason for incarceration (Allen and Dempsey, 2016).

There is little research to be found on the differences (if any) in educational achievements among individuals who have been charged with a sexual offence compared to those charged with other offences. There may be many reasons why there has not been any significant research in this area. For example, there may not be any differences in educational achievements between individuals who have been charged a sexual offence than those who have been charged with other offences. Another reason may be due to low numbers of individuals being charged with a sexual offence in previous years. Research from the Office of National Statistics (ONS) (2017) illustrates there has been an increase of 48 per cent of individuals who have been charged with a sexual offence in the past 10 years. In the year April 2006 to March 2007 there were 56,042 individuals and this has increased to 116,012 in the year January 2016 to December2016 (ONS, 2017).

Prisons in England and Wales offer educational programmes, which include functional skills: literacy; numeracy; information and communications technology (ICT). The reason for provision of these three subjects is because they are considered to form the core skills offenders will need on reintegration into mainstream society (Owen-Evans and McNeill, 2006). All prisons provide different qualifications and courses with each prisons' education curriculum being different. The minimum levels of education classes provided through the educational offer in prisons ranges from entry level (equivalent to pre-secondary school level) to level two which is the equivalent to a GCSE A-C. The Skills Funding Agency (2016) show that 101,600 individuals participated in prison education in the year 2014-15, an increase of seven per cent from the previous year. However, the number of offenders achieving a level one or two qualification has fallen by 37 per cent in English and 34 per cent in maths in the same year 2014-15 (Skills Funding Agency, 2016). Therefore, this suggest that although offenders are attending education classes the number of qualifications they are achieving is falling.

Prison education programmes may offer wider opportunities and benefits to the individual participating in them; for example, through growth and development as the offenders may also be gaining new social skills through the interaction of learning. Wider benefits from education may also include the development of character and resilience which are important life skills (Stickland, 2016). Also with gaining new knowledge offenders can gain soft skills such as increased self-confidence, or an enhanced sense of purpose. Education, then, can be noted as a constructive way to spend one's time (Wilson and Reuss, 2000).

There are immediate benefits of participating in education for the offender; these can include communication with teachers and communication with other people in the class. Other personal benefits may come from showing positive behaviour in class such as not being disruptive and therefore not engaging in anti-social behaviour (West, 1997). Indeed, having a positive attitude has been noted as more important than having technical skills for a role in the employment market (CfBT Education Trust, 2011). Prison education, therefore, also has the potential to provide personal growth and development for an offender. Building up personal skills along with confidence has been identified as crucial for long-term desistance from crime (Terry and Cardwell, 2015).

There are no official statistics that show the differences in education levels between individuals charged with a sexual offence and those charged with other offences. It is through personal observations by working in a prison education department that anecdotal differences have been noticed. Through personal observations individuals charged with a sexual offence present with education qualifications at level 2 or above; as a result, this has the potential to limit the learning opportunities available to them within the minimum educational offer.

In several prisons, but not all, there are opportunities for prisoners to study at level 3 (equivalent to an A-level qualification). Level 3 qualifications are only provided at certain prison establishments and research suggests that the attainment for these qualifications is relatively low. In the year 2014-

15 only 200 offenders achieving a level 3 qualification which is a 1,000 fewer than in the year 2011-12 (Skills Funding Agency, 2016).

There are also opportunities for offenders to study at degree level through distance learning programmes, largely provided via the Open University. The number of prisoners studying for a degree, however, has fallen by 37 per cent since 2010 (Allison and Sloan, 2015). This demonstrates that while higher levels of education are available in prisons, the number of people studying for these qualifications are decreasing. This may result in many offenders studying for qualifications that are below the levels that they have already achieved. Taylor (2014) shows that 43 per cent of offenders with a degree and 41 per cent of those who have achieved a level three qualification were studying for a level one qualification. Coates, following her review in 2016, recommended that governors use their budget to fund qualifications at level three and above.

Although education can be one of the pathways out of reoffending in England and Wales (NOMS, 2005) various factors inside a prison establishment make attending education an option that is only available to 25 per cent of offenders because of the often-limited courses that prison education must offer (Schuller and Watson, 2009). There are many challenges that offenders face when wanting to study for a distance learning course. For example, some offenders are unable to apply for student loans because they would only be eligible for this funding if they were within six years of their release date (Darke and Aresti, 2016). Although there is a demand for distance learning courses in prisons, access to, and application for these courses is dependent on the prison establishment and whether they support and encourage distance learning (Clark, 2016). Other challenges that distance learning brings is the access to ICT. Access to the internet is very limited in prisons, if at all; this adds further challenge if studying for a degree via distance learning. ICT facilities are often not made available for offenders who are studying or the ICT facilities are out of date. Another negative aspect that offenders who are studying for a distance learning course encounter are the often-negative attitudes by some of the prison staff towards the offender (Darke and Aresti, 2016).

Individuals who have been imprisoned for a sexual offence may come across barriers because of their offence. For example, they may not be able to go back to their previous employment. Anyone convicted of a sexual offence in England are now added to the sex offenders register and this will show up on any Disclosure and Barring Service (DBS) application. The DBS provides a mechanism for safer recruitment for employers to make decisions about employees and aims to prevent unsuitable people from working with children or vulnerable adults (gov. uk, 2017). Therefore, offenders convicted of a sexual offence may need to re-skill to find alternative employment on release. Gaining appropriate educational qualifications at a higher level than a level 2 therefore becomes significantly important for this prison population.

Individuals who have been convicted of a sexual offence also have the added social stigma of being a 'sex offender'. Employers may discriminate against ex-offenders and refuse to employ someone with a criminal offence, generally regardless of the nature of that offence. In a survey by the Ministry of Justice (2014) one in five employers (19 per cent) said they would exclude or are likely to exclude ex-offenders from the recruitment process. These effects are exaggerated when the offence is considered a particularly heinous crime such as a sexual offence. Therefore, ex-offenders who have been convicted of a sexual offence may find employment much more difficult as they are not only labelled as offenders but they may also identifiable as a sexual offender because of the sexual offender's register. Subsequently, those convicted of a sexual offence may face a more difficult time in re-establishing any sort of positive identity within society (Manza, Brooks and Uggen, 2004). Becoming isolated from mainstream society via employment opportunities, and potentially being shunned by society may lead to the issues that caused the sexual offence in the first place, potentially triggering a relapse (Hudson, 2005, Tofte, 2007).

The employment market is constantly changing, with a growing demand for higher levels skills. It is estimated that by 2020, 16 million more jobs will require high level qualifications, while the demand for low skills will drop by 12 million jobs (Hawley *et al*, 2013). Thus, emphasis should be placed on prison education to offer higher levels of learning opportunities beyond level 2 to all offenders; offering recognised qualifications that will help the offender to gain employment, training or education upon release.

Research has shown there has been a constant increase in individuals convicted of a sexual offence in the past 10 years (ONS, 2017). This provides an abundant amount of research to be found on the differences in educational achievements among individuals who have been charged with a sexual offence compared to those charged with other offences, which in turn, will see a wider range of learning opportunities becoming available for this growing prison population.

HORTICULTURAL THERAPY:
developing a path to recovery from addictions

JOHN NOBLE
Project Co-ordinator, H.M.P. Rye Hill Master Gardener Project

Involvement in organic horticulture is used as a tool to promote personalised rehabilitation at H.M.P. Rye Hill. The prison's garden project is delivered by Garden Organic's Master Gardener team, working in conjunction with the Drug and Alcohol Recovery Team (DART) and G4S. Since its beginnings in 2013, the project has set out to provide an environment to support offenders who have a background of drug misuse, with the aim of assisting their recovery, wider health and well-being.

From the outset the project's ethos has been to encourage offenders to take responsibility for the project and they have designed, built, planted and now maintain the space, while their learning and development has produced a culture of ownership, shared responsibility and investment within the project, which is something normally difficult to instill with the prison population, and even more seldom among those who are fighting addictions and dependency. Participants develop team-working skills and have built a 'community', because they need to work together to overcome project issues. This is learnt through skill sharing, workshops and regular team meetings where they can collectively govern the project.

As a substance misuse intervention, it is important that participants learn to step into the confines and social complexities of a community, because it was through addiction that they have stepped out of society. Stepping into the unknown can be a daunting and scary time and the project, with its participant-centered approach, offers the opportunity to do this within a safe, supportive space, which was highlighted in an H.M. Inspectorate of Prisons report as an, "important asset in assisting prisoners recovering from drug misuse."

While working on the project, participants learn about and take part in various levels of physical activity, which over time brings improvement in areas such as sleep patterns, appetite, diet and overall fitness. These things are of particular importance when moving away from addiction and dependency as years of abuse can leave the body depleted and worn and simple things such as regular sleep can help re-regulate the circadian rhythm, which can possibly reduce vulnerability to relapse. The project is also seen to 'complement the limitations of the prison health service' in terms of offering additional support for misuse offenders who may be awaiting appointments.

One of the major roles of the project is to reduce the negative impact on mental health produced by addiction. The garden offers the opportunity to divert attention away from the pressures of living with mental ill-health and also alleviates many of the symptoms of anxiety and depression by giving prisoners a feeling of freedom in a safe, secure and supportive environment. Prisoners working on the project have also attributed reducing their self-harming to involvement in the gardens.

Working with nature can have a positive impact on an individual's well-being and one of the most successful of the project's interventions is involvement with and learning about beekeeping. Learning about bees in a 'hands-on' way not only introduces the participants to the concept of giving something, in terms of caring for the bees without necessarily getting anything in return (except the pollinating benefits) but also gives prisoners a sense of connecting with the natural world beyond the prison wall.

Participants have attended weaving workshops and learnt the skills necessary to build their own hives. The creation of sun hives (originally designed by German sculptor Guenther Mancke) has not only helped prisoners to develop restraint and self-control strategies - since weaving the hives is a fiddly and time consuming business - but has also instilled a sense of achievement and success upon their completion. It has also led to the creation of community interest company with the intention of selling the hives, which has provided opportunities for the prisoners to learn new skills in business, alongside being part of something constructive and positive within the prison system.

The bees are also contributing to the garden project in other ways. The comings and goings of the bees have attracted the attentions of a variety of bird species and the garden is now home to starlings, blackbirds, wagtails and house martens. This adds another dimension to the project that participants to discuss and reflect on shared interests in the natural work and happenings outside of the prison.

The garden project is affiliated to the Natural Beekeeping Trust, which puts the bees at the forefront of beekeeping in the sense of not harvesting the honey produced by the hive but allowing the bees to keep it for themselves. Six healthy hives are currently housed within the prison estate (the first in the form of a Warre hive, donated by Gareth John of the Natural Beekeeping Trust and populated by some of his Oxfordshire bees; further hives were populated by collecting the swarms from the original Warre hive).

In summary, the project shows that not only does horticultural therapy benefit the individuals on the programme, but also the wider prison environment too. It allows those in recovery from addiction to gain confidence, a greater wellbeing and a positive attitude towards life.

What do I need to learn for my release?

ANONYMOUS
H.M.P. Downview

I need to stick to my recovery by going to drug related groups like NA meetings. Volunteering in the drug services. I am more determined to stay clean because I don't want to come back to prison as I have learnt so much about myself. I have learnt that I have grown in confidence and my self-esteem has increased. I have also learnt that I have the ability to help others and I am more focused in my recovery. I am trying to put certain steps in place so I don't set myself up to fail! I have spoken to my drug team outside and I have spoken to resettlement.

My aim is to become a Recovery Champion and help others in recovery and with the same issues I have had. I feel so passionate and determined to stay clean because there will be so many different opportunities for me. I can continue with my peer mentoring related drugs. I can identify the issues that can stop me from achieving my goals.

I am now four months clean and I will be five months clean in recovery when I get released and I don't want to throw away five months clean time. That is a big achievement for me and staying clean for a day is hard enough. There is a saying in NA meetings, 'One is too many and a thousand never enough.' I'm going to finish off this essay with the serenity prayer. Also I managed to stay clean by thinking I will not use for five minutes and that's how I stayed clean before relapsing in the community and coming back to prison.

God grant me the serenity / To accept the things / I cannot change / The courage to change / The things I can / And the wisdom / To know the difference.

INSIDE RECOVERY:
peer support in mental health and addictions

TREVOR URCH

Birmingham and Solihull Mental Health NHS Foundation Trust H.M.P. Birmingham Inside Recovery Team

"The peer groups run by experts by experience made recovery real for me. My way of thinking really changed at this time as this work enabled me to deal with problems and setbacks better. I can now take things in my stride. As where previously I would get angry act out and isolate myself. The peer work made me aware of my actions, behaviour and consequences. The experience of peer to peer groups inspired me to want to train as a SMART Recovery Group facilitator and run other groups myself. There is nothing more powerful than people with lived experience coming together.

What surprised me most was that people like me CAN help others to understand themselves and are needed to do just that. The rewards I get from helping others are fantastic; I get a real sense of self-pride, worthiness and belonging. So now when I see someone begging on the street, roughing it, struggling or looking depressed the least I can do is say 'hello mate', give them a smile, maybe a handshake and wish them luck, or even just say 'I know what it is like, I've been there – there is a way out'." (former B wing resident, H.M.P. Birmingham)

Peer support interventions can directly aid the recovery of others as it demonstrates the personal experience of mental health and/or addictions is valued. This experience and knowledge can help to transform the view of an illness experience - as well as self-perception. Peers often utilise their own personal experience of accessing services as source of motivation to help others. As they bring a unique set of skills and know-how to the support and advice that they provide. Exhibiting a high level of empathy peer work is invaluable when supporting people who may be experiencing similar hardships that peers can recognise or relate to.

Peers are an approachable and credible option for individuals looking to take their first steps upon their own recovery journey. A journey of continual growth based on individual strengths and away from formalised treatment interventions. Peer support and mutual aid can enable people to take back control of their life and become responsible for their own self-care and participate in all decisions that affect them. The message of peer support is to motivate others to a better future.

Peer support is largely considered a recent advance in healthcare services. As a range of peer support options were implemented in the 1990s as part of the mental health service user movement. However, peer support has its roots in the late 18th century France as it was introduced by Pussin and Pinal. Pinal the chief physician and Pussin the superintendent of Bicetre Hospital in Paris enlisted the help of service users in this institution to help and support their peers. As the following quote from a letter in 1793 from Jean Baptiste Pussin to Philippe Pinal, illustrates, "They are at any rate better suited to this demanding work because they are usually more gentle, honest and humane."

There are three types of Peer Support to aid recovery:

Mutual self-help groups: Focus on lived experience and a shared identity. Groups are delivered in an open and relaxed atmosphere that allows all participants to contribute. Leaders within self-help groups are visible role models. Hearing the experience of others can be inspiring and promote hope.

Peer support specialists: Peers support specialists are people with their own lived experience of mental illness. People who are in a position to aid the recovery of others as they share learning, offer hope, choice and opportunity. There is an abundance of evidence to suggest that Peer support when implemented effectively can enrich the service user and staff experience of services while aiding recovery. It creates a common ground between those that access services and those responsible for delivering them.

Consumer operated services: Peer run services directly communicate the message the experience of mental illness is an asset. The goal of consumer operated services is to support people and engage them towards determining their own future. A peer run programme is staffed by people with lived experience of mental illness with the purpose to promote recovery through its values and operating practices.

Birmingham and Solihull Mental Health Foundation Trust has a shared understanding of the three types of peer support to aid recovery and supports all aspects of their introduction. Experience-based co-design (EBCD) supports a developing and supportive culture that values the role of peers across services while complementing the work of staff. EBCD is an approach that enables a range of stakeholder groups to work together in partnership to co-design services. EBCD is designed to be used in the NHS to develop simple solutions that offer service users a better experience of accessing a particular service. Similar service user design techniques have been used by international companies for a number of years. The co-design process involves identifying an area of service provision or delivery that you wish to improve. Key stakeholder groups are identified to take part in the EBCD process. The process of giving back to others and learning new self-management skills can be developed and work related skills enhanced:

"I haven't found it easy to resettle back into the community. However I have overcome difficulties that have come my way and my prison experience has really made me appreciate my freedom and independence. I am looking for new challenges and have just started a peer mentoring

course which probation signposted me too. I hope to take up this kind of work and give something back to others. If I can help one person not to use (mamba) or to turn a negative experience into a positive one especially in the prison system I would be happy. I have maintained contact with Inside Recovery since my release 12 months ago. I have contributed to a number of interview panels for perspective new healthcare staff which I find rewarding. I have provided consultation on how healthcare services can be improved based on my own experience of using them and attended conferences. These are all opportunities to take back control of my life and I hope will lead to some form of paid employment. Hopefully I can find paid work in peer support across the criminal justice system as it is needed and effective." (former K Wing resident, H.M.P. Birmingham)

LIBERATION AND TRANSFORMATION IS POSSIBLE, EVEN IN PRISON

NORMAN ANDERSON
Artist and Quaker

My story I feel can offer at least information, at best inspiration. My life of drug addiction and crime lasted 40 years, through heroin and crack cocaine and stories that could fill volumes. I will concentrate on my last prison sentence. In 2004 I was sentenced to 18 years in prison for drug importation. I was 54 years old and on entering prison I was a heroin addict, and continued to use heroin for the first two years. Standing in my cell one evening a letter came under my door. This letter was a reply from my eldest daughter who I had written to saying sorry for not being around and would not be for a long time. Her letter began, "Dear daddy, you are our daddy so we forgive you."

This struck me to the core of my being and became the catalyst for change. I realised how selfish and wrong I had been, what I did to myself was one thing. All the casualties of my chaotic lifestyle was another. I stopped using and then I found myself in a very vulnerable state. What do I do now? The cloud and comfort of losing myself in drugs was gone. I was lost, years of prison ahead of me. I started with yoga and meditation that I had tried in the seventies, I saw a counsellor for two hours a week for six months. This woman was a Sikh, her name was Bali, she was someone

I felt empathy with and could be very open with. Bali Batal wherever you are thank you.

Around this time I went to a weekly art class, watercolour painting, during our first demo of clean water a brush was dropped onto the paper, the mystery of this mark really took hold of me and something in me was transformed. Art then became a journey from then till now.

I started to exhibit yearly with The Koestler Trust. The gift of being able to attend full-time art classes for the next five years was helped by the Koestler's feedback and prizes. This was a big chink of light in my transformation, engaging with a creative community was invaluable. Shortly before I moved to an open prison, by chance I met through art a Quaker chaplain, during that first conversation with her I was intrigued to find out more about Quakers, this I did. It turned out to be one of the best things I ever did, I am now a Quaker. A big shout to the Prison Phoenix Trust who also supported me with books letters and especially light.

In the open prison I carried on with Quakers, art and yoga and lots of advice from the art tutors. At this time I asked for, and was allowed to attend Doncaster College to do an adult access course. Also, during this time, I was offered a place on the Fine Art and Craft Degree. This, I was allowed to do, even from prison. After the first semester I was released from prison and I chose to carry on with my degree. But also from open prison I attended Doncaster Quaker meetings where I eventually became a member.

Upon reading Quaker literature, I came across two words which were: 'applied mysticism'. For some reason, I was like a dog with a bone and couldn't let go of these words until I found out what they meant. The simplest answer was for me the best. It was that the mystical part is what you find in a Meeting for Worship and the applied part is how you use it in your daily life. Having become a Quaker while in prison, the day I left I went to live in the Quaker community in Derbyshire for four years. I now have a degree in fine art and am about to finish a Master's Degree. Creativity and being open to the transformational qualities of spirit can and does change our lives.

Philosophical Dialogue:
education in philosophy as a means to engage with and relate to others

KIRSTINE SZIFRIS
Research Associate at the Policy Evaluation and Research Unit, Manchester Metropolitan University

"I cannot teach anybody anything. I can only make them think."
Socrates

"With philosophy you can bring out your own ideas and then, through the group you can rework it, remodel it, change it, look at it, to get to somewhere. So it's your part in building that and, I suppose, it's more empowering in that sense because you are doing it yourself."
Michael, H.M.P. Grendon

"My time these last 12 weeks have been, what I can only describe as a journey, a journey into who I am and what I stand for. At times I've sat in my cell overwhelmed at the depth of thought I've entered. Ultimate introspection you could possibly describe it as but with guidance and enlightenment."
Jason, H.M.P. Full Sutton

Education encourages personal growth. Through education the individual learns about themselves and develops their understanding of the world.

To be successful, education ought to strive to meet the learner where they are and facilitate the individual to pursue their own interests. To achieve this, education must cultivate a safe environment; learners must feel comfortable exploring new ideas, testing out emerging personal philosophies and feeling able to persevere, get things wrong, change their minds and develop. Education also involves interaction with others: fellow learners, tutors, teachers, administrators and examiners. The nature of these interactions (the way in which the learner is treated and reacts to the different players in their educational journey) can be fundamental to the learning experience.

In this summary, I describe a philosophy course I delivered in two prisons in England. In the Socratic tradition, philosophy is an activity to be conducted in the company of others. Dialogue, conversation and debate are seen as central to discovering knowledge and advancing both shared knowledge and personal philosophical thought. Through a method of Socratic inquiry, over the course of 12 weeks, I cultivated an environment that developed relationships, fostered trust, and provided a mechanism for self-reflection and personal exploration. During this time, we covered a range of philosophers, schools of philosophy and philosophical paradoxes. We discussed the work of some of the great Western philosophers, exploring their ideas, developing our understanding and gradually building a shared experience of philosophical dialogue and personal reflection. My work focused on developing the strengths of prisoners, looking (and largely succeeding) to provide a space where for a short time their status as prisoner could fall away and they could be philosophers for a while.

I begin by describing the philosophy course, the pedagogy I employed and the content of the discussion. I then go on to discuss how the pedagogy proved appropriate for cultivating a positive learning environment before briefly outlining some of the findings of my research. Before doing so, it is important to note that what I describe here formed part of a five-year research project culminating in a PhD thesis. In this short piece, I provide a snapshot of what I found and of the experience of teaching philosophy to prisoners. In particular, I focus on one aspect of the findings: the role of this type of education in fostering trust and positive, pro-social relationships.

All quotes provided are from participants of a philosophy course I delivered in Grendon and Full Sutton prisons. Pseudonyms are substituted for the participants' real names to protect their anonymity and confidentiality. All participants were informed of the research and given clear guidance on use of data and findings and their right to withdraw at any point.

What did I do?

Delivered through the medium of a Community of Philosophical Inquiry, half of my participants resided in H.M.P. Grendon, a democratic therapeutic community, and the other half in H.M.P. Full Sutton, a maximum-security prison. The purpose of a Community of Philosophical Inquiry (henceforth, CoPI) is to engage participants in philosophical conversation (Murris 2000). The classes involved participants, including myself, sitting around a circular table and engaging in collaborative, non-adversarial conversation on a range of philosophical ideas.

My philosophy course was rooted in the practices of a programme called Philosophy for Children (P4C), a programme in which I have been formally trained and have experience of delivering in secondary schools.[1] In moving my teaching into prisons, I moved away from the official pedagogy, developing my own method of teaching philosophy, thereby ensuring the programme was appropriate for my participants.

Participants would arrange themselves at desks, seated so that all participants faced each other. I would also place myself, seated, as part of the circle so that I could facilitate the discussion as a co-inquirer. The start of the first session involved a brief discussion around the purpose and expectations of the dialogue as I introduced the topic. Following this, the class had a round of introductions where I asked each participant (including myself) to state their name and tell the group an interesting fact about themselves. In subsequent weeks, I began each session by asking for comments or feedback from the previous session and for a brief recap to get the dialogue going. At this stage, participants would occasionally have written some reflective thoughts for me to read and respond to, or would bring along questions and new ideas.

Once introductions and feedback had come to a close, I would introduce the day's topic. As the time allotted for each of the sessions was substantially longer than a normal class time (which is usually around an hour), it was important to ensure there was sufficient material to maintain conversation throughout. I therefore introduced the stimuli in stages, drawing participants through the philosophical ideas. I took care to introduce each stage naturally, allowing conversation and dialogue to flow, but using each new stage as a means of redirecting and reinvigorating the conversation. After handing out each stage, I would ask participants to give each other a moment to read and reflect on the content in their own time before starting the discussion. Some participants would take notes while others would sit and think for a moment. The purpose of this was twofold: first to allow those with more limited reading skills time to digest the stimulus without feeling pressured and second, to allow all participants time to consider their own initial opinion. After a suitable pause I would openly ask for contributions usually saying something like, "Any thoughts?" or "What's our opinion of this?" and the discussion would get underway. At the end of each session I gave participants a handout with optional further reading to take away.

I based each session on a different topic. Some of the sessions focused on a particular philosopher such as Kant or Descartes. These sessions introduced the philosopher's ideas in stages, drawing the participants through their arguments, demonstrating how a philosopher builds from first principles. Sessions based on a school of philosophy, such as the Stoics or Utilitarianism, introduced participants to the ideas of several philosophers, which provided opportunity to discuss arguments for and against a philosophical school of thought. The final 'type' of session focused on classic philosophical problems such as the Ship of Theseus or the Trolley Problem.

As an illustration, figure 1 displays the stimuli used to discuss Kant and the categorical imperative. This session was paired by a second session on Bentham, Mill and utilitarianism. This allowed my participants time to discuss and reflect on two opposing philosophies of moral action.

Compassion, Kant and the Categorical Imperative

Stage 1: An example

It's wartime and two women volunteer to be nurses. Anne is motivated by compassion; by nature she is sensitive to the suffering of the wounded and she feels a mild personal satisfaction in helping someone's recovery. Sue, by contrast, lacks compassionate sentiments (she has lost a close relative and is consumed with grief). Nevertheless, Sue rouses herself and works just as hard as Anne because she can see that there are important reasons for tending the wounded that have nothing to do with her personal feelings (she has worked as a nurse before and knows that anyone with her background would be useful to the community in this situation).

Stage 2: Kant's response

Kant claimed that if you do something just because of how you feel that is not a good action at all. Therefore, although it is of benefit that both women have volunteered only Sue can be said to have acted out of moral motive because her actions have nothing to do with her feelings.

Stage 3: The Categorical Imperative

Kant thought that morality should be based on rational thinking. As rational beings, we have certain duties. These duties are categorical which means they are absolute and unconditional; they apply at all times and in all circumstances and to all people. This is what Kant called the 'categorical imperative': moral rules that an individual is obliged to do as their duty. "Act only according to that maxim by which you can at the same time will that it should become a universal law." Immanuel Kant, *Critique of Pure Reason* (1781). So, Sue is acting morally because she has volunteered as a result of her duty to do so. In other words, she has acted in a way that all people should act given the same situation.

Stage 4: An example

There's a knock at the door. You answer. It's your best friend who looks pale, worried and out of breath. They tell you someone is chasing them, someone who wants to kill them. He's got a knife. You let your friend in, and they run upstairs to hide. Moments later there is yet another knock at the door. This time it is the would-be killer and he has a crazy look in his eyes. He wants to know where your friend is. Are they in the house? Are they hiding in the cupboard? Where are they? In fact, your friend is upstairs. But you tell a lie, you say they have gone to the park. Have you done the right thing?

According to Kant, you have not done the right thing. It is morally wrong to tell a lie and this is always the case. Therefore, it is morally wrong to lie to the would-be murderer. This is an example that Kant himself used and demonstrates the length to which he took his 'categorical imperative'.

Developing community and building relationships

The environment of a CoPI provided opportunity for stimulating conversation around a variety of issues. Participants made contributions and formed opinions, received feedback from their peers and gained new knowledge as the sessions progressed. Throughout, as discussion progressed, participants would change their minds in light of what they heard; turn over ideas; consider them from different angles and take account of a variety of factors and perspectives. As such, they developed more nuanced opinions:

"There are basic principles one must rely on to guide your life but consequences matter. You have to think about consequences as well because if you don't you can end up committing a large wrong because

you don't want to commit a minor wrong. Sometimes, the right thing to do is commit a small wrong in order to ensure a greater wrong does not occur."
Alex, H.M.P. Grendon

"You got the opportunity to express what you thought, even if it was wrong and everybody else thought it was wrong. It was a situation where you could do that openly and feel confident that what you were saying wasn't gonna be vilified, it wasn't gonna be repeated everywhere, and that's rare in here."
Keith, H.M.P. Full Sutton

"In an educated circle … you can learn enough… And that was the first and foremost reason why I started…Then, seeing the subject matters as well as the diverse amount of thinking … people's rationale and that, I thought yeah, I think I should stay here, I'll definitely benefit by opening up my horizon, expressing my ideas, taking in new ideas."
Jason, H.M.P Full Sutton

"The best thing is discussing your own perspective in light of other people's opinions. It's good to get other people's ideas on things."
Cady, H.M.P. Grendon

"[Philosophy's] changed worlds innit, it's changed ways of thinking in whole continents so if we can learn to kind of like … make that a microcosm, we could do that in out our lives personally."
Charlie, H.M.P. Grendon

Conclusion

I found that my prisoner-participants were deep thinkers, fully capable of intellectually challenging conversation, and with perspectives that often proved insightful. Many were earnest in their attempts to find meaning in the prison environment and engaged in philosophical conversation with a passionate interest in self-improvement. My participants articulated their arguments, expressed their thoughts and feelings, and engaged in critical reflection on the thoughts and feelings of others. Through these interactions, my participants got to know, and learned to tolerate, each other. They became more willing to listen to different points of view, express their own views in the company of others and learned to trust the environment of a CoPI as a safe space for open, honest dialogue.

I opened this summary with a statement on the purpose of education, to encourage personal growth. I have provided here a brief description of a philosophy course I delivered in two prisons and given some comment on its role in developing relationships and fostering trust. I chose to focus on this aspect of my experience for a key reason: the environment of a learning space is fundamental to how the learner engages with the learning experience. If we want education to encourage personal growth, then cultivating a positive learning environment that allows for this seems necessary. A community of philosophical inquiry not only provides a suitable pedagogy to achieve this but also encourages learners to learn and think together.

THE MAN OF SORROWS AND THE DIGNITY OF THE PRISONER:
reflections of a Catholic prison chaplain

Mgr ROGER READER
Catholic Bishops' Prisons Adviser

Often, at Mass, even the most devout of Catholics can feel got at. The Scripture readings can induce feelings of guilt, of sins of omission or commission. There are times, however, when the Scripture reading lets us feel that we are doing something good, when we feel encouraged in our Christian lives. For those of us who work in prisons, therefore, I have to confess we feel greatly affirmed by Matthew 25 v 35ff,* part of the great discourse of Jesus on the Last Judgment and the virtuous ask, "When did we see you sick or in prison" and the King answers, "I tell you solemnly, in so far as you did this to one of the least of these brothers of mine, you did it to me." This is a deeply affirming part of the Gospel for anyone who works in prison. You could say that it is the heart of what we do, and it is because of these words of Jesus that we are empowered to give human dignity to those who are in prison.

I have been in and out of prison since 1986. I started, as an Anglican visiting minister, working part time in H.M.P. Pentonville in north London. It is a huge Victorian prison, built in the early nineteenth century.

It looks like every prison you've ever seen in the films. Long wings with small doors set into thick walls on either side of landings with netting stretched across them. The wings are five stories high, and each cell is designed to hold two people. The window is set high up in the cell so that the only way to see daylight is to stand on a chair. Pentonville houses well over a thousand prisoners, and when I worked there they were nearly all on remand, awaiting trial, wondering just what would become of them. It was a place where, among the smell and the jangling of gates and keys, you could sense the anxiety of so many men as they feared what would come out in court, what the jury would say, and the numbers which the judge would eventually decree – days, months or most probably years of their lives handed over to the justice system. I worked there for six years and got to know many of the men well, as they kept returning for relatively petty offences with the need for alcohol or drugs at the root of their offending. On the whole they were the most pathetic of people, whose lives were utter chaos, and prison was the only place where there was any safety or routine.

My next assignment was to H.M.P. Whitemoor, a high security prison in the middle of nowhere. The contrast between the two establishments could not be greater. In Pentonville, I can remember one man who could point to the windows of his sitting room in the flats built near to the wall; in Whitemoor the nearest building any sort was about a mile away. One was a crumbling nineteenth century warehouse of despair, the other opened only in 1992, and a state of the art high security prison, housing 500 of the most dangerous men in Britain. Here I encountered on a daily basis people who had, in various ways, utterly destroyed the lives of others. Maybe through straightforward murder, or through organised crime, or by various horrific sexual crimes. Sitting and listening to them talk about their lives and their crimes was often a harrowing experience.

Finally, in what many of my colleagues thought was a moment of madness, I applied for the post of Catholic chaplain at H.M.Y.O.I. Feltham in west London. Madness, because it is well known that young offenders between the ages of 15 and 21 are in many ways the most difficult group of prisoners to work with. Put together chaotic home lives, drug dependence, alienation and violence with normal adolescence and this can become the perfect storm.

"I tell you solemnly, in so far as you did this to the least of these brothers of mine, you did it to me". These words of Jesus both encourage me, but they also disturb me, they bring me up short. Indeed, anyone who works in Christian prison chaplaincy will tell about how often fairly unambiguously they can daily encounter Christ in their ministry. In the man who stole to feed his family; the boy who travelled thousands of miles to get money for his sick sister; the woman whose heart is broken as she is separated from her child because she could not stay away from alcohol and all that stems from that addiction. People whose lives have been ruined by poverty and deprivation of every sort, who have been victims themselves of the greed of the drug dealer or sexual predator. It can, however, be a lot harder to see Christ in the man who makes tens of thousands of pounds out of the misery of others, in the person whose violence has destroyed the confidence and happiness of others; the person who has killed a child. And yet we are called as Christians to see Christ in all of these people, and to afford them dignity.

Seville in southern Spain is crammed full of beautiful churches; a priest told me that only Rome has more. These, in their turn, are filled with some of the most beautiful art which the Catholic Church possesses. To borrow a phrase from an exhibition held a few years ago, here the sacred is made real. Artists, sculptors in wood from the seventeenth and eighteenth centuries created statues of such almost photographic reality that they moved those who saw them to worship and to tears. Among all the statues I saw of the weeping Virgin and the suffering Christ there was one which caused me to stop, sit, wonder and to pray. It is in the church of El Salvador. It is among many beautiful things, and is in a setting of sumptuous gilt luxury. And it was maybe this contrast between the setting and the subject which first drew my attention to it. It is of The Man of Sorrows. There, sitting, virtually naked, with one hand supporting his bruised head, is the Saviour of the world. This would be after Jesus had been handed over by his apparent friend Judas, brought before two courts, convicted and sentenced and then tortured and humiliated by his guards.

The parallels between this image of Jesus and the prisoners in modern jails are so clear. (I am indebted to the work of W. H. Vanstone for clarifying my thoughts on this.) In the gospel account, Jesus is a man of action, whose words and deeds evoke strong reactions both of love and of hate. He teaches, he heals, he confronts, he feeds, he exorcises, he calms the storm, he visits the sinner, and he eats with prostitutes and tax collectors. In all the gospels we see a dynamic figure who engages the crowds around him. And then it all changes. He is handed over by Judas, and his passion begins. Particularly in Mark and in John's gospels he becomes the *object* of events instead of the *subject*. After he has been handed over he barely speaks, and when he does the words which used to forgive, to heal and to calm storms, are now ineffective or misunderstood. Words which used to change people now have no effect at all on the hearers except to arouse anger. "Are you the King of the Jews?" asks Pilate the judge, "It's you who say it." Jesus replies. In John's gospel, Jesus moves from one who does mighty works, to one who is restrained. On the cross itself Jesus cries, "I thirst" in stark contrast to the man who assuaged the thirst of the Samaritan woman.

"When I was in prison you visited me." The parallels are clear between what happened in the passion of Christ and what happens to thousands of men, women and children in our prisons today. The moment of arrest and imprisonment are moments when the active becomes passive, the subject becomes the object. I was talking to a man who knew he was going to prison, and I could see the fear coming into his eyes as I outlined the very basics of prison routine. He was a businessman, used to controlling his life and the lives of others. I think it really came home to him when I explained what access he would have to the telephone. No texts, no emails, no voicemails. He would have to compete for the phone with maybe fifty other men, supervised by the officers. He would have maybe two or three five minute phone calls a day, if he had enough credit. And only to people on his list of approved numbers. He would have to ask those he trusted to look after his affairs. The active becomes passive. People in prison, by definition, lose so much freedom. Freedom to move, to buy, to meet, to eat, to choose: the list is almost endless. They move from active to passive, and in this we can see Jesus Christ as he endures his passion. And the passion of Jesus Christ is for Christians a manifestation, a showing forth of the divinity of Jesus Christ. A radical departure from traditional ideas of the Divine. In the words of the centurion, gazing up at the Cross, "Truly this was the Son of God." In his passion, his divinity is revealed. "In so far that you did this to the least of these brothers of mine you did it to me" – to Jesus Christ, the Word made flesh. Little wonder these words motivate me and many others who work with people in prison.

I met a former prisoner recently and I showed him this extraordinary image of the Man of Sorrows and immediately he associated with it, and told me how it expressed the waiting and the patience which has to be part of every prisoner's life. Waiting for almost everything, above all for the moment of release which could lie days, weeks, months, years or even decades away. Now, waiting is of course part of all of our lives, from waiting for a bus through to waiting for the results of tests for cancer, but it is particularly part of prisoners' lives; people who have become almost completely the object of life, not the subject. You ask anyone in prison what they are waiting for, and a long list will emerge with varying degrees of frustration: for a phone call, for a letter from home, for a solicitor's visit, to get on the list for education, for a job in the gym, for a transfer to another prison. Some wait with real patience, some will smash up their cell and their prized possessions in frustration.

To see even more clearly how the dignity of the prisoner is identifiable with the Man of Sorrows, it is helpful to look at Jesus' whole attitude to those who sin. Because while it is maybe easy to see Jesus in the prisoner whose crimes are perhaps understandable in some way, it is much more difficult to see him in those whose actions have outraged society. While I do feel affirmed by the words, 'In so far as you did this to one of the least of these brothers of mine you did it to me', this can also be extremely challenging. And this Christian attitude to those who have outraged society in its turn can outrage society.

In his book Jesus: *An Historical Approximation*, Fr. Jose Pagola helps us to investigate Jesus' attitude to sinners. We are so used to reading about how Jesus associated with sinners, with tax collectors, with prostitutes that we have maybe lost the huge significance of these encounters. In much of the Old Testament, sin provoked God, and his prophets, to wrath. Sinners would need denouncing, warning and purifying. Jesus' approach is utterly different, new and revolutionary. So often he says there is room for them in God's kingdom. This is at a time when notorious sinners had to live apart from everyone else. Some were 'publicans'. These were tax collectors whose activities were so shameful that they were shunned by everyone. Jesus is also the friend of prostitutes (even as I write this I can see how this can even now be shockingly misinterpreted). These were women who may have been widowed or abandoned and who had no other way of living – and we cannot underestimate the scandal that involved. And yet we see Jesus mixing with, talking and listening to these folk. Even more amazingly he eats with them and dines with them. This in an age when whom you had to your house, whom you chose to eat with was known and assessed by all. The scribes and Pharisees are outraged by this, "Why does he eat with tax collectors and sinners?" And Jesus responds, "It is not the healthy who need the doctor but the sick. I did not come to call the virtuous but sinners." (Mark 2 v.16).

It is also clear from the gospel that Jesus is at the table of the sinner not as severe judge, but as reassuring friend. He does not demand repentance before he will walk in through the door, but rather he evokes love from those with whom he is eating. If you have ever been to the Middle East, you will know that a meal is not just about eating and getting up and going away. With a guest a meal is about chat, fun, wine and maybe even song. This eating with sinners gives them back their lost dignity, and with no threat they can open themselves up to God's life changing forgiveness. Whenever we have a baptism or confirmation in the prison where I work, we always have a celebration afterwards. We sit down together, with the prisoners' families, and eat, drink (weak orange juice) and even sing together. Here, I hope, in a small way, we bring people face to face with God's love and tenderness.

I would now like to share another image with you, Piero della Francesca's gripping picture of the Resurrection. Again, I shared it with the former prisoner. He knew it well, and he said that it speaks to him of the quiet authority of Jesus, of the hope which comes from the Risen Christ, of the fact that we can never dismiss the possibility, the hope of transformation in human beings. Hope has to be a crucial motivation of all that is done in the name of Jesus in prisons. In Gerard Lemos's *The Good Prison* (2014) we read, "Whether criminals should be punished, condemned, rehabilitated or forgiven, or indeed whether they are criminals at all, are questions embedded in one of the definitive moments of Western Christian cultural history, when Christ on the cross tells the repentant crucified thief, tonight you will join me in paradise. In this way, to the Christian mind, Jesus Christ gave every human being the hope of redemption, even the wrongdoer; especially the wrongdoer repentant but facing intolerance and condemnation."

I would hand in my keys for the last time and walk out of a prison never to return if I lost hope in what I was doing. If I ever felt that my role was truly hopeless, if I gave into cynicism of a few who work in prisons who see nothing but despair in what they do, that would be it. The resurrection of Christ gives me hope that even from death itself hope can come. If we give dignity to those in prison, in whom we see Jesus Christ himself, then we give them hope, the hope which stems from the resurrection, 'a hope which is not deceptive, because the love of God has been poured into our hearts by the Holy Spirit which has been given to us.' (Rom 5 v.5). Indeed, there have been times when, as for anyone who works with damaged humanity, situations seemed so overwhelming, depressing and frustrating, it is tempting to lose hope, but, by God's grace I have not. I have seen relationships, self-knowledge and potential flourish among the dross.

Calvin is a young prisoner who has made a deep impression on me. After seeing him for several months cleaning on his unit, one day he asked if he could come to Mass. He was a boy of few words and few friends: rather withdrawn. He began to attend our small prayer group as well as Mass, and it was most moving over time to see him become confident enough to take part in discussion, speak his own mind and read aloud from the scriptures. Small things so many take for granted, but which for him were enormous steps. I think he found in the group both dignity and hope.

In so many ways, prisons can be seen as warehouses of despair, but I well remember one governor having in his office a mock-up of the front page of *The Sun* newspaper with the headline 'Well run prison has a good day'. Among all the despair, there has to be hope, and among the indignity some dignity. In *The Good Prison* you will see many examples of how things can go well. I know this, I have seen it. Of course, this is not the sole preserve of chaplains – in education, in the workshops, in the gym, in good caring work by officers and other staff; there are signs of hope always.

The first witnesses to the Resurrection were overcome by the most normal of human emotions: fear kept them behind locked doors, grief at the death of their friend brought them to tears, and shock at what had happened made them doubt the power of God. But Hope broke through, and lives were transformed.

A while ago I was on the tube and I spotted a young man in painters' overalls propping up the door of the train. He called out to me, somewhat to the surprise of my fellow commuters, in a clear Polish accent "Hello Fr. Roger." I replied, "Hello, Lukas, how are you?" "I'm fine" he said, "now I work as painter and earn honest money." Then he added, much to the consternation of everyone else, "When I was in Feltham prison, I was bad boy, but you made me good boy." Of course, I can claim little responsibility for making Lukas a good boy. But, in that I am part of a tradition which finds its source in the life, death and resurrection of Jesus Christ, a tradition which knows the dignity of every human being, 'even the least of these brothers of mine.' I was pleased to hear those words from Lukas.

THE WAY I SEE IT,
I SEE IT THIS WAY:
in the style of a chain-link writing

ANONYMOUS
H.M.P. Low Moss

This essay and the following charts are part of 'Inside a Lifer's Journey: an anthology' (courtesy of the Koestler Trust).

Experience

I write to express. I express my hope. My hope is that you will understand. Understand my hopes and fears. My fears drive the storyline. The storyline is driven by my passion. My passion is to inspire. I am inspired by those who teach. Teach me how to write.

I have read great fiction. Great fiction based on facts. Facts based on discovery. I discovered a new skill. A skill to convey meaning. Meaning distilled from experience. My experience of imprisonment. Imprisonment for life. A life behind bars. Bars that separate. Separate me from family. Family who support me. Support my will to survive. I survive by staying occupied. Occupied with learning. Learning about how to live. To live is what all people want. What they want is that which prevents it. I am prevented from forgiving. Forgiving those who loved me. Those who loved me, abandoned me.

I was at the top of my game. My game is actually business. Business fulfils my needs. My needs are very simple. A simple man is what I am. I am so disappointed. Disappointed that I fucked up. I fucked it up with my lady. My lady who believed in my future. My future is not so certain. Certainty is a luxury. Luxury I cannot afford. To afford it, I need to move on. To move on I must forgive and be forgiven.

Forgiveness

I am the one who decides. I decide what goes down. Down I fell into her arms. Her arms were so strong. A strong woman is the fantasy. A fantasy is not real. The reality was we had it all. All the dreams we loved. Loved and lost. Well, that is now all over. Over debt and time. Time I did not spend with her. Her, the perfect partner. My partner blamed me. Blame split us apart.

Choice is what it's about. About now I have choose. I choose to accept I am the cause. Cause and effect. The effect is that I will receive. Receive and be forgiven. Forgiveness intones the priest. A priest of the old religion. Religiously I observe it. It is really only tradition. Traditionally I would have married. Marriage was not an option. Options drive my decisions. Decisions that define who I am. I am a broken man. A broken man needs a new dream.

I Dream

I read to escape. Escape from reality. Reality is my life. My life was full of work. Work to pay the bills. Bills that just kept growing. Growing children demand more resources. Resources I did not have. I had a good house. A house, wife, child and car. The car gave me freedom. Freedom is what I crave. I crave the opportunity. Opportunity to create and build. To build you need money. Money is just a tool. A tool to do your bidding. I bid on my future. A future of innovation. Innovation is the key. The key to my success. Success is my dream. A dream, with flights of fancy. I fancy another chance. A chance to make my dreams come true.

A Simplified Chart – *a Graph of Concepts:*
the reasoning behind the effect of education in prison

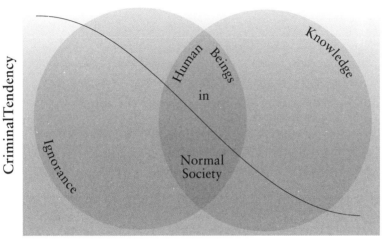

Education

On the Effect of Prison Education – *a poetic Venn diagram:*
a condensed realisation in the style of Brian Bilston

Less   **More**

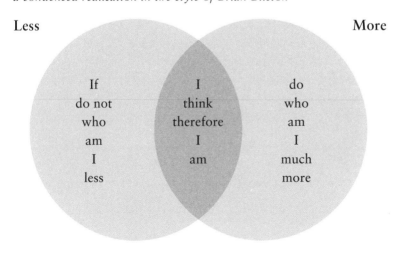

LGBT PRISONERS:
being true to yourself

PHIL FORDER
Community Engagement Manager, H.M.P. and Y.O.I. Parc

I am an openly gay man though that hasn't always been the case. For the larger part of my life, a lot of which was during a time when being gay was illegal and at best unacceptable, I was what is known as 'living in the closet', trying to be something I was not. This caused a lot of pain for myself and for others around me who had to deal with my mood swings and what must have seemed like irrational bouts of depression. Pretending to be someone you are not, 24/7, is bound to have consequences. Eventually, I just had to come out no matter what. Strangely the place where this took place was in H.M.P. Parc in south Wales, which like most prisons at that time was probably one of the most homophobic places in the U.K. What I hadn't realised was that my coming out effected a lot of other people and wasn't just about me, although it did feel like it at the time. Prisons are enclosed, inward looking places, where information circulates faster than the internet. An incident in one corner of the prison is known throughout the estate in minutes. Surprisingly, I found I was able to be more effective in my work, being true to myself and also more supported and respected as a result.

Similarly, many prisoners arriving on the wings for the first time feel they have to be something other than themselves to prove who they are. This involves displaying a macho and tough persona. Many a time the person you talk to in public, on the wing, is quite a different person to the one you speak to alone in their cell. I guess we all feel we need to wear masks at different times depending on who we are with, but I have learnt from personal experience, that to have to wear one all the time is difficult. Unfortunately, the idea that the more macho and violent you are, the more looked up to and respected you are, seems deeply embedded in prison culture. This puts enormous pressure on those who are not that way inclined. Traditionally, we are conditioned from a very early age into roles depending on our gender (for instance, boys have cars, toy soldiers and guns; girls have dolls, ponies and tea sets). Subliminally, we are meant to fit stereotypes, which if we don't inculcates failure and inadequacy. Although there has been much headway in what is acceptable for girls-such as women's football, women engineers, female prison officers - the emancipation of boys lags behind.

With this in mind, when considering the gay community in prison many feel they need to go back in the closet once they are past the gates. We at Parc (at the time of writing) have 25 gay men in the Vulnerable Prisoner Unit and eight on the Mains; it's the most we have ever had. But by the use of anyone's statistics compared to the percentage of gay men in the community at large, this is low. There are nearly 1,800 prisoners here. Either gay men don't commit crimes (Hah!) or, more likely, there are a lot of men in prison who are afraid to be who they really are. Obviously nobody should be forced to be 'out', that is a personal choice, but neither should anyone be forced to hide if they don't wish to. The challenge is to create a non-judgmental environment and 'normalise' the gay man in the eyes of the general prisoner population.

When the general prisoner population takes responsibility for what they say and do for themselves, then we will know we are on the right track. A recent example occurred when I attended a prison event in the role of photographer for a visiting rugby celeb who was giving a talk. There were

36 prisoners in attendance. During the presentation the visitor made a few wise-crack allusions about Gareth Thomas, the gay rugby player, that were mildly offensive. I thought, 'do I say something here?' The audience were laughing, the mood was upbeat; so I let it go. Later that afternoon I had a visit in my office from the gym teacher who asked if I was OK. He said, "A lot of the boys felt uncomfortable about what was said and asked me to check out with you that you were alright." What had made me feel awkward and isolated had been rescued by the prisoners themselves. It was as if the bad situation had given opportunity for prisoners to show concern. The shift is already happening.

So there is a two-pronged approach: one is to offer support for those who wish to be out and the other is to challenge the homophobic culture on the wings. Although different, a lot of events work both ways. Here are a few things we have put in place to help do this.

- As in all prisons, the gym is the most popular place for prisoners. It's where you get more macho, it's where you pump iron and it's a good place to start if you want to make a difference. I began by inviting in probably the most well-respected, most-loved rugby referee in the world, to come and talk. Yes, Nigel Owens, who by the way just happens to be gay. This is Wales and rugby is god and here was god's messenger on earth saying it's OK to be gay. Nigel spoke for about an hour and a half, about rugby. But also about the pain he went through as a gay man struggling to be himself, under the spotlight, in a macho sport. The audience was empathetic. They felt what he was saying.

- I then invited in the Cardiff Dragons, a Cardiff based football team, to come a play a few matches against prisoners and staff. Brilliant! I didn't tell the players till afterwards when we all sitting around sharing refreshments that the team were gay. The prisoners were so shocked (in a nice way). One said to the captain of the Dragons, "Good God! You don't look gay" to the amusement of everyone there. I took a few after match photos. When the Director asked if it had been a success I showed her – the prisoners had their arms over gay men's shoulders – it spoke for itself. This led on to visits from the Swansea Vikings and Cardiff Lions, both gay rugby teams with the same effects.

- I also run an annual literary event called Hay in the Parc in which I always try to include writers who come from a variety of backgrounds. I was lucky enough to get Peter Tatchell to come in and give a couple of talks. Peter spoke openly and directly about his various scrapes with the law and the suffering of gay men around the world. Again, by being himself he won the audience over. They listened and were amazed at his courage and commitment.

- The list of people who have come into the prison is extensive. I strongly believe the more you can bring in, the more opportunity there is for influencing others. We have had so far the Terrence Higgins Trust, Ddraig Enfys, Cardiff Pride, Iris Film Festival, Swansea Sparkle, Jenny Anne Bishop, Cardiff Gay Man's Reading group, Unity Group, Lou Englefield, Pride Sports and many more.

- We have also introduced a Compact for Sports orderlies whereby to get the job you have to agree to challenge homophobia as well as support any LGBT individual who feels uncomfortable in the gym.

For those prisoners who are out, I run various LGBT support groups for anyone who wishes to attend. They are opportunities to spend time together. I always say 'this is your space' and shun too much agenda-led discussion. Peer support is so important in not feeling isolated and alone. Not surprisingly many men attend out of interest - 'not because I'm gay' - but later realising it is a safe space in which to come out, at least initially for the short time they are in group. Ironically, the reverse can also happen. At one time, I had more Irish Traveller young men in the gay group than I did in the Traveller Support group, which I also run. Sadly, they felt being in prison, away from their outside culture was the only opportunity they had to be themselves. This is also true of others who attend from fundamentalist religious groups. Unlike the majority of gay men who hide when coming to prison, these prisoners seem to do the opposite.

In my opinion, however, the most effective intervention of all, are two prisoners we presently have working with us who are very obviously gay. They are not macho, they are not aggressive they are just themselves. They live on the Mains and they also man the internal prisoner helpline. Their job is to take calls from prisoners and sort out problems/ find out information for, in many cases, some of the most difficult prisoners on the wings. They have gained a 'super enhanced' status which allows them to walk freely about the prison-visiting prisoners to sort out their problems. They are the bravest and yet the softest men in the prison. Just being themselves, being highly visible, has broken down so many barriers and is probably the most effective catalyst for change of all. Like children we learn by example and being true to yourself is essential if you want to be taken seriously.

Learning in the 'Restorative Prison'

GARY STEPHENSON
Chief Executive, Restorative Solutions CIC

The concept of the 'restorative prison', which is has been piloted at H.M.P. Buckley Hall and H.M.P. Peterborough has provided significant learning opportunities for those engaged in applying a restorative approach to addressing and resolving conflict in prison communities. Staff, prisoners, visitors and families are all engaged in a 'whole prison' approach. Prisoners have embraced the restorative approach to conflict resolution, which has resulted in many positive learning outcomes for them including, respect for others needs and feelings; a sense of responsibility for their own actions; and the ability to reflect on how those actions impact on others. The programme, managed and delivered by Restorative Solutions and funded by The Monument Trust, will be evaluated by Birbeck, University of London. In the meantime, I believe that the concept is helping to change the culture within the prison environment and equip the prisoners involved with skills to change their own and other's lives.

A truly 'restorative prison' would ensure that staff and prisoners are empowered to resolve issues restoratively either through an informal restorative conversation or a formal restorative conference. This approach leads to timely interventions, while also preventing escalation and retribution. The essence of the restorative approach is, by using proven techniques, to get to the core of the conflict and repair the relationship and significantly decrease the possibility for the conflict to persist. Our input includes awareness raising, a communications strategy developed by prisoners, training planning, senior leadership development, process change, joint briefing sessions with staff and prisoners, resource commitment from the prisons and integrating the approach into their regime. The flexibility of the approach allows it to be applied to all situations involving conflict anywhere in the prison (between prisoners or between staff and prisoners) with the understanding that appropriate notification of the interventions must be made and that the processes put in place are adhered to.

The role of leadership is of key importance to the implementation of the programme. It is essential that the senior leadership team (as well as prisoners and staff) are fully committed to the transformation. Prisoners have been courageous in stepping forward and making themselves available; selected individuals needed to command the respect of their peers and staff. The ability to demonstrate that as a former offender while imprisoned you were able to lead, change and influence the behaviour of staff and other prisoners is a significant achievement and learning experience. The whole team (prisoners and staff) needed to take some risks, act as advocates and ensure that they are known and available to answer any potential questions and provide ongoing support.

The restorative approach works well in conjunction with the adjudication process, providing the adjudicating officer with an additional option rather than punishment alone. It gives the adjudicating officer the option to defer action and provide the parties with the opportunity to have a facilitated restorative conference between all parties involved in the conflict, which would lead to a better-informed outcome aimed at solving the problem or resolving the issue. The participants learn of the human consequences of their actions that they are unlikely to have been exposed to in our adversarial justice system. The parties concerned enter into an agreement between themselves which they construct; the 'outcome agreement' is intended to make things better.

When adopting the restorative approach, people begin to view situations differently and are equipped to solve many of the issues that arise within the prison, which leads to a change in their behaviour, attitude and mind-set. The Prison Officers Association recognise the benefits and value of the approach and have proven instrumental in winning over the hearts and minds of staff. The approach has been equally effective in the female estate, where the first ever group of female prisoners have been trained as practitioners, demonstrating themselves as true pioneers.

The attitude and dedication of the prisoners, many of whom have troubled backgrounds, who are practising the approach has been impressive. They have achieved respect from fellow prisoners and support from staff, displaying a 'can-do' attitude, proving themselves as true role-models. The prisoners have learnt a diverse set of new skills which will stand them in good stead for the future. These include the ability to listen and display empathy, they are equipped with a problem-solving tool that will assist them in resolving conflict before it gets out of hand and leads to violence. They have learnt that staff and prisoners can work together as a team to make the prison environment a better place to live and work. The prisoners are learning to recognise the vulnerability of others in the prison and how to respond formally or informally; they are learning of the benefits of mutual respect and humility. They are recognising that they have been trusted to make decisions and take actions. This level of responsibility and trust is new to some of the prisoners.

Those prisoners who have been exposed to the restorative approach either through an informal or formal restorative conference are beginning to see that there is another way to gain respect other than violence and coercion. They are seeing and experiencing the emotional impact their behaviour, whether intended or not can have on others. (This is particularly so with cases of bullying). Typical cases involve, verbal altercations, bullying, debts, assaults, drugs and fighting. Respect for other people's needs and feelings, a sense of responsibility for one's own actions and the ability to reflect on how those actions impact on others have been identified by prisoners as key learning experiences that will help them to reintegrate into society.

It is our ambition that once those who have received training gain further experience in applying the restorative approach, they may progress to our accredited course, where they would achieve a BTEC Level 3 in Restorative Practice. This would be a major educational achievement that could put them on the path to professional development and potential future qualifications. Many prisoners have demonstrated an interest in continuing to practice after their release and may look for opportunities in either a voluntary or professional capacity. Some have said that they would be grateful for the opportunity to meet their victims and be held to account for their actions by those they have harmed.

The approach is not something that can be taken out of the box and simply applied. There have already been considerable changes from what we set out to do at the introduction of the programme due to our ongoing learning. The key lesson has been that there must be a change of the culture from the inside, which then needs to permeate across every layer of the prison regime. A leading governor has spoken of how impressed he has been with the enthusiasm for the approach from staff and prisoners, acknowledging the considerable improvement to the environment of the prison to a level that appeared unimaginable at the outset.

The short-term and long-term benefits so far have seen a more safe, secure and supportive environment for prisoners and staff alike. Individuals are developing a strong sense of responsibility for their own actions, while also reflecting on how these actions might affect others, leading to a growing respect for the needs and feelings of others. The measurable benefits for the participating prisons are: a reduction in the numbers and types of complaints; reduced numbers and types of adjudications; reduced numbers of staff misconduct and discipline investigations; decrease in levels of staff sickness; decrease in numbers of assaults and use of control and restraint; improvement in perceived quality of prison life according to MQPL indicators; improvement in perceptions of the prison environment and relations; reduction in self-harm; improvement in well-being of staff and prisoners; creating an environment where rehabilitation can occur safely and effectively.

A longitudinal study will evaluate the impact of this approach, but walking around the participating prisons and encountering people from the prison community who have been affected by the programme, my personal intuition and experience indicates that this approach works and contributes to the learning and development of prisoners, staff and their families while helping to make the prison a safer place, which will allow prisoners to learn and develop and prosper in their future lives.

RE-IMAGINING THE PRISON EDUCATION PARADIGM:

identity transitions, social learning and 'de-othering' in a climate of penal inexactitude

Dr ANNE O'GRADY and Dr PAUL HAMILTON
Nottingham Trent University

With MARK DERBYSHIRE
H.M.P. Lowdham Grange

The question What Do Prisoners and Ex-Offenders Need to Learn? is interesting because it seems to consider this 'community' homogenously, rather than capturing the inevitable heterogeneity within these discrete populations. Equally, there appears to be an implicit assumption about what 'they' (prisoners and ex-offenders) need to know. That said, one could reasonably argue that those who are incarcerated (prisoners) and those who have been exposed to the criminal justice system (ex-offenders) have much to share about their experiences of the system, and are well-positioned to provide learning opportunities for other members of society. Arguably, the notion of prisoner and ex-offender learning may therefore be best seen in the broader context of challenging societal narratives of 'offenders' and providing opportunities for individual self-reflexivity and agency (Vaughan, 2007). Opportunities to learn while incarcerated have been part of the 'prison offer' through a legal framework for centuries (Forster, 1998). What that education offer is, and the resultant learning opportunities, have evolved and altered over time, often reflecting changing political foci, economic imperatives and social tolerances.

Contemporary prison education is funded through a framework of adult learning, with funding provided through the Skills Funding Agency, facilitated by the Offender and Learning Skills Service (OLASS). The focus of prison education is largely targeted at a limited suite of courses, including English, maths and computing, and mostly at a level of competence expected of a pupil completing GCSE qualifications. This may seem a reasonable basis for the provision of prison education, not least because of the significant evidence demonstrating the high proportion of prisoners who have neither qualifications nor capability in these areas (ONS, 2012).

There are a range of imperatives for learning, which can be grouped into two distinct groups – economic and social. Indeed, lifelong learning for all adults has been identified as the key to the development of a society that is both economically successful and also inclusive and just (Hodgson and Spours, 1999). Economically, one can observe, in our knowledge economy, the need for a base knowledge in English, maths and ICT. These subject areas are required for the majority of employment in contemporary society, regardless of whether the job is deemed to be low-skilled, semi-skilled, skilled or professional. There is a reasonable argument to be made, therefore, that prisoners need to learn this information, particularly when we consider the persistently low levels of employment for those individuals transitioning back into communities after serving a custodial sentence (Schmitt and Warner, 2010). Indeed, government funding formulas support such learning opportunities within the framework of prison education; funding is provided to support prisoners develop their capability in these subjects to the expected national minimal level for adults (Level 2), and achieve recognisable qualifications for future potential employment.

The second group of learning – social learning - which is synonymous with adult education (Yeaxlee, 1929) is much less in evidence within the majority of prison education. However, there is a growing body of evidence from employers that these sorts of skills are much needed, and less present among potential future employees. Such social skills can include, but are not exclusively, team work, communication skills, presentation skills, independent thinking. So, while learning these skills can be regarding as being of economic value, evidencing these competences can be tricky.

For prisoners and ex-offenders, like all members of society, learning relevant and appropriate knowledge and skills which can contribute to personal and national economic prosperity can only be of value. We argue, however, that a focus on the development of social skills – for all members of society – can result in a strong sense of social responsibility. This is significant when one considers what we know about the path to redemption and the 'road from crime'. Ultimately, placing learners at the centre of a learning experience, acknowledging their diversity and their multiple literacies (Newman *et al*, 1993) may be a more effective approach to the consideration of what prisoners and ex-offenders need to learn and may ultimately lead to a reduction in recidivism and enhanced rehabilitation opportunities. Put simply, we argue it is not what prisoners or ex-offenders need to learn that should be of paramount focus, but rather what is it that we as a society need to learn. As Maruna (2004: 273) points out 'not only must a person accept conventional society in order to go straight, but conventional society must accept that person as well'.

This core argument is exemplified in a recent piece of work between Nottingham Trent University and H.M.P. Lowdham Grange (a private, Serco-led prison). This partnership brought together learners from both institutions to study a higher education module: the intersection of social justice and criminal justice, and the role of prison education. While the programme was situated within the prison, all learners (university and prison) were invited to engage in the academic content of the module. The aim of the project was to explore opportunities to develop a shared learning community for knowledge exchange, and to invite participants to consider, challenge and be exposed to stereotypical assumptions often attributed to these groups (i.e. higher education students being considered elite and prisoners being considered the antithesis of this – the worst in our society), and examine their legitimacy. Throughout the course of the module, participants were offered opportunities, through a participatory dialogic model of delivery, to reflect on these assumptions and collectively co-construct new meanings; and to build new understandings of their own agency, roles and responsibilities to, and within society, in relation to social justice and civic engagement. The module was built on Griffiths (1998) proposed model for social justice – that being a process of ongoing checks and balances, which consider the interests of both the individual and the community, as the participants examined the economic, social and political imperatives associated with prison education. Furthermore, the philosophy of Freire's (1996) pedagogy of hope, encapsulated as 'dialogue' drove the pedagogic approach; enabling meaningful and purposeful learning to occur, allowing participants to become critically conscious of their reality, and recognising that one's participation in the world is at its most effective when undertaken through action and reflection. Such an approach to learning is not without its challenges. Firstly, and perhaps most importantly, it is not funded, so has relied on a lot of 'good will', belief and support from both institutions to allow the project to proceed. Secondly, it is not credit-bearing; this module was built on the principles of informal adult learning (Rogers, 2003). While the benefits of such an approach to learning seem insurmountable, the opportunity to evidence one's personal growth and achievements through engagement in the course is only recognised by a certificate of participation. In this regard, while the content of the module was important, of equal importance was the model of delivery, and this is something to be considered when answering the question posed above.

Coates (2016), in her final report which, arguably, can be regarded as a blueprint for the future of prison education, concluded that prison education should be the central activity around which the prison day, and prison activity, is organised. She presents a justification for good quality education (too much provision is woeful, see Wilshaw, 2015); for rigorous assessment and for more accountability of governors for high quality education provision. It is hard to argue against these recommendations. If this model of education were to be adopted, learning opportunities could be more wide-ranging to meet individual needs, governors could use budgets innovatively to incorporate a wider range of formal, and informal adult learning opportunities. There could be opportunities for more appropriate, up-to-date technology to facilitate the learning offer, allowing learning to go beyond the prison classrooms, and actually link to education providers beyond the prison walls so that learning can be continued once a sentence has been served.

A system of education, which provides appropriate and meaningful learning opportunities for prisoners is absolutely vital and a valuable contribution to prison activity; and has a significant role to play in supporting the transformation agenda. It must, however, take into account the diversity of the population it seeks to provide for; there is no one thing that a prisoner or ex-offender needs to learn. If learning opportunities are to be provided, we need to be able to cater for what each individual needs to learn. That requires access to highly qualified staff across the prison estate. All too often prisoners report commencing programmes only to transition to another institution where the course is not being delivered and therefore cannot be continued, or they are released and there is no mechanism to support prisoners to enrol with local education providers. Often, it can be perceived that bureaucratic barriers are actively put in place to discourage prisoners from enrolling onto courses.

Even if one was able to come up with a 'list' of knowledge and skills one might feel prisoners, or ex-offenders 'need to learn', of course there is the question of individual motivation to learn. Seen through the lens of desistance, Loeber *et al* (1991) point out, that it is attitudes towards learning rather than educational opportunities *per se* that are more obviously correlated with shifts in internal narratives.

We argue the question should not be what do prisoners and ex-offenders need to learn, but rather what do we, as a holistic society, need to learn. Considering this question allows us to consider our individual and collective social responsibility, enabling those who have served their sentence to re-enter into society with the same equality of all citizens. Potentially this reminds us that 'a reformed identity' inevitably necessitates a process of pro-social labelling (Maruna *et al*, 2004). Learning is the key to liberation for all; it has the capacity to be transformative. We, as a society, need to learn to transform our relationships; and have acceptance of each other. Prisoners and ex-offenders need to be able to transition into mainstream society: obtain employment; access education; source accommodation and open bank accounts. Therefore, it is imperative that they have the requisite knowledge and skills to be able to achieve this; and the role of prison education has an important part to play here. Equally, in order for such transition to be achieved, society more widely needs to accept individuals with a criminal past into these spaces without oppressive scrutiny. We are in danger, through this question, of homogenising people into narrow groups, diminishing individual learning needs, ambitions and goals. It is only with this perspective one can achieve social justice, recognising that criminal justice has been served.

University students and prisoners learning collaboratively:
the inside-out prison exchange programme

Dr KATE O'BRIEN, Professor FIONA MEASHAM,
and Dr HANNAH KING
Durham University

"Inside-Out moves beyond the walls that separate us. In a more literal sense, it moves, actually, through the walls. It is an exchange, an engagement— between and among people who live on both sides of the prison wall. And it is through this exchange, realized in the crucible of dialogue, that [the walls that] separate us from each other – and sometimes, from ourselves – begin to crumble. The hope is that, in time, through this exchange, these walls—between us, around us, and within us—will become increasingly permeable and, eventually, extinct—one idea, one person, one brick at a time. All of our lives depend on it."
Lori Pompa, Inside-Out founder, 2013: 7

The Inside-Out Prison Exchange Programme is based on a very simple concept: people come together to talk about and wrestle with issues that are important to them. However, it is the setting in which classes take place, behind the prison walls, that makes it profound and for many participants, a transformative experience. It is a pioneering prison education programme because it brings together 'Inside' (prison) students and 'Outside' (university) students to learn collaboratively through dialogue and community-building exercises within the prison walls. Challenging prejudices and breaking down social barriers, the programme provides students from diverse backgrounds with a unique opportunity to study together as peers and as equals behind the prison walls. Drawing on the critical pedagogy of Paolo Freire (1996) and the teaching practice of bell hooks (1994) and Palmer (2007), Inside-Out instructors engage in "teaching to transgress", enabling students to build academic knowledge together while simultaneously learning experientially the various ways in which identities and commonplace environments are shaped by privilege, difference and inequalities. More broadly, Inside-Out develops a dynamic partnership between universities and prisons which deepens the conversation about, and transforms our approaches to, issues of crime and justice. It is a model of prison education, therefore, that invites us to rethink the purpose of prison education; to prioritise *how* prisoners, ex-offenders and those at risk of offending learn, over *what* we think they should be learning. When delivered ethically and when adhering to the hallmark features of the programme, outlined below, Inside-Out is a powerful means through which men and women from both sides of the wall can build knowledge about the world and themselves within the unique prism of the prison setting.

Prison education and criminology at Durham University

Durham University has a long history of engaging in prison education, beginning with Stan Cohen and Laurie Taylor in the 1960s. Their seminal study, *Psychological Survival: The Experience of Long-term Imprisonment* (1972) is the product of their experiences of teaching sociology classes to men serving life sentences at H.M.P. Durham during the late 1960s. The School of Applied Social Sciences at Durham University has been delivering undergraduate modules in the sociology of crime and deviance since 1965, launching its BA (Honours) Criminology degree in 2007 and its

MSc Criminology and Criminal Justice degree in 2011. In October 2014, following eighteen months of planning and partnership building with two local men's prisons; H.M.P. Frankland (category A) and H.M.P. Durham (category B); Durham University criminology staff delivered the first accredited Inside-Out Prison Exchange Programme in Europe, at H.M.P. Durham to a student community made up of equal numbers of 'Outside' (Level 3 undergraduate criminology) students and 'Inside' (imprisoned) students'. In 2016, following a request from the then Minister of State for Justice and Civil Liberties the programme expanded to the local women's prison, H.M.P. Low Newton, at post-graduate level. Inside-Out is now delivered annually at all three prisons, with an Inside-Out alumni men's Think Tank established at H.M.P. Frankland in early 2015 and similarly a women's Think Tank at H.M.P. Low Newton in 2016.

Inside-Out: History, pedagogy and ethos

The Inside-Out programme was founded 20 years ago by Temple University criminologist Lori Pompa in collaboration with incarcerated men at Graterford State Correctional Institution (SCI), Philadelphia, in response to the racial injustice and mass incarceration that characterises the U.S. criminal justice system. Following many years of taking criminology students into prison for tours and discussion sessions with prisoners, Pompa was keen to develop a more meaningful form of education and engagement for individuals on both sides of the walls through dialogue about criminological issues. After several years of negotiation with different prisons, Pompa piloted the first Inside-Out Prison Exchange Programme at Graterford SCI. That cohort of men went on to establish a 'Think Tank', the first of its kind, developing Inside-Out into a national model and Instructor Training Centre. Over the last twenty years, the programme has grown into an international movement with over 100 prison and university partnerships, 700 trained instructors and 22,000 graduating students across the globe (www.insideoutcentre.org).

Back in the mid-1990s, the challenge Pompa and the Think Tank faced was to create a liberating learning process and space within a repressive context. This required a pedagogical approach that was distinct from the didactic methodology most often used in university settings. Inside-Out offers something quite different: a learning environment that encourages students to engage in "challenging debates on the use of incarceration by offering alternative, more rigorous, observations on imprisonment and the overall consequences" (Ridley 2014:20) . Inside-Out is not research, voyeurism or activism aimed at or about those in prison. Rather, it is an educational approach that prioritises the insights and perspectives of every student in the classroom, enabling them to build knowledge collectively. Students are not objects that teachers do something to, rather, Inside-Out facilitators listen, ask questions, welcome students' insights and encourage them to always learn more (Freire, 1996; bell hooks, 1994; Palmer, 2007).

The course is challenging, intensive and demanding, for students and staff, with students required to engage fully in classroom discussions and to reflect critically on their own learning in their written coursework. There are a number of 'signature' pedagogical components of Inside-Out, which together combine to characterise Inside-Out as a distinct prison education programme with a focus on dialogical pedagogy at its heart:

- Programme conceptualised and designed with imprisoned men – initially with Graterford Think Tank and subsequently with Think Tanks across the U.S.A.
- Transformative, transgressive and egalitarian in ethos: a pedagogical approach rooted in the philosophies of Freire, hooks and Palmer
- Instructors trained experientially by imprisoned men
- Inside-Out mandatory rules – no sex offenders, no contact outside of the classroom or after the course finishes, no research on Inside students
- The 'teacher' as 'facilitator'
- Dialogue-focused learning
- The group establishing its own guidelines for dialogue within the classroom
- Foregrounding of ice-breaker and community building activities
- All students and staff seated together in a circle

- Experiential activities to illustrate and explore key concepts (e.g. theories of crime)
- Reflective papers (that integrate academic readings, class observations and personal reflection)
- Group projects with real world significance to consolidate collective learning and community building
- Closing ceremony celebrating the achievements of the class.

At Durham University, Inside-Out is consortially taught with approximately 24 students meeting together weekly for a three hour class within the prison and engaging in the same readings, assessments and discussions that prioritise the collective building of knowledge through dialogue. The programme is delivered weekly across a 10-week term. Each class begins and ends with students seated in a large circle in alternate seats so each Outside student sits next to an Inside student. This seating arrangement makes a powerful statement about our common humanity and fosters a shared sense of equity: students have an equal voice and stake in the learning process. In this shared learning space, we can be who we are and say what we know; it brings out the best in all of us. The circle provides a space of liberation, not only for Inside students who regularly say that they 'forget' where they are for those brief hours, but for Outside students to feel free to speak without the competitiveness that some feel in an elite university classroom, and where all participants are recognised for their unique contribution. In this circle and in small groups we explore topics such as prisons and penology, drug policy and drug harm, and theories of crime and criminal justice. Using community building exercises we grapple with issues together; emphasising that everyone has the capacity to be both a teacher and a learner, and together we create criminological knowledge.

Levelling the playing field

From initial recruitment through to assessment and graduation, Inside-Out engages with individuals in a way that seeks to level the playing field within the constraints of the prison estate. All prospective students are asked to write a letter of application, be interviewed by the instructors and obtain individual security clearance to attend classes by the prison establishment. We require our Inside students to have broadly similar levels of educational ability by requiring an estimated minimum Level 2 educational assessment, equivalent to age 16. While recognising that this excludes the majority of prisoners, it enables the programme to operate as a genuine higher education module and allows all students who successfully complete the module to receive equal Durham University accreditation. Outside students understand without question that the programme is not an opportunity for them to 'help', 'research' or 'adopt' a prisoner, an important component of this is using first names only. This protects the identity of everyone involved and reduces the likelihood of Outside students being tempted to conduct internet searches on the offending histories of their co-students. Related to this, student interaction is limited to the time that they are engaged in the programme and contact is not allowed outside of the classroom or after the programme has finished. All students understand the importance and necessity of these rules and boundaries in order to ensure a safe and nurturing environment and to protect the programme and those involved. It is notable that in 20 years of Inside-Out courses around the world there have been no security incidents of concern.

Concluding remarks

At the end of each module, and in their reflective essays, Inside and Outside students routinely comment on the importance to them of the unique educational space and learning community that Inside-Out creates. For Inside students, the classroom becomes an 'oasis', or 'third space'; an environment within the prison setting that allows them to be and feel 'normal' and 'human', not to be treated like a 'prisoner', a number or even an 'animal', and to forget that they are in prison (see also Braggins and Talbot 2003 and O'Sullivan, 2017). For some, the Inside-Out classroom becomes an 'emotion zone' (Crewe *et al.* 2014): a caring and nurturing space that allows prisoners to show their emotions, facilitating a temporary respite from the reality of imprisonment back on the wings. Equally, many Outside students comment on the Inside-Out learning environment as being a 'safer space' than their regular university classrooms. Away from the pressure and hyper-competitive nature of their academic seminar room, Inside-Out, despite being located inside a prison, is perceived as a less threatening space to learn in. Students are more able and willing to speak up and to share their thoughts, ideas and perspectives. And yet, as Pompa (2013: 132) points out, "it is an interesting, albeit ironic, twist that we are able to create a space of freedom within a context that is often the antithesis." A 'good prison', therefore, should focus its energies not on educational content or educational attainment *per se*, but on devising programmes that embrace collective and transformative learning; to create learning spaces that inspire greater educational and personal ambition; provide opportunities for men and women to recognise their capacity as agents of change in their own lives and in the broader community; and support students in taking a step towards building positive lives outside prison, thereby avoiding a return to incarceration.

LEARNING YOUR VALUE IN SOCIETY

GARETH EVANS
Researcher and former prisoner

There are many institutions and individuals who believe that the key to moving away from crime lies solely in the 'pathways' to desistance i.e., employment, education, housing and so on. While these areas do cover important conduits for remaining pro-social, it is this author's suspicion that these are by-products of something much more fundamental. Understanding the theories gleaned from studies, such as the Cambridge Study in Delinquent Development (CSDD)[1] and the Sheffield Study of Desistance,[2] are valuable and useful to practitioners working with those who are at risk of offending and reoffending and can offer useful guidance when learning what differences exist between a person who successfully avoids crime and one who does not.

The CSDD, in particular, sheds light on a broader concept in the context of likely delinquent development. If we try to reduce the causes of crime, both psychological and sociological, we are left with a common denominator that speaks to the disconnect one may have with a pro-social way of living. For example, an increase in probability of a boy growing up to be delinquent relies on dysfunctionality and limited access to social resources. Isolation and, more generally, distance from a social contract in which they are valued by and responsible to and for their peers.

For people who grow up in environments where confirmation of their separateness from society is blatant and enduring, it seems logical to assume that the most basic thing needed to be learnt is that they still have a role and, therefore, a stake in abiding by the law. Value, ability and uniqueness are all areas in which the production of belief would surely yield an 'at-risk' person's drive to invest in our country's shared values.

This is not to say that the importance of strong foundations within a community are not vital for sustaining a crime-free existence. A secure home makes a person feel like their engagement with their community is voluntary and, on the whole, on their own terms. This means that anxieties around safety, for example, are less likely to culminate in subtle manifestations during social interactions with a person's peers. A reduced feeling of threat and danger will reduce defensiveness and impulsivity which, according to offending behaviour programme literature, contribute to criminogenic attitudes. Employment, although also intrinsically linked to ideas of security, can provide routine and purpose. Structuring a typical day in the absence of criminal activity must be done so with meaningful replacements. Similarly, education has the potential of installing attention and diligence ethics within a person that could transfer in meaningful ways to what their life will look like if they were to remain crime-free. Education also begins to address the connectedness a person must feel with their society, if they are to adhere to and respect its laws.

Education, however, in any old form will not suffice. In fact, reducing education to a means of an 'at-risk' person reaching economic validity may have a diametric effect on whether they feel invested enough in society to honour its values. In environments in which socio-economic deprivation is obvious and 'othering' is widespread, a person may find solace either in working towards social mobility, or rebelling against the involuntary, subordinate role i.e., start offending. Good education, (both in prison and before a person might usually enter prison) ought to be mainly founded on broadening any connective channels a person may have with society. To teach someone the reasons to follow the law is to teach them why it matters, why it is in their best interest and why its respect and complexity is often contested in spite of its value. The intrinsic value in learning must be at the core of how someone moves away from crime.

As a learner in the 'at-risk' category, I must thank those who have taught me new ways of communicating frustrations, anxieties and ideas. To gain confidence in being able to express these complicated concepts in positive and productive ways has almost certainly been the primary contribution to my desisting from crime. The power of understanding the world at a deeper level and coming to understand that my own dysfunctional background is neither completely unique to me nor unsurmountable, means that I now feel less alienated from the society I was once banished from. This has allowed me to empathise both with those who have experienced similarly traumatic formative years and those who had become the targets of my, formerly, unspeakable frustrations. Being able to relay feelings, such as anger and fear, have been almost accidental to studying in Higher Education. I did not begin this journey with a particular vocational aspiration, I wanted to understand the world which had rejected me. And, by doing so, I learned that I could rightfully claim a role within it upon my release.

It is very easy to assume that basic respect for society will flourish when someone has a job or a qualification – or even a house – but unless feelings of disassociation and resentment are addressed these feelings will be cherished by those who have matured in the most impoverished conditions. These pragmatic resources, that are important, will only be received as something compensatory for the unequal access they had previously experienced. They will not change the fundamental attitude of a person teetering on the point of offending.

The final academic point to be made is one which draws out the quality of this type of learning. Using the same premises as those in 'Intergroup Contact Theory[3]' it is not enough to establish opportunities for exposure purely on its own sake. There is a risk of assuming that to know the conditions of connectedness which contribute to an 'offender's' efforts to desist means a model of Offending Behaviour Programme can teach these conditions in an overt way – therefore creating an intervention for those involved with the criminal justice system. Gill Valentine explores this when trying to create community cohesion between different cultural and ethnic groups.[*(ibid)*] If the point of the intervention is so explicitly focused on connection and mutuality, engaged groups tend to remain obstinate to change. Similarly, in a report which evaluates evidence on the effectiveness of 'Reducing Reoffending' strategies states, "A recent UK review of the quality of offender supervision highlighted that accredited [offending behaviour] programmes cannot operate effectively in isolation, without addressing the broader context in which offending takes place and the multiplicity of offenders' needs."[4]

The reasons people become at risk of offending are wide-ranging and complicated. Hopefully, however, this article has managed to highlight something in common with almost all shifts away from the social contract. If one does not feel part of society then it is not a stretch to consider why they fail to respect society. The ultimate lesson for a person considering either a beginning of a criminal lifestyle or a continuation of offending is to understand how they relate to others in their community. Being able to empathise with those who we may harm through illegal activity comes with a more general expansion of understanding around how society is constituted. Coming to know that social deprivation is something that can be survived and diminished feels comforting and hopeful. By showing would-be offenders that their efforts to remain free from crime have *for them* an inherent personal value which allows them to share in the economic and social resources we all need, will be the biggest lesson someone can learn.

MUTUAL LEARNING THROUGH MUSIC AND SONG FOR PRISONERS AND YOUNG DISABLED MUSICIANS:
Orpheus goes to prison

Sir RICHARD STILGOE OBE, DL
Director, Orpheus Trust

There is hardly a human being who hasn't at some time been moved by a song; most of us have a library of songs in our head that we heard, often in our youth, that have cheered us up, given us comfort or simply expressed a feeling we would have found it hard to put into words. Music and songs are in a different part of the brain from speech, and seem to unlock emotions more easily. For many years I have been encouraging young people to write songs, and the results they come out with surprise them. If they are then brave enough to sing the results to an audience, they surprise that audience as well, and I have lost count of the number of times I have heard, "I didn't know he/she could do that" and "I didn't know he/she felt that way".

This has been particularly striking when working with the students at the Orpheus Centre, a residential college where young disabled people preparing for independent living through a variety of life-skills courses, with particular emphasis on the performing arts, which we use as a tool for improving self-confidence and understanding. They have produced work of great passion and insight – as well as humour – and amazed and enlightened many audiences.

A chance meeting with Peter Dawson, then the governor of Highdown prison near Banstead, set me wondering whether we could do this work with prisoners.

And since then we have been regularly taking groups of our students into prisons to work with young offenders and get them to write songs.

The idea is to get the prisoners to let some of their emotions out through song-writing, perform those songs to their fellow prisoners and prison staff, and record the songs so that they can send a CD home to a parent, partner or child as a reminder that they are thinking of them.

On our first visit to Highdown I took with me five disabled students, and two other song-writers; Birgitta Kenyon, who is fearless at working with tricky young people, and Emmanuel Imuere, who is a rap artist and writer. We travelled to the prison in the Orpheus bus every day.

On the Monday we got our first taste of locked gates, jingling keys and a world of concrete and steel gates. After much examining of the underside of the bus, we reached the education block where we would be working. The prisoners were playing a number as we arrived, and there were obviously good musicians among them who were keen to impress. So after being introduced to them (Reuben, John, Ivano, Jonny, Malcolm, Jermaine and Wolfie, and our officers Clive and Sian) I organised a small concert of Orpheus songs to show that we knew what we were doing as well.

Next we had a brainstorm of ideas, and produced the bare bones of two songs.

Each afternoon each tutor held two individual sessions, each with one prisoner and one student, which produced six partly completed songs.

We shared these at the end of the day. By the Thursday we had 11 new songs, which we recorded. Getting each song right for the recording makes them secure for Friday's performance.

On the Friday we moved into the chapel to rehearse. We had to go back to our normal room between 11.30 a.m. and 2 p.m. during Muslim prayers. During this time we sang and played games. The sight of seven hard men singing, 'The Grand Old Duke of York' with ludicrous actions will be with me forever. At two o'clock we moved back into the chapel and were joined by the audience – about 40 other prisoners and twenty guests (relations, staff, supporters). The concert had a varied musical mix, with much innovative genre-mixing – several songs were half-song, half-rap, which was new – and there was some good choral harmony work. In all modesty, the quality of invention and performance was far higher than the audience expected. They cheered at the end, and we handed out Orpheus certificates to everybody. For one prisoner, this was the first paper indication of success he had ever been awarded.

Observations

- Every one of the prisoners had problems with concentration. Lots of good ideas, but getting them organised and finished was hard for them.

- Several prisoners said they had never spoken to a disabled person before. "I avoid them because I wouldn't know what to say. But now if I see one in the queue at the post office I'll go up and have a chat." It will, sadly, be some time before the prisoner in question gets to stand in a queue in the post office.

- I should love to think all prison officers were as enthusiastic and helpful as the two we had with us, who appeared in the choral numbers and sang lustily.

- The Orpheus students made thoughtful comments as we drove into the prison each day. It was sobering for them, and I believe made them feel privileged – privileged to be free, and to be working as enablers. This they certainly did, having more song-writing experience than the prisoners.

- The end of these high-energy weeks is always tricky, but this was especially so. We drove out of the prison, the prisoners went back to the cells with a much duller week ahead of them than the one they had just had.
- You could not have had a more diverse group, mixing abilities, races and genders in real co-operation.

I believe this was a useful week, and not just a diversion. A lot of pain and anger was represented in the songs the prisoners wrote, and this pain and anger might otherwise have been more violently expressed. The prisoners sang their songs with real passion – a passion usually suppressed by their situation. In addition, Stephen and Ed from Orpheus each wrote a song about their impressions of prison from the outside. When each of them first performed these they produced much emotion and many tears from prisoners and officers alike. The bringing together of the two communities was enhancing and educative for both.

A final thought

'There's always somebody worse off than yourself.' Prisoners in general believe they are the worst off of all. For their belief in themselves to rise they need to meet people they think are worse off than them. This is one of the jobs of the Orpheus students – to appear to be worse off than other people, and then inspire them by displaying what they can do. Being apparently at the bottom of the heap can make you the object of derision or bullying, but in my experience the presence of the Orpheus students always brings out the best in others. I do not believe that the prisoners would have behaved so well had we had just the tutors and them. Orpheus is a catalyst for the release of the good in people; I have seen this often enough to be convinced of its truth.

A selection of lyrics written during the week at H.M.P. Highdown

My Little Girl

By Ivano
I have a picture in my mind
Of my little girl, my little girl
I see guys around me fight for no reason
I have a reason not to fight
My little girl, my little girl.

Operap

By Angus Morton and Jonny
I struggle to get through, keep my head low.
You're the one that keeps me going.
Keeps me going.
You left me all alone, you hang up the phone.
I know you feel it's over with me.
Open your eyes and see.
I just fell apart
Please, darling, mend this broken heart.

It's Not What I Expected / Inside

By Steven Rann and Malcolm
We were sitting on a bus on the way to prison,
I as nervous – would I find fear and fighting.
I was trying to keep calm but I was frightened.
It's not what I expected, it took me by surprise.
A gang of friendly faces, right before my eyes.
No need to be nervous – no need to run and hide,
I guess they're just like me – inside.

It's All Right For You

Group work
It's all right for you

Your time is your own
Anytime you like
You can pick up the phone.
It's all right for you
You can sit in the sun
It's all right for you.
It's all right for you
You've got acres of space
Not just four walls
And this God-awful place.
It's all right for you
There's a handle on your door
It's all right for you.

Brand New Eyes

By Ed Percival
Brand new eyes see people for people
Not just men in chains.
You spend an hour with them
And learn to feel their pain.
What do you find when you look behind
Those closed doors.
Humanity
I hope we all can see
With brand new eyes.

I Send You This Song

Group work
I send you this song – it isn't a lot
I did something wrong, so it's all that I've got.
I'll see you again – I hope it's not long
Until then all I have is this song ...
Each of these is on a CD, and played in the homes
the prisoners will eventually return to, as a link and a reminder of a
connection that might otherwise fade.

ART AND CREATIVITY:
'much better than any drug'

KATE DAVEY
Communications and Engagement Officer, National Criminal Justice Arts Alliance

As the national body supporting and promoting arts in criminal justice, we asked our members to contribute to the question: 'what do prisoners and ex-offenders need to learn?' Key ideas from our members included the importance of knowledge and the provision of activities that promote soft skills and aspirations, alongside formal education opportunities. Our members want prisoners to be encouraged to look forward and visualise a future that's realistic, and at the same time, they want prisoners to feel more confident in their skills and abilities. On a more practical level, healthy coping mechanisms and creative and financial skills were seen as important for prisoners to have on their release.

Our 800 plus members practice arts within the criminal justice system in many different ways. They take place in education classes within the prison system, via innovative voluntary sector organisations, and are practiced by individuals with positive results. Arts and creativity in criminal justice settings can support improved well-being, awaken an interest in learning and can help people build new positive identities. Engaging in the arts can also lead to new skills and employment opportunities, as well as equipping participants with a desire to engage actively in their community and culture.

"The purpose of participation in arts, whether by individuals or groups, is that it gives latitude in self-expression, allowing the individual even in a group, to explore themselves, engage positively with others by expressing through the various forms their own ideas without fear of derision or criticism. I have seen many individuals blossom through art, not to become great artists, but to become more fulfilled individuals."
NCJAA survey respondent, 2014

Learning to test and create new identity

Learning about creativity and how to be creative is central to enabling offenders to test new identities in a safe space, giving them the ability to try new choices and make new decisions. There is a clear link between taking part in arts-based activities and entering into a non-offending future, and there is evidence that arts projects can enable individuals to redefine themselves positively, while giving them the opportunity to engage in productive activities and learn to co-operate with others: skills that can all be utilised in their new, non-offending life.[1]

"Creative writing has made me a calmer, more reflective person, whereas before I was more impulsive which is part of the reason I got into trouble in the first place."
NCJAA survey respondent, 2014

Re-discovering self-worth is vital for prisoners when preparing for a new life of desistence, and it is even more vital that this worth is confirmed externally on their return to their local community. In light of this, the arts can give prisoners and ex-prisoners a tool for expressing themselves, something which is powerful when mending damaged relationships, sharing journeys and stories, and creating a new identity. Creative activity can be a socially engaging platform for individuals, helping prisoners form friendships based on something less destructive that drugs, crime and gangs.

"Within writing, I have learnt to express emotion and also feel emotions through poetry. It has helped me express my feelings, and my emotional understanding is better."[2]

Learning to use arts as a way into education

There isn't a right or wrong answer with creativity, something that makes arts activities less daunting for prisoners with a fear of - or reservations about - education or learning. In 2013, the National Criminal Justice Arts Alliance ran a creative writing programme specifically aimed at engaging 'hard-to-reach' offenders with education and arts opportunities during their time in prison. An overwhelming majority of participants said that the workshops helped them to think about themselves differently, and the evaluation shows that creative workshops are a catalyst for change and can offer a pathway into engagement with more formal learning opportunities.[3]

"Since I went to the workshop, I have started a 'moving on' course, voluntarily it's about skills and getting on with life... I'm starting to write short stories and poems. I've never done anything like that before."
Write To Be Heard participant

Dame Sally Coates' review into prison education acknowledges that prisoners often need encouragement and support when initially dipping their toe into the waters of education – and the review goes on to suggest that increased provision of creative arts activities could support prisoners who have had negative experiences of education in their past.[4]

Learning that arts are for everyone

The arts can often be seen by communities and individuals as something that is 'not for them.' This is particularly key for much of the prison population. It's vital that there are no additional barriers within the prison system that prevent people from accessing the arts. This requires prison staff and arts organisations to recognise the culture within prisons and other criminal justice settings and understand the potential barriers. For example, who gets to attend arts workshops or performances? And how can external organisations shape this through building relationships and asking the right questions?

Learning that arts can reduce stigma

Showcasing the impressive work created by prisoners and ex-prisoners has a huge impact on the public's perception of people who have been through the criminal justice system. We have previously conducted surveys amongst the prison population which have highlighted that prisoners agree that works produced in prison should be shared with the public. The strongest reasoning for this is that by showing work to the public, we can alter pre-conceived ideas about prisoners and things like talent, ability, motivation and commitment. Acceptance and celebration of the work produced in the criminal justice system is affirmation for prisoners that they have good in them. Additionally, this point links back to community ties – exhibiting or showcasing work by prisoners in their local communities can create a bond between the prison and the community and encourages acceptance towards people leaving the criminal justice system and returning to their communities.

"It's diverted all my efforts into something that I'm more happy with, and people are certainly more interested in me as a person when they see me play. I've always been one of those people who tried to draw attention to myself with outrageous (criminal) behaviour, but I've realised there are better ways of doing it – which is why I took up art."
NCJAA survey respondent, 2014

Learning that arts can provide meaningful activity

Arts activities take many different forms in prisons. They can be undertaken as part of an organised education class, as part of a one-off session delivered by an external arts organisation, or by prisoners in their own time in their cells. We asked prisoners for their thoughts on the arts in criminal justice settings and had responses from people who noted that the arts – both in cell work and organised classes – had provided them with something to productively fill their time with, and had a positive impact on their mental health.

"The main value for me has been to be able to keep mentally active and to occupy my time constructively. I think this has given me a psychological advantage compared to those unable to fill their time and, therefore, prone to slip into negative patterns of thinking about their situation."
NCJAA survey respondent, 2014

"I put down the bottle and picked up a pen."
Artist at a Women's Centre in Gloucester

"It is a great help for someone like me who has attempted suicide in prison, and I am a self-harmer at times. Art relieves me of a lot of my stress and is also a form of escapism. Much better than any drug."
NCJAA survey respondent, 2014

"I know there are other ways to spend my time instead of drinking and using drugs."
NCJAA survey respondent, 2014

Conclusion

It is not enough to only think about what it is that prisoners need to learn. We need to consider, too, other stakeholders within the criminal justice system. What do prison staff need to learn? What do ministers need to learn? And what do artists need to learn? For us, certainly, a change in attitude towards what the arts are, who they are for, and what they are capable of is an important initial step. Rather than an undeserved indulgence, the arts should be seen as hard work, because amidst all the discipline of learning lines, pitching up to play a role, or rehearsing a score, you have to work with others, build trust, take responsibility, play your part and face your demons. The arts should be an essential part of a whole web of interventions applied in criminal justice settings, because if we overlook it, we do a disservice to people who do – and could – really benefit from the empathy and lasting change that can result from participating in arts projects.

THE BIG ISSUES:
an art gallery working with prisoners

KARA WESCOMBE BLACKMAN
Head of Learning, Watts Gallery

Alongside the 2008 restoration programme for Watts Gallery in Compton, Guildford, Surrey, the Watts Gallery Trust wanted to resurrect the Art for All ethos and heritage of G. F. and Mary Watts. The Watts Gallery director saw an opportunity to bring the Watts' social enterprise and Art for All ethos and vision back to Watts by working with prisons. Prison reform was of interest to G. F. Watts (his painting, The Good Samaritan, is dedicated to Manchester philanthropist and prison reformer Thomas Wright) and Surrey has one of the highest prison populations.

G. F. Watts painted about the great social issues of his time – poverty, equality and justice and Mary was a potter, illustrator, designer and teacher. He and Mary believed that art could transform lives and they set about widening access to seeing art and making it for those who might not otherwise have a chance to do so – especially people whose lives had gone down the wrong track due to unemployment, poverty, mental illness and addictions. In addition to opening up their studios to local people, building a free admission public art gallery and working with others such as the Toynbee project to found galleries on the then outskirts of

London (Whitechapel Art Gallery, South London Gallery), they worked on transformational community public art projects – Postman's Park and Watts Cemetery Chapel. Mary trained out of work local people in pottery. This resulted in the setting up of the Compton Potters' Art Guild, a social enterprise that continued until the 1960s. In their time Watts was the Grayson Perry of the art world – eccentric, multi-talented, controversial and loved and known equally by wealthy cultured circles and local families living in the village that he and his wife came to retire to whilst setting up their creative colony and social enterprise that helped to regenerate the local community.

Our Big Issues programme model is simple: a professional artist brings reproduction images of the Watts' collection of paintings, sculpture, ceramics, decorative arts and uses these to introduce conversations about the themes, about life, creative thinking and technical skills. The participants (we call them artists) make their own art and design which we exhibit annually. They are invited to sell their work if they choose to. Some of the income goes to victim support but the rest they can keep or donate back into the programme – which most of them choose to do voluntarily. The exhibitions have also toured including to the RSA and many of the prisoners' families attend.

Since 2008 we have worked with about 10,000 prisoners. We regularly work with H.M.P. Send, offering a weekly studio led by a professional artist. The professional artist is like an Artist in Residence in the sense that they work, by choice, for a minimum of a year with the women. Some have worked there longer. Sandy Curry was the first artist who really got the group going and stayed for just over five years. In the past month, the women artists at H.M.P. Send have for the first time curated their own exhibition in the prison under the guidance of the current Art Tutor, Sophie Artemis, the Watts Team and the supportive funder of the project, Sally Varah from the Michael Varah Memorial Fund. This is a real first for the country we think and an example of really creative and positive working with the prison governor and authorities.

In addition to H.M.P. Send, we have carried the model into H.M.Y.O.I. Feltham and H.M.P. Bronzefield, and we also worked with H.M.P. Downview. At Feltham, we deliver Arts Awards and work with around 60 different young men over the year. Our work with young offenders is funded for three years until September 2018 and we hope to continue it. All the work made is exhibited at Watts Gallery Artist's Village.

The Watts Gallery Trust Art for All programme seeks to engage people with art who might not otherwise have the opportunity to do so. About 18,000 people participate in our Art for All programme from children to adult learners and in our work with prisons and Surrey Youth Support Service working with young people at risk of offending, we have seen incredible outcomes that have proven that Art can transform lives – reduction in reoffending, improved literacy, re-entry to education, training and employment, reduction in self-harm, improved commitment to rehabilitation and lifelong learning, reduction in depression – more happiness and well-being. The list goes on, but is better said by the participants and partner organisations:

"I gained an insight into how I feel about my life and what gives me strength, hope and optimism. It has helped me to think about the kind of changes I need to make when I go outside of prison... I learnt a lot about my identity and the type of person I'm becoming and who I'd really like to be and the values I'd like to stand for."
Bhavini participant, H.M.P. Bronzefield

"I enjoyed taking part and getting my hands dirty. Working on the art makes me feel relaxed. It helps my mind become more creative. I chose the colours to reflect my heritage which is very important to me; it's good to express it in a non-violent or contentious way."
Tendai participant, H.M.Y.O.I. Feltham

"For any funder to commit finance to a community arts project for more than a three-year cycle, the programme itself must be a true exemplar of best practice. What it delivers must demonstrate a real impact on the lives of those taking part, over a sustained period....When the project takes

place inside one of Her Majesty's Prisons – never the easiest environment in which to operate as an external third party, however much a scheme has the blessing of the incumbent Prison Governor – keeping the flame alight for eight years is nothing short of a miracle."
Sally Varah, The Michael Varah Memorial Fund.

In addition, some of the professional artists working on the programme have responded to working in the prisons through their own work:

"I created a large-scale installation at Watts Gallery that spoke directly about my experience of working with the Watts group at H.M.P. Send. I talked through and shared my ideas with the women along the way and listened carefully to their comments and suggestions, which helped me to conceive the piece and evolve it. Like the women in the group, it was tough to reflect my feelings. The work has a truth within it that I feel couldn't have been able to communicate unless I had witnessed the reality of prison life close-up for a brief moment each week. These women have given me a window into their world and so the piece that I created felt like one of my most powerful works to date."
Mary Branson, Artist in Residence H.M.P. Send, 2014

The programme is by no means simple to run. For a small heritage organisation with a learning team of three people with no prior experience of working with prisons, the prison work alone can take up much of our time not only in the delivery but acting as ambassadors for the participants – sending their work into other exhibitions and competitions and dealing with their collectors! Every year we worry about whether or not we will find artists willing to work in prisons, whether they will be safe, whether we will have enough money to pay the artists and for materials (the participants use a lot of paint!), whether we will meet the expectations of our funders - particularly in the face of reduced prison resource/staff, lock-downs, closures of classrooms/art rooms - and whether we have the adequate expertise and skills to give participants the best and most appropriate experience. Yet, because we are a small team, this gives us the flexibility to be honest about the challenges and face them; to be inventive, responsive and collaborative with prisons and with incredible funding trusts and foundations willing to share expertise of working in criminal justice. From personal experience, the close relationship we share with our partner organisations and funders and our ability to rearrange programmes with short notice is less likely to be feasible in a large museum organisation.

We are keen to share our experiences and learn from others and have initiated a programme of continuing professional development. We plan to focus our next one on Museums and Young Offenders in February 2018 in collaboration with National Criminal Justice Arts Alliance and publish a collection of essays and ideas in a toolkit for other museums and organisations to use.

To celebrate 10 years of the programme, work by 2018 artists will be shown in a large show at Watts next summer. This is the first time we will curate an integrated show where work by prisoners is shown alongside work by other adult learners, young people, children and schools. We feel this is an important step change. The Big Issues project is no longer a project – it's an integrated part of our programme and the artists involved can also make a contribution to society through showing their work, even though they are 'inside'. The Art for All exhibition will coincide with the opening of our historical exhibition, James Henry Pullen, an artist, designer and maker who spent his life in an asylum.

SHAKESPEARE AND WOMEN PRISONERS:
finding a voice

PHYLLIDA LLOYD CBE
Theatre, film and opera director

In 2012 a report was published saying that for every woman working in British theatre there were two men. Two girlfriends of mine, Kate Pakenham and Josie Rourke, had just become the first female heads of the Donmar Warehouse and asked me to suggest a production in their opening season. I proposed an all-female production of *Julius Caesar* with Harriet Walter as Brutus.

I decided to set *Caesar* in a women's prison. I thought it would help the audience and the actors believe the action of the play and in prison uniform they would immediately become androgynous. We went into Holloway - and asked the prisoners what they thought. With their obsession with freedom and justice, their apprehension of danger, their superstitions, they regarded the choice of *Julius Caesar* 'highly suitable'.

The group of actors I brought together at first glance could not have been more unsuitable for their roles. They felt like refugees from our culture, apparently ill equipped to serve up the crown jewels of our dramatic literature. They were the 'others' – outside the mainstream of classical theatre.

We joined forces with Clean Break, a company who work with female ex-offenders, using theatre as a tool for rehabilitation. I cast two of their members, Carrie Rock and Jennifer Joseph. Jen, who had been in prison was to become a core member of the company, helping us to create an authentic prison world and to build up prison characters. Robert Harries the writer came to talk to us and told us that to the conspirators in Julius Caesar's Rome was a prison. We worked on the pressure cooker of fury and fear that a prison can become and we used the uncertainty that attends any event or class or workshop in prison. We found that we could never depend on keeping the space or the people in it for a whole session. People would be whisked away for medication, for meetings with governors, social workers and there were always people clamouring for the space we were occupying.

When we opened, audiences familiar with the plays said they heard the text as never before. It was a like a familiar score being played on unfamiliar instruments. And young people especially began to come forward saying it was changing what they saw as the possibilities for them, not just on stage, but in life itself. By now prison was not just a framing device for our play it had become fundamental to our mission. We felt our prison characters were in fact real people whose stories we were carrying onto the stage. We were bearing witness to their lives. Our mission was not just feminist it became about class, diversity. Who feels voiceless in our society.

We chose a second play, *Henry IV*. It was a play about change. Could a person reform? We went into Askham Grange prison near York and asked the actress playing Prince Hal to stand up and read his famous soliloquy about all his bad behaviour being actually part of a master plan to make him look more impressive when he turns over a new leaf. And one resident put her hand up and said, "Oh, the governor has heard that speech many times in her office." We said, "How?" She said, "Well, we are all claiming we can change aren't we? That we've got it all in hand, and that we'll kick the habit - but can we?" So we said, "OK, you play the governor and come up here and interrupt Hal." And suddenly the speech took flight. After one workshop a woman turned to me and said, "There are people in here who will get out of here sooner because of this." "How could that work?' I said. "Getting out of prison is hard. You have to be able to speak to the Parole Board. Some of these women came here not able to speak. Now they've found a voice. They know what it's like to have Shakespeare's great words in their mouths."

Every Tuesday night (thanks to a brave governor and passionate staff) we had an audio phone link from our London rehearsal room to the prison drama group in Yorkshire. We would read a scene and say, "What's going on here?" And they would say, "Well, the Earl of Northumberland feels guilty. He's converting his guilt into rage and violence. That's what happens." We were learning from them and they felt their voices were being heard. When we came back from New York we were able to tell them, "You know that gag we tried with you that day, that idea you had? It went down a storm in Brooklyn."

To find a third play to set in a prison was not hard though it was not one I had ever thought to direct. We had been to visit the prisoner on whom Harriet Walter had based her character, Judy Clark in prison in upstate New York. Arrested for her part as the getaway driver in a robbery in which three people had been killed she was now 33 years into her 75-year sentence. She had spent two years in solitary confinement and decades pursuing deep study of religion and philosophy. We realized we were sitting across the table from Prospero in *The Tempest*. Judy made us realise that being thrown into prison is a tempest. That prison is an island and you feel you've been shipwrecked on it. You've lost your friends and family and the isle feels indeed 'full of noises'. You've nothing left but your troubled dreams. You spend the time in the world of your imagination.

From these women, so apparently powerless, we had learnt so much because they had lived literally Shakespearean lives. Loss, abandonment, betrayal, murder, loyalty and honour; goodness they knew honour because when you've lost everything else that is all you have left. When we first went into Holloway prison we had felt physically afraid of these women who we quickly found were very similar to us. But for a stable childhood and good luck we might have been here too. They reminded us that it was too easy to make assumptions about people and their potential. Just because you looked or sounded one way it didn't mean you should be automatically excluded from the centre of things.

Since we began the project there had been great changes in the world. Everywhere there was talk of the threat from 'others' from outsiders (or as Shakespeare would call them 'strangers') on our shores, in Europe and across the Atlantic. We had voted to leave the Europe Union and the U.S. had elected a President proposing to build a wall to keep out the 'others'. Division seemed everywhere. Yet our journey had been an opposite one. Thanks to the genius of Shakespeare and our prison communities we had come to feel not less connected to others but more, so much more. Not more afraid of strangers of 'others' but less, much, much less. We had stopped striving so hard to define the differences between us and come to appreciate our common humanity. As Harriet said when playing Prospero, I felt neither a man nor a woman, just a human.

'Inside':
invitation to submit artwork for the Koestler Awards

Sir ANTONY GORMLEY OBE
Sculptor

*A*ntony Gormley wrote this invitation to people in prisons and secure
establishments to make art on the theme of 'Inside'. A small selection
*of these works, subsequently made and exhibited at the Southbank in
London is reproduced in this publication courtesy of the Koestler Trust.*

I want to celebrate this great resource: the imaginations of the 85,000
prisoners currently in UK prisons and those in secure establishments. Art
is a place in which you can do what you like; it need not be for or about
anyone else but the artist. In the words of a prisoner, 'in our minds we can
always be free'.

The future has always evolved from exploration. Firstly, by those who
discovered the remote parts of this planet, then by astronauts who
explored the moon and the possibility of human life migrating to other
planets. This looks unlikely, so perhaps the 'psychonaut' – or explorer of
the mind – is the explorer of the 21st century.

This show gives you the opportunity to communicate passionately
expressed inner truth with the outside world.

Please contribute to the exhibition 'INSIDE' and share the thoughts and feelings you have buried deep inside. I am not so interested in works of high technical ability but in the truth you find when you look inwards.

The works can be about your situation now, a cherished dream or a terrible nightmare. Dark or bright, hopeful or despairing, strong or fragile, large or small and in any medium – from a small piece of paper to a sound work, from drawing to model making, film to calligraphic poetry – please help make this exhibition a bold testament to what is happening inside of you.

Play Time (drawing), Camden and Islington Probation

Authentic HMP Collage Greetings Cards (handmade greeting card), Camden and Islington Probation

First Light in February (watercolour and gouache), H.M.P. Channings Wood

Cornflower Blue (needlecraft), H.M.P. Leyhill

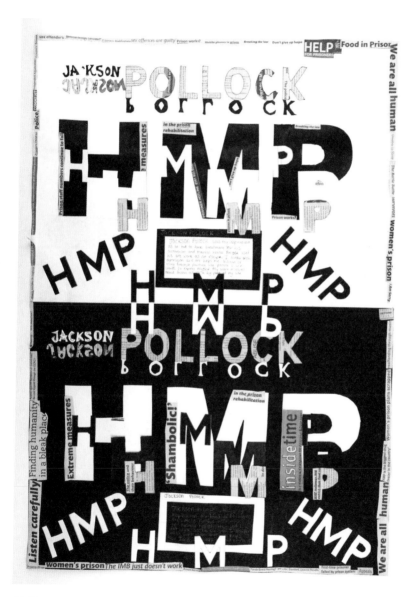

It's Transparent in Black and White (mixed media),
H.M.P. and Y.O.I. Styal (women's establishment)

Trapped ...Inside (mixed media), H.M.P. Peterborough

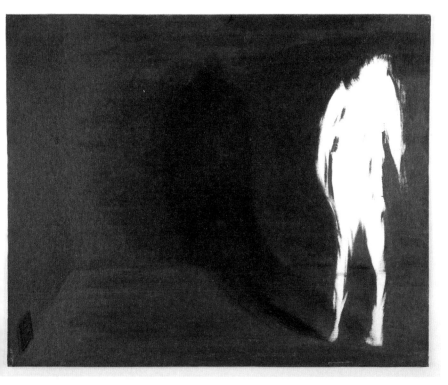

The Dream Door is Too Small (painting), Katherine Price Hughes House

PART THREE
RETURNING TO THE COMMUNITY

Overcoming trauma, building emotional resilience

ELAINE KNIBBS
RISE prison team leader

MOLLY WRIGHT
RISE prison team member

Something is clearly wrong with our prison system. Ministry of Justice figures show there were 119 self-inflicted deaths in prisons in 2016, the highest number since 1978. In the same period, there were 37,784 incidents of self-harm and 25,049 incidents of assaults on both staff and other prisoners. According to the chief executive of the Howard League for Penal Reform, suicide rates in prisons are 10 times that of those among non-offending community populations. Add to this a first-year reoffending rate of 44.7 per cent for adult and 37.9 per cent of juvenile offenders released from custody and this assertion becomes compelling (MoJ, 2017). So what are the factors driving this situation? For many prisoners and ex-offenders, addressing incidents of trauma in their past and learning to develop greater emotional resilience in the present may need to happen before they can be expected to build a positive future for themselves. I will therefore discuss research around trauma and emotional resilience within the criminal justice system, and RISE's mission to deliver specialist, innovative trauma-centered offender rehabilitation services. This will include looking at the work we are doing at H.M.P. High Down, and in connection with the Mayor of London's 'Gripping the Offender' scheme.

The word 'trauma' is derived from the Greek word for 'wound'. It is a phenomenon which requires both a particular kind of event and a particular kind of reaction to that event. It defies simple definition: trauma can result from a single, shocking event, or multiple, repeated and/or extremely frightening experiences that have had a lasting adverse effect on an individual's functioning and well-being, (Beyond Youth Custody, 2014).

There is evidence to suggest that offenders have a disproportionate amount of childhood and adolescent trauma in their background. This includes abuse, neglect, bullying, domestic violence, abandonment, bereavement, and witnessing violence (Beyond Youth Custody, 2014). Of those offenders committing the most serious offences under 18 years old, 72 per cent had experienced some form of abuse as children and 57 per cent had experienced traumatic loss (Boswell, 1996). The link between traumatic experience and criminal behaviour is clear, well-established and much researched (Ardino, 2011; Foy, Furrow and McManus, 2011).

Organisations that work with offenders are confronted by the signs and symptoms of trauma every day and yet often fail to see it or make necessary connections (McGlue, 2016). Within such services, many behaviours that are indicative of unresolved trauma such as poor emotional management and affect regulation, self-harm, substance misuse and impulsive aggression, may be disregarded and viewed as just anti-social behaviour, attention-seeking, or non-compliance. This is exacerbated by the fact that trauma precludes engagement in offence-related programmes and is associated with treatment non-compliance. Trauma is therefore a clear responsivity barrier (Benedict, n.d., Miller and Najavits, 2012) and it is unsurprising that offenders with unresolved trauma are referred to as being the 'revolving door', given their high propensity for returning into the criminal justice system (Clark *et al*, 2014).

Additionally, traumatic experiences that offenders bring into the custodial setting remain unaddressed and unresolved. The custodial environment itself can exacerbate underlying traumatic symptomatology and many routine occurrences can serve as triggers for trauma survivors, including control and restraint techniques and body searches. Prisoners may also experience repeat traumatisation through being victimised, witnessing violence and peer suicide attempts to name but a few.

Across social systems, the term 'trauma-informed' is trending (Becker-Blease, 2017) and care professionals consider being 'trauma-informed' a new touchstone in the advancement of understanding people with complex needs. RISE is placing itself at the forefront of this by establishing itself as a leading provider of trauma-informed interventions and services within the criminal justice sector. Youths involved with the juvenile justice system represent one of the most complexly and pervasively traumatized populations (Abram *et al*, 2003). This is why RISE is delivering trauma-based interventions as part of the Mayor of London's pilot initiative 'Gripping the Offender' (GTO): an enhanced whole system response to those young adult offenders causing the most harm to communities and the greatest demand on the broader criminal justice system. We also work with H.M.P. High Down, delivering both the T.I.G.E.R (Transforming Inside Growing Emotional Resilience) programme and the R.E.A.D.Y (Resilience, Engaging, Awareness, Decisions & You) programme. R.E.A.D.Y is a two-day personal development and self-enhancement programme that helps offenders reflect upon their lives and build emotional resilience to leave low self-esteem behind and move towards a positive future.

The heart of RISE's trauma-informed approach is the T.I.G.E.R programme: an intervention for offenders aged 18 and over who continue to experience the legacy of trauma as a barrier to moving forwards. The T.I.G.E.R programme offers offenders an opportunity to explore this aspect of their past and subsequently benefit from the development of greater emotional resilience. The programme uses an eclectic therapeutic model, with Solution Focused Brief Therapy techniques supported by Jungian ideas of creative therapy, image making and symbols. It also draws upon Cognitive Behavioural Therapy (CBT) techniques.

The use of an eclectic model ensures that the T.I.G.E.R programme can be customised to meet the unique needs of each offender. Additionally the use of creative therapy enables facilitators/therapists to be responsive to offender needs by employing a range of verbal and non-verbal activities as a means of exploring feelings and deciding on goals related to addressing the trauma. Creative therapy strives to incorporate the social, emotional, cognitive and spiritual aspects of the person.

The T.I.G.E.R programme has four key objectives: (1) To provide participants with the opportunity to acknowledge the legacy of their trauma in a safe environment and receive peer support; (2) To provide participants with an opportunity to identify helpful and unhelpful coping or survival strategies; (3) To provide participants with an opportunity to identify possible future alternative survival skills and the resources needed to develop greater emotional resilience; and (4) To raise individual motivation levels to participate in other regime opportunities relating to criminogenic and non-criminogenic needs.

While implementation of the T.I.G.E.R programme is in its infancy, early work taken place indicates promising outcomes for offenders who engage in the programme. However, one of the key challenges for staff delivering trauma specific interventions which are relatively short in length, is working in a way which achieves the right balance between promoting an offender's psychological growth and their safety. Traumatised offenders will feel safe in an environment which feels protected from further trauma or from people or situations which trigger traumatic memories. An over-emphasis on developing psychological growth may lead to interventions that are delivered in a too intense or fast-paced way. The effect of this may be recognised in an offender's resistance to engagement in the intervention. Of greater concern however, is the risk that challenges designed to promote psychological growth, may instead recreate initial trauma and a subsequent diminishing of the offenders ability to cope (Wright, S. and Liddle, M. (2014).

Case study

One offender who positively benefited from a trauma-based intervention was Jane, who took part in an early previous version of the T.I.G.E.R programme within a women's prison. Jane, had been in and out of prison most of her adult life. Within the prison she often displayed confrontational and challenging behaviour; outside of prison she was a sex worker and had multiple addictions and problems. At the time Jane joined the group she was self-harming and was extremely low and depressed. Although she put herself forward for the group she was hesitant about how it could help her and very nervous about expectations, and what may be discussed. The programme is set up in a way to make everyone feel relaxed and calm. A lot of work is done on the first day to create a safe environment - a mentally and physically comfortable space.

During the second day of the programme we considered personal journeys and personal experiences. Jane told her story, revealing that from eight years old she was subject to horrific abuse and neglect. She described strangers coming to the house to sexually abuse her, and the betrayal and confusion she felt as a result of realising it was orchestrated by her parents. She described being given drugs including crack cocaine to pacify her so she would be more complicit in the abuse, and how, as she went from childhood into adulthood, her reliance on drugs and alcohol to numb her feelings and deal with the difficulties in her life led to addictions, sex work and crime. Jane sat in the group room and spoke for the first time in her life about her memories and her trauma; she always thought blocking it and pushing it from her consciousness would help her cope, when in reality it was not allowing her to move on.

Jane said she had never spoken about this before as she felt shame and guilt, labelled as a drug user, sex worker and criminal she had such low self-esteem because of the abuse and neglect she suffered as a child.

Talking in the group was the first time in her life she felt able to sit with people who weren't judging her, and she was finally able to recognise that not only was it not her fault but that she can have some control over her life and she didn't need to supress the memories to survive.

Jane transitioned from this quite aggressive, challenging prisoner and by the end of the third day she had set herself goals, thought about her future, and she was able to self-reflect on her behaviour, exploring where her aggression was stemming from. After completing the programme she grew in confidence, engaged with courses in prison and started basic numeracy and literacy skills courses, as well as engaging with support workers and the sex work team.

Jane's story is just one of many personal stories heard in custody which focus on past experiences of abuse, neglect, self-harm and domestic violence. It is a reminder that while past experiences of trauma amongst offenders are difficult to escape, given the right focus, intensive targeting of issues, as seen in interventions like T.I.G.E.R, even the most trauma affected lives can be transformed.

———————

Research clearly highlights the widespread and disproportionately high experience of past trauma among the offending population. These experiences have been shown not only to create ongoing suffering for offenders but also increase their propensity for offending. To date criminal justice agencies have generally failed to identify and respond to offender experiences of trauma in a way that meaningfully addresses the issue. It is the firmly held contention among those working at RISE, that the issue of trauma must be a regular consideration in the provision of services for offenders.

Learning about their own experiences of trauma, the way in which it has shaped their lives and the means of extricating themselves from its effects will not only empower offenders, but also create a foundation on which they are able to make an increasingly positive contribution to society.

THE VOLUNTARY SECTOR APPROACH:
we always have something to learn

NATHAN DICK
Head of Policy and Communications, Clinks

I f there was one thing that Clinks would recommend we teach people in the justice system it would be that support is out there. It is difficult to make sure people know where services are available in the community, or in a police cell, or in the court room, in a prison, or if you are a worried family member at home. How would you know where the services are and who has the right support for you? There are services available and many are well known, but there is more we can do to integrate services and make it more commonplace that our public sector partners work alongside voluntary organisations to make sure people have easy access to (and knowledge of) the type of support they might need. That way we can make sure that people know where the services are and how they could help.

The other thing that 'offenders and ex-offenders' need to learn is that this label of offender that our system so readily applies is not a permanent one, and neither is it a useful one. The only people for whom the term '(ex) offender' is useful to are policy makers who want to encapsulate complex human beings in a single word, or perhaps people who do want to stigmatise, discriminate against or demonise people who have at one time broken the law and been caught. The term dehumanises people who pass through our criminal justice system, and those that are labelled as an offender or ex-offender need to learn that this does not define them and it never should.

Learning from people with lived experience

Voluntary organisations are saying we have as much, if not more, to learn from people with lived experience of the criminal justice system than we have to teach them. This is an exciting approach and I think we should embrace it. Asking people caught up in the criminal justice system what *they* want gives voluntary organisations delivering support a head start. Forward-thinking voluntary organisations are closer to finding solutions to crime and reoffending because they have refused to see people as (ex) offenders and have instead viewed them as individuals with hopes and aspirations, as well as needs. They have recognised that people in our criminal justice system are experts, and this logic extends to their families and the communities within which they live. This doesn't mean to say they can replace trained professionals, who can and do support people in a range of ways, but they can challenge existing practice and policy.

Our police, courts, prison and probation services are starting to embrace the idea of involving people with lived experience, and good practice examples are becoming far more common.[1] Those working in criminal justice settings are often far too hesitant (or unwilling) to listen and learn from those with direct experience of the system. This hesitancy also, inadvertently, shuts out a vast amount of experience from within voluntary organisations (both small and large) because they are all too often viewed as well-meaning amateurs rather than seasoned experts.

In 2016 Clinks' surveyed voluntary organisations in the criminal justice system (our *State of the Sector* reports) and asked to what extent they involve their clients in the design and delivery of services.[2] Over a third reported that they had consulted people on the design of services, a similar number had recruited service users as staff or volunteers, just over 20 per cent had a service user council or forum, and just nine per cent had recruited service users as trustees. This looks unimpressive, but in 2017 our survey saw a remarkable change. 80 per cent had consulted service users about the design and delivery of their services, 58 per cent recruited service users as staff and/or volunteers, 41 per cent have a service user forum or council, and 20 per cent had recruited service users as trustees. I believe this upsurge in service user involvement reflects a change in the way the voluntary organisations are approaching their work.

Clinks' state of the sector research also found that service user need is becoming more complex and more immediate – people are increasingly arriving at the office door in crisis, or not accessing services at all. They are also in need of different types of support to tackle various issues, with no one service being able to provide all the necessary support. Furthermore people in the system are experiencing difficulties accessing services and struggling to fit into state support services with increasingly narrow criteria and high thresholds for support. So what's the solution? One approach has been to move away from a service that does things to people, to one that asks people what they want to do. A service that moves away from simply assessing needs to one that also thinks about aspirations. A service that can see someone's life as a journey, not simply a series of interventions and risk factors.

"I didn't choose to wake up on a morning, right, and think 'I'm going to fuck me whole life up here'. I'm going to continue doing this until I am dead. I did not make a conscious decision to do that… you don't wake up on a morning right, 'I'm gonna be a heroin addict, I'm gonna be a crack head, I'm gonna become an alcoholic'. You don't do it. Anyone in their right mind wouldn't do it just like millions of people in their right mind don't do it."
MEAM solutions from the frontline participant

The quote above is taken from the Making Every Adult Matter (MEAM) Coalition's 'solutions from the frontline' report[3]. They reached out to people with 'multiple needs' to inform policy, getting ideas and opinions from people who have been through it. When I say 'multiple needs' I mean people who are experiencing a multitude of complex issues, such as contact with the criminal justice system, homelessness, drug and alcohol misuse, and mental ill-health. MEAM's work is comparable to the Big Lottery Fund's 'fulfilling lives' project which has funded eight local partnerships to work with people who have complex needs and improve their access to services. The Fulfilling Lives projects and the 'MEAM Approach' areas have been pioneering new ways to embed service user involvement by employing people with lived experience, developing forums to gather their views, getting commissioners to hear their views, and challenging local services to do things differently by offering service users more voice and influence. This sort of work has many advocates, such as Revolving Doors Agency[4], Agenda[5], and foundations such as Lankelly Chase[6] and Calouste Gulbenkian[7]. The desire to do things differently and the approach voluntary organisations are taking in these examples feels more like a movement than just another service.

People with lived experience learning from each other

"Those people that are in, or still around the madness, if they've got someone who's been there, seen it, done it, I've even used with them, they can trust them, d'you know what I mean? That element of 'right, what are they out for here?' is taken away, the person can relax and tell an honest story because I know myself, when I was in there, I was bullshitting."
MEAM solutions from the frontline participant

Peer support is one of the ways that voluntary organisations have challenged the idea that people in the system are always the recipients of pre-defined services. The voluntary sector is over-flowing with examples. The Samaritans[8] in prisons across England and Wales recruit and train prisoners as 'listeners', allowing them to support the emotional wellbeing of people inside. User Voice have established service user-led councils in prison and probation settings so they can directly influence how those services run.[9] The Shannon Trust's reading plan has trained up prisoners as mentors to help other prisoners that can't read[10]. St Giles Trust have provided prisoners with a level 3 certificate in advice and guidance so they can support people into more stable accommodation.[11] Clean Break

Theatre Company involve women in the justice system as writers and actors in plays that challenge public opinion and portray real life stories in a way that's accessible and incredibly moving.[12]

"The Listener scheme was viewed with suspicion by prisoners and prison staff at first, because it was something new and there was an uneasiness about that. You need to build trust in that environment... In the early days, prison staff didn't really understand how the scheme worked and if someone was kicking off, they would just open up the door and throw me in to try to diffuse the situation. I found that prisoners responded to me because I'm just like them. ...When you first come into prison you feel worthless but becoming a Listener helps you feel as if you are giving something back. It gives you some dignity again."
Lynn, 47, a Listener for 22 years[13]

It is no accident that the voluntary sector has pioneered these approaches. They are seen as 'risky' by a system that constantly assesses people's likelihood of reoffending or whether they might harm the public. We accept that prison and probation services need to assess these risks, it is logical and necessary, but they should not override our ability to understand someone's assets, aspirations or their needs and circumstances. At the moment consideration of risk tend to override our ability, as a whole system, to understand someone as an individual. Risk assessments drive the system, and that's why many parts of the criminal justice system don't ask themselves, what can I learn from those at risk of offending, prisoners and ex-offenders? Instead they continue to wonder what we need to do to people to stop them from reoffending.

"I think they have to step out of their comfort zone and start doing things that feel uncomfortable. They have to. It's going to feel uncomfortable for them to do this because it's all new and different, but they've got to feel uncomfortable."
MEAM solutions from the frontline participant

We often feel uncomfortable in our professional lives when we are being challenged. Yet sometimes we exist in an echo chamber within our own organisations, or even within our sector. Genuine service user involvement should be uncomfortable, and this discomfort needs to extend from our services to our funders, commissioners, and policy makers. The trend is heading in the right direction but it will not naturally occur without champions who are pushing for change.

Learning from the voluntary sector's experience

Voluntary organisations have shown time and time again that they are change makers. We need only to look at the increasing recognition of the need for women-only services, or the now accepted need to work with the children and families of prisoners, the growing recognition that young adults (18-25 years old) have distinct needs, how we need to change our approach to an ageing prison population, or that racism and discrimination against black, Asian and minority ethnic communities exists in our criminal justice system today.

The reason why voluntary organisations are at the forefront of these reforms in the justice system is because they have listened and learned from the people in the criminal justice system. RECOOP have developed services for older people by working alongside them and asking what is needed[14]. The Transitions to Adulthood Alliance have piloted services, researched the issues and engaged directly with young adults to look for solutions[15]. The Young Review talked to young black men and young Muslim men to understand how the criminal justice system needs to change if we're to address their needs[16]. These are just a handful of examples of where the voluntary sector is leading the way.

Learning that life is not binary

When it comes to the care and rehabilitation of 'offenders' the mind-set of the system has often been to 'do-unto'. That approach arises from the assumption that 'we', or the systems in play, have the answers. As a consequence the criminal justice system offers processes for people to follow, assessments that need doing, ways to manage risk or harm, accredited programmes, and measures to see whether or not the service providers did what they were supposed to. The voluntary sector is inevitably part of this system, but it is also a disruptor, an agitator and an interrogator.

The voluntary sector has often been naturally inclined to put into practice what has now been coined as 'desistance theory'.[17] In practical terms this means talking to a person and understanding what they need - in the round - whether they are willing to make changes, what they aspire to be, what matters to them, and how a service might be able to help. It recommends that we orbit the service around the individual, rather than trying to fit them into a pre-defined or prescribed service.

To put desistance theory into practice voluntary organisations have had to learn how to co-produce support packages alongside their service users. This challenges us to see the person as a whole and to understand their situation more fully.

A stumbling block to this approach is the fact that commissioners of criminal justice services continue to base success on a binary measure of whether or not someone reoffends (or rather whether or not they are convicted of a further offence). Sometimes it will also consider whether someone got a job or got accommodation. But these are rarely useful measures of someone's success or failure to change their life, those changes are far more nuanced and take often take a long time to be realised. You can have a job and a place to sleep but have not tackled underlying mental health issues that also lead to problematic drug use. You may have ticked a box and services might have 'succeeded', but do they know whether that person is well enough to prevent future reoffending – or whether they are ready to change their life? The answer is: probably not.

The take-away lesson from this is that no one service will ever be able to fulfil the complex needs of people walking through the door. Better collaboration is probably the answer, and this means that service providers, commissioners and policy makers all need to work better together. We have to acknowledge that collaboration is by no means simple, straightforward, or resource neutral. Even so it is worth seeing how we can change the systems that have developed so they no longer revolve around the needs of different organisations and sectors, but rather that we all fit around the service user and their aspirations, hopes and needs. Once again, it's most likely that people with direct experience of how the system works (or doesn't) that will be able to advise us on a new blueprint.

I AM NOT YOUR LABEL

PENELOPE GIBBS
Director, Transform Justice

Prisoners and ex-offenders don't need to learn anything except that they are not a label. As they themselves know, they are people who have been in prison, or people who have been in trouble with the law, not prisoners and ex-offenders. The more society labels people who commit crime as bad people who have chosen to do wrong, the more difficult it will become for those individuals to rebuild their lives.

No-one wants to see themselves as a criminal, but our whole approach encourages those who commit crime to take on a criminal identity. Most crime is committed spontaneously with little, if any, planning. There is no excuse for crime, but many who commit it are socially excluded, addicted to drugs, poor, have mental health problems, have no formal education or any combination of these. They do not set out to be criminals and may commit many crimes, not because they have embarked on a life of crime, but because they can't see an alternative. Again I am not excusing any crime, however 'minor'.

By labelling people as prisoners, offenders and ex-offenders we distance ourselves from them and imply that is all they are. Unfortunately our whole criminal system is based on the idea that people commit crime deliberately. And, having committed a crime, are at risk of committing another one for ever more.

Look at our criminal records system: it decrees that if you were convicted of shop-lifting twice aged twelve, you need to declare those crimes when you apply for a job as a teaching assistant or a traffic warden aged 52. No matter if you have led an upstanding life for forty years. You are labelled a potential offender because you went a little off the rails before you even hit your teens. You may get the job as traffic warden, but you have to suffer the humiliation of declaring something which has no relevance to your current life while research shows that those who are convicted of crimes are more likely to commit another one, this is only true for the years immediately after conviction and, even then, may be because we make it hard for people to rebuild their lives.

Look at the way we name and shame children for their crimes. Children are immature. They have every chance of rebuilding their lives, if given a chance. But our courts can and do name children in trouble with the law – whether for anti-social behaviour or for serious crimes. Once a child has been named they are vilified in the press and on social media. And that hatred stays on the internet forever. A child who had been imprisoned googled himself: "I read all the reports and that. I scrolled down to see people commenting – one of them said "monkey see, monkey do". If we publicly label children as evil monsters, we risk making it impossible for them for rebuild their lives and identities. Mary Bell, who killed two children when she was 10 and 11 was named when convicted, but given a new identity later. She has gone on to lead a law abiding life under a new name, and to have both a child and a grandchild.

Naming and shaming is done to punish and deter. Our system of sentencing is based on the idea that people make a rational choice to commit a crime, so we need to use ever harsher punishment as a deterrent. There are a few people, such as those who commit internet fraud, or big-time drug barons, who plan crime and might be put off by the prospect of a long spell in prison. But most of those who commit minor crime don't think about the consequences. Once they are serving a community sentence, or on parole, they know they may be imprisoned if they don't turn up for appointments. But they often lead chaotic lives and just forget. I would rather people serving sentences complied with their orders, but I don't view non-compliance as defiance, as courts often do.

Most people who commit crime do not see themselves as criminals or offenders and don't want to. Anyone who has committed a crime needs to understand the harm caused by their action, even if it was unintended. But then be allowed to move on, and be seen as themselves, not an ex-offender.

I have never been convicted of a crime, so can't speak for those who have, but there are glimmers of hope for believers in rehabilitation. There are employers who don't see those in prison as prisoners. We could all help through never talking about prisoners, offenders, criminals or ex-offenders. I find the term 'people with convictions' a bit clumsy, but there are lots of alternatives – people who have been in trouble with the law, people who have been convicted, people who have committed a crime. Language matters and labels are currently a millstone round the neck over those who want to turn their lives around.

LEARNING TO LIVE INSIDE AND OUTSIDE

GORDON
Koestler Trust Award Winner; Founder of 'Banged Up',
H.M.P. Guernsey's first-ever magazine

I will break this down into two main areas: learning to live in prison and learning to live outside of prison. I learnt a lot about myself while serving 18 months of my three year sentence. My learning experience was a mixture of pain and pleasure. And some stuff in-between. I guess all of my experiences inside prepared me to some extent for living crime-free on my release.

The first thing I did to enable me to use my time positively was to get clean and sober. I needed the rock bottom of being ill and going to jail again. I needed the pain of physical and mental withdrawals. Then I needed the 12-step meetings to help me recover. This was not the easy option. I could have easily carried on using drink and drugs. The 'sentence buster' as my mates call it. However, I wanted change, and real change does not come quickly or easily. I had to put time and effort in.

I participated on some good courses. 'The Decider' is one. Tag-line, 'For living a more skilful, less impulsive life'. This is a powerful CBT/DBT informed resource. (Writing this has motivated me to revisit some of the coursework, so that's all good!) Having encouragement from members of staff was immeasurably helpful. Some prison officers, my probation officer, a psychotherapist and the prison chaplain in particular. Of the 150 books I read in prison (I listed each one), 35 were self-help books, 20 biographies, 17 history and the rest non-fiction. I got a job in the prison library which suited me. I went to the gym as often as possible. I was given help but it seemed that it was down to me to put the effort in.

Not much was ever really said about how I was going to avoid reoffending upon my release. On 'The Decider' course we acted out some scenarios which we felt could be challenging on release and attempted to use new skills to deal with the situation better. I got some benefit from this by looking at ways to repair my relationship with my children.

I remember early on my prison probation officer asked me to talk her through the reasons I had ended up in jail. I said I didn't know what to say. She said, "just be honest!" I took her advice. Best advice ever. I wish I could be so positive about my experience with probation whilst on licence. I had five different probation officers over 18 months. All but the first one seemed to be over-worked. Because I attend 12-step meetings every week I think they just let me get on with it. Which is kind of OK. But when I asked for some help e.g. with accommodation, none was forthcoming.

I have been out of jail for over a year. I am still clean and sober. I have a full-time job. I feel great that my employer trusts me. My friends and I often say that to get into and stay in recovery from addiction a person only needs to change two things. Everything he/she thinks and everything he/she does. This also applies to staying away from reoffending.

On getting out of jail I started rebuilding my life on solid ground. I started to learn while in jail how to maintain high hopes and low expectations. Soon after my release I started voluntary work with an organisation that works with ex-offenders. That lead to an interview for a full-time post which went well and I was given the job. Brilliant! I was so pleased. Six weeks later they sacked me on the basis that they had not fully understood the criminal convictions which I had fully disclosed. I was disappointed. And that was with an organisation that claimed to want to help ex-offenders! I feel they handled the situation clumsily. I got over it.

One day a very helpful man at the local job centre put me onto an organization called Blue Sky. They help ex-offenders find work. I put in a CV online and forgot about it. A few weeks later they called me and said could I start on Monday! I worked with them in commercial gardening for ten months. It was hard work and low paid but the routine was good for me. And it kept me busy. Myself and five others who were also on probation, started together at that job. A few months later I was the only one of us still there. I think three of those lads relapsed on drugs and the other two didn't like getting up early. I left the job after eight long months and took a few weeks off before looking for another job.

One day a mate of mine who is also in recovery said that the company he worked for needed workers. I had to go through a recruitment agency first. I had to disclose my convictions and the woman who interviewed me was very relaxed about it. I started the job two days later and I am still there. People at work have been very friendly. I am a trusted employee which feels great. I drive the company vans and I am given company credit cards to buy goods with. That level of trust has really moved me.

I say the serenity prayer every day. It helps. I don't always think or say the right things but what matters is that I try always to do the right thing regardless to how I am thinking or feeling.

Race against crime, crime against race

GERARD LEMOS CMG
Partner, Lemos&Crane

M illions of people arrived from the Caribbean and the Indian sub-continent from the late 1950s onwards, some of them via east Africa. Though they had marked cultural differences with each other as much as with the longstanding denizens of the British Isles, all had a sense of historical belonging in Britain, even if it was an unfamiliar place. They felt entitled as well as grateful to be in Britain. The society in which they arrived also felt some obligations towards them. They were welcome as citizens of the empire, carrying the freight of more than a century of international traditions. Just as the influence of Africa can be heard in Bob Marley's bass line, the harmonies of Anglican Church choirs come through in the Wailers' songs. An integrationist consensus towards the new arrivals was promulgated by all parts of the establishment, although many simultaneously failed to conceal their racist attitudes about these citizens of empire.

Diversity soon made its presence felt in the world of law and order. Perhaps reflecting an underlying ambivalence beneath the public consensus, almost from the beginning of large-scale immigration black and minority ethnic people found themselves disproportionately on the wrong side of the law. Alongside a growing black consciousness which stressed pride over deference, the harsher depredations of racism in the criminal justice system provoked a sustained reactive outcry against police harassment, unfair and discriminatory sentencing, deaths in prison and a discernible reluctance on the part of the authorities to deal with growing evidence of racially motivated hate crimes, most memorably following the racist murder of Stephen Lawrence in 1993. Prisons still contain a disproportionate number of black and minority ethnic people and racial tensions within the prison population notably surfaced in the events surrounding the death of Zahid Mubarek, who was murdered by his racist cell mate in Feltham Young Offenders' Institution in March 2000.[1]

A new and different form of immigration and diversity was to emerge in Britain in the 1990s. Many people, mostly white, came from former Warsaw Pact countries newly acceded to the European Union, seeking work and betterment. Before the locals' very eyes, towns and cities all over the U.K. were transformed into polyglot communities where hybrid cultural forms flowered even more rapidly than reggae and Tamla Motown had before them. Resistance soon sprang up in the forms of protests about these large groups of immigrants – but all too late. Accession to the European Union had come with the promise of free movement. These new arrivals also cast a shadow into criminal justice and prisons. The European arrest warrant means that offenders convicted of crimes in other European Union countries can be picked up in the U.K. and imprisoned here while awaiting extradition. One prisoner I met told me he had been told he was to be sent back to Poland a few days later. He was dreading it. "You're banged up for 23 hours a day. You've got six or twelve men in every cell."

Diversity in modern society never stands still. Attention has also turned to Muslim communities in Britain since the rise of radical Islam, said to be borne in part by Western and British foreign policy in the years after 2001, and its arrival in the U.K. in the form of terrorist attacks in London in 2007, in Manchester and again in London in 2017. This has inevitably led successive governments and the criminal justice authorities to create new terror-related offences for what are undoubtedly new forms of attack, including the willingness among some attackers to accept that their own death will result from their actions. One of the consequences is that the prison population of Muslim heritage has grown. In the ironic hall of mirrors that is post-modernity the rise in the number of Muslim people being imprisoned has also increased official concern about the possibility that prison, instead of being a corrective, may be a place of radicalisation for some. And, in the predictable and depressing interdependencies of cause and consequence that race in Britain sometimes seem, public debate about terror, some of it irresponsible, appears also to have sparked a rise of intolerance and hate crimes towards Muslim communities in the U.K., most vividly expressed in the attack on worshippers outside the mosque in Finsbury Park in June 2017.

The great and unabated surge in post-1960s youth culture aided and abetted by the shocks and energies of cultural diversity has created an individualised and expressive culture distant from the old British norms of stiff decorum, rigid social pecking orders and Albion's other perfidious traditions. Men and women of all backgrounds now speak about their feelings, seek out a unique place in the world, which may have little to do with their family histories and seek to build professional and social lives in which they 'can be themselves'. Ours is an age of identity. It is the post-modern form of liberty while fraternity and equality have, alas, each in turn receded as general social aspirations. Those identities are multiple and situational, not fixed by personal history and natural heritage. Identities can be invented and reinvented; and when a new identity is adopted the old one need not be abandoned, just slipped into and out of more or less at will, like re-ordering a slide show. This expressive culture can bring the social margins, including criminal sub-cultures, into the cultural mainstream. Gangsta rap is the most egregious example: crime is glamour and celebrity and vice versa.

From the point of view of the offender emerging from prison contemplating what they might need to learn, they will of course want to pursue such opportunities as exist to join the hardworking meritocracy of jobs, family life and community. After the experience of prison that is likely to stretch both their talent and their effort. However, it is more important and more durably beneficial to understand that, although the mutability of identities in the society into which they emerge may be confusing, it is an opportunity to accelerate rehabilitation and social acceptance. If one can master the modern techniques of self-expression and re-narrating your own story by shuffling the deck of experiences into a different sequence with different interpretations and meanings, the ex-offender can start to become someone new in their own and everybody else's eyes. On the other hand the young man in and out of prison, aggressive, violent, unrestrained, insensitive and irresponsible is not just someone likely to reoffend. It is an outdated cultural trope with no accepted place in contemporary social discourse, except as a permanent delinquent outsider. That is the heart of the matter when it comes what all offenders need to learn. If not an offender, then what?

LIFE SKILLS

SHIRL TANNER
Operations Director, Sussex Pathways

Sussex Pathways has been working in Lewes Prison for over nine years mentoring offenders 'through the gate'. The question of what prisoners and ex-offenders need to learn raises a great many thoughts, ideas, personal opinions, organisational options that have been tried, tested, failed and succeeded, but basically, it comes down to this: prisoners and ex-offenders need life skills. Most of us gather life skills as we grow and develop from childhood. These are assembled learnt behaviour, school, parents, siblings, and being in and part of the community.

We have learnt how to work the latest mobile phone; we have upgraded from a basic PC to a Blackberry to an iPad; we have gone from paper bills to everything being online, including internet banking. Now, very few people pay by cash or even carry cash. New laws are put in place on a regular basis - for example using your mobile whilst driving is now banned, there is no smoking in public places, and a lot of towns now have a no-street-drinking laws. It's difficult to keep up with the changes and adhere to them, so as we live in the community we learn to adapt and develop new life skills to aid us to live peacefully. Even if we don't agree with these changes, we have developed the skills to accept and adjust to them.

When a prisoner, however, is locked away for a period, he (or she) will find it much more difficult, when released into an unfamiliar society, to adapt to these changes, as he hasn't developed the life skills to be able to process the changes. Think about it! If you have been away for a while or moved to a new town and you go back to visit and there is a new road layout or housing estate has been built, you can easily be disoriented and confused and feel that you don't belong there anymore as it's not how it was when you left. You have to find your way round again and this takes time. It makes you feel a tad cross or even angry for a while, but your learnt life skills help you adapt to the changes so that after a short while you see the changes as positive.

So what are life skills and how are they achieved? Life skills can be as basic as, Saying No; Paying Rent and Bills; Keeping Safe; Shopping for Food and Clothes; Cleaning; Making and Keeping Appointments; Problem Solving; Cooking; and Laundry; to Taking Responsibility; Accepting Changes; Making Changes: Maintaining changes; Looking to a Positive Future; Keeping Boundaries. Without all these life skills, no one can survive on a day-to-day basis.

While in prison, prisoners don't need these life skills. Bills don't need to be paid, little money is required, taking responsibility is not an issue. The government insists that 'prison works' and that locking people up does not deprive them of these essential skills. But life in society moves on, changes and evolves with new technology; experience of these changes and developments is lost to the offender while in prison. So when he is released much has become alien to him. This emphasises the fact that he does not have the basic skills needed to survive and remain offence free and law-abiding. This situation is, obviously, more prevalent for long-term prisoners, but can also be attributed to prolific offenders who return to prison on a regular basis, as their life skills have not evolved with the changes in society.

Mentoring is the way forward. It teaches these skills, builds confidence, reduces the likelihood of reoffending and helps the free person to move forward rather than backward. Mentors can bridge the gap between prison and society, offering the offender the time and space to learn and adapt, by acting as his advocate until his is empowered to take responsibility for his own and his family's life. It enables him to learn the vital new life skills that will help him adapt to our changing society. The mentor and the person leaving prison can develop a respectful adult working relationship. That relationship enables the person leaving prison to learn, without feeling patronised. Our experience is that the mentor also learns, gaining from the respectful adult working relationship, though in different ways from the person leaving prison.

EXPERIENCE OF POST-SECONDARY LEARNING AFTER PRISON:
reintegrating into society

Dr ANNE PIKE and RUTH McFARLANE
The Open University

Our focus is on what prisoners need to support their learning once they leave custody and this article describes a pathway of support, starting in prison and continuing beyond release, which we feel is crucial to enabling prisoners to reintegrate into society. This project is based on substantive research by Pike (2014) in which a group of male and female prisoners took part in a longitudinal study before and after their release from prison, focusing on their experiences with higher level (post-secondary) learning. Prison, probation and education staff were also interviewed as part of the study, along with family and friends to provide a complete picture of post-release experiences.

The encouraging finding was that those who had successfully studied at a higher level in prison had developed a positive attitude, characterised by their:

- determination, confidence and self-esteem
- positive student identity

- hope
- aspirations for a better crime-free future
- resilience and reflection.

By contrast, those who had not studied lacked any comparable aspiration or positive identity and their hope lacked substance.

For all concerned, however, early post-release findings indicated a combination of frustration and disillusionment. They lacked the information they needed to overcome the huge hurdles of reintegration and all strongly felt the stigma of having been in prison. This was compounded by the lack of access to technology. Old laptops, forgotten passwords, poor internet access and availability of quiet study spaces led to an erosion of the confidence and positivity that had been established by students during their time in prison.

One young woman, who had been a university student before her imprisonment and continued her studies during her time in custody said, "I actually don't see myself as a student anymore". This made her feel worthless and a "loss to society". Another, who felt desperate about the lack of support and structure on release said, "There have been days when I've thought "sod it" ...I'll just go and do something that'll send me back to prison, it'll just be easier". However, he did not go back to prison. The reflection and skills he had developed through his study enabled him to see beyond his difficulties and provided him with a resilience which enabled him to persevere.

A follow-on pilot study in Milton Keynes showed that with the right support, students were able to regain their positive identity and to continue with their studies. The findings from the research are summarised in figure 1, below. This pyramid shows the pathways of support required for successful integration into society.

Figure 1: Requirements for easier post-release integration into society, Pike (2014)

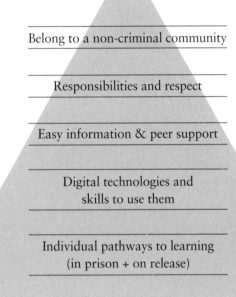

Belong to a non-criminal community

Responsibilities and respect

Easy information & peer support

Digital technologies and
skills to use them

Individual pathways to learning
(in prison + on release)

Beginning with individualised learning, which allows for progression to higher level study if appropriate (both in prison and post-release), the pyramid highlights the importance of access to technologies and the digital skills that are required to be a citizen in this fast-paced digital world we live in. Easy-to-digest information is also vitally important to those who are due for release, providing specific local information that arms the newly-released prisoner with the means to contact the right people and organisations they need to continue their learning. The guidance and support of peers, who have been in their shoes, helps to provide confidence to tackle the huge problems that they will face in the quest to gain responsible roles in society which help them to 'give back to society' and can provide the self-esteem and respect from others, that they desire. Ultimately, belonging to a non-criminal community, such as a learning community, is of supreme importance and we believe is key to continuity of learning and more successful integration into society.

The Open University, in partnership with St Giles Trust and Futures Unlocked, is developing a new project (Transform Ed) which aims to provide these pathways of support through community hubs for learning (in London and the Midlands). These two partner charities already offer Through-the-Gate support, and therefore have significant experience of supporting people with convictions. Together, we will promote contact with post-secondary education level students in prison prior to their release and provide a learning community hub which is a safe space for learning with the necessary digital technologies and designated study partners.

We hope, initially, to capitalise on connections made via the PUPiL project (PET, 2017) to provide students to act as study partners in this learning community, with appropriate training and support provided by the partner charities. As ex-prisoners progress with their studies and develop their post-release stability, some will be trained as peer supporters to act as expert study partners for newly released prisoners, so providing sustainability. Two project champions (who have recently completed their OU degrees in prison) will act as advisers and champions on the project.

The key focus will be on establishing a learning community to which all participants feel a strong sense of belonging. This will involve providing the necessary digital technologies and regular face-to-face study sessions, with discussions about digital skills and key study skills such as note taking, referencing and assignment planning, as well as about wider student experiences of time-management, stress and anxiety. While these sessions will initially take place at the premises of the charity, in the longer term they may move to a college or university communal area, library or café so that the ex-prisoners will have the opportunity to integrate into this wider learning community. By engaging in this way, we anticipate that students will be able to continue with their existing studies, and also recognise that mainstream college or university life (and wider society) is open to them. The ultimate goal is for ex-prisoners to move into well-paid permanent employment. We believe that many post-release barriers to employment can be reduced through this transformative project, with students developing increased confidence, relevant digital and vocational skills and engagement in a social community of successful peers. We will promote integration pathways with engaged employers to encourage a more open approach to recruitment.

The project aims to be scalable and sustainable, with the model being shared for wider adoption at relatively low cost. It is already planned for the project to also engage with those at risk of offending through connections with police-led projects such as DIVERT, run by the Metropolitan Police which targets young people who have been arrested, offering them an alternative to custody if they agree to engage in specific projects. Our project also has significant interest from many of the police forces in the Open University police training consortium. In this way we hope to encourage those who have given up on education, and are in danger of offending, to return to the learning community.

We believe that this project adds an educational dimension to established desistance theory. Our evidence shows that progression to college-level education enables ex-prisoners to develop the cognitive ability to make their own decisions and to reflect on difficult situations; taking on roles of responsibility, such as peer support, increases their confidence, while belonging to a learning community promotes hope and a positive sense of identity, which can help them to resist the easier path back to prison.

By the end of our first year, we hope that some students will have progressed through the whole process from ex-prisoner to trained peer-study-guide with employment, and can act as ambassadors. They will appreciate the project's strengths and help to develop the solution. Our project evaluation will provide hard evidence of its benefits, enabling expansion to other study and employment pathways. In terms of what prisoners need to learn, this project provides the necessary support for ex-prisoners to complete their qualifications, maintain their positive identity and find appropriate employment following their release.

LEARNING FOR PEOPLE WITH MULTIPLE COMPLEX NEEDS

JENNIE McCREIGHT
Employment training and education co-ordinator/operational manager, Touchstone

At West Yorkshire Finding Independence (WY-FI) peer mentoring programme, we have had the opportunity first hand to develop and deliver an accredited peer mentor learning/employability programme for people with lived experience of multiple complex needs (homelessness, offending, addiction and mental health). This pathway includes a significant proportion of learners who have experience of offending or have been involved within the criminal justice system (between 80 and 110 learners who have started the programme have declared some involvement with offending or peers who offend).

The course covers accredited units on mentoring skills, negotiation skills and conflict resolution at level 2. The aim is that after the twelve week course individuals will become a volunteer peer mentor and support the beneficiaries on the project to engage with their own rehabilitation and recovery needs. In addition, the course and placement offer pathways into employment and opportunities for individuals to access further training and transferrable employability skills, on a practical level, applying what they have learned through the course at their placement role (and often also within their personal life circumstances).

Two employed peer mentor training support workers guide the learners in identifying their personal support package, which in itself is a process of learning. This learning includes the individual identifying with the tutor what happens when things 'go wrong' and developing strategies they need to know or do (in their own circumstances) to maintain their recovery. The tutors combine practical educational support, to aid completion of the level 2 accreditation, while also ensuring additional guidance and information is provided to the learners to teach other skills such as budgeting, managing emotions, accessing services and keeping themselves engaged with meaningful activities.

This learning and support is continued through the placement where individuals (supported by a wider workforce of staff of which many have their own lived experience) develop skills in team work, risk assessment, support plans, negotiating with other professionals, participating in supervision and a whole range of other areas crucial to the individual remaining well and active in their recovery and rehabilitation.

For those who progress into employment, ongoing support/learning is provided. This is as a direct result of feedback identified from a working group led by the WY-FI project focusing on 'people with lived experience succeeding in the workplace', with experts by experience noting that taking up employment is a further challenging time for individuals. Key areas, identified as 'learning and development needs', we revise or learn a fresh the process of applying for a role, learning the etiquette and expectations of the workplace and making transitions in personal routine to accommodate for work responsibilities.

Some of the key educational areas that we support and teach peer mentors about are:

- Navigating the benefits system – particularly around the transition back into work and what they are entitled to
- Access to Mental Health and Crisis services – who and where to go when things go wrong

- IT skills and confidence in using IT and social media – in addition having the opportunity to practice and maintain skills
- Reflective practice
- Utilising supervision
- General communication skills; for example, what to do if you are going to be late, how to tell your manager you are finding things difficult, how to identify your own training needs
- Going through the DBS (Disclosure and Barring Service) process; this has included the development of a DBS guide for peer mentors co-produced by a peer who had to go through a Route 4 for his DBS and addresses some of the concerns learners may have about declaring their offences.

In addition to the accredited learning units we have tailored the course to address problem solving, self-resilience and self-development. Examples of these softer learning outcomes include the following: (1) Why we lie and learning to be honest: exploring the habit of distorting the truth in the addiction/offending cycle and considering how honesty is important to the workplace for personal support needs and in line with workplace expectations. This aspect involves a large aspect of peer learning/peer support around choices and changing behaviours. (2) Constructive and destructive behaviours: understanding past behaviours and how these have impacted on decision making. (3) Learning about services and what they can offer. (4) Utilising peer support to identify and address challenges and solutions to recovery and reoffending. This extends to areas such as understanding about positive relationships, boundaries and identifies role models and influential figures.

We have had the opportunity to carry out some action learning research with two areas, focusing on the WY-FI male prison leaver engagement worker and the WY-FI female prison leaver worker aspect of delivery. In prison, the following issues were identified as important to the support/learning that offenders needed: budgeting skills; self-esteem workshops and workbooks; managing own well-being; prison listener service.

In the community, these issues were identified: budgeting and managing spending; a buddying/peer mentoring service; an independent ETE service. When we asked a peer mentor forum (eight peers) about the topic, they came up with some aspects which complement that noted in the action learning research above. They were: NHS counselling techniques; how to run a household and budgeting for this; life skills; speaking on the phone and making appointments; basic computer skills; mutual aid groups - where they are and how to find them; cooking skills and food technology/hygiene basics; links to voluntary work/college courses .

In summary, we have found that learners from offending backgrounds have benefitted best from learning skills, aimed at boosting their employability goals, while facilitating their own personal development, self-esteem and rehabilitation strategies. This has included one peer who completed the conflict resolution module and then applied these skills to resolve a long term feud with a neighbour – in which she stated she previously had been dealt with in an aggressive and confrontational way.

A balance of IT, literacy and communication skills with softer skills around recovery needs, practical life skills, finding and knowing how to access services and understanding and maintaining recovery and rehabilitation has proved successful for many of our learners.

The benefit of visible recovery that comes with a diverse workforce of volunteers and paid staff with lived experience has promoted informal learning for the peer mentors around choice, opportunity and hope for learners with offending backgrounds. This has often been the most valuable part of the learning for some of our peer mentors who have identified a shift in mind set from feeling trapped in the offending cycle and in turn looking to a future which includes rehabilitation, improved well-being and opportunities of employment.

Learning and support for young people as they leave prison

JESS STUBBS
Researcher, Centre for Mental Health, South Bank University

RICKY and JLBJ
Project Future

This is written in collaboration with young men and staff from Project Future, a holistic well-being service that has been co-produced with young people labelled as 'gang members' and 'offenders' who have varied and often multiple experiences of prison. It is written with Centre for Mental Health who have been facilitating youth-led research at the project. The young men are experts in this field whose life experiences offer invaluable knowledge in reforming prisons and in how to stop young people from reoffending. In responding to the question, there are undoubtedly important skills and lessons that would be helpful for people leaving prison to learn, which will be discussed. This piece will also consider how services and systems surrounding these young men need to learn from them and consider the role they play in limiting a young person's chance of moving forwards in life.

The society we live in tends to find all the problems in the individual. Yes, a crime has been committed and people have to take responsibility but we often neglect the context in which young people offend. You see your mum struggling to buy you school shoes, new trainers, pay the rent, put food on the table and you live in an area where there are no jobs, no opportunities – how are you going to make money? Or you're constantly looking over your shoulder worrying about who might be there, worrying about how you're going to protect your kids, how you're going to avoid getting hurt at on your way home – how do you protect yourself? 'What you see is not what you get'. The reality is there is a complex interplay of health, racial and social inequalities that contribute to offending, which get neglected when we just focus on individuals. Therefore, this debate will consider more broadly what needs to be learnt when someone leaves prison.

There are some skills that you need to have when transitioning back to the outside, which prison could help to equip you with. People 'go in small and come out tall' and especially for those serving a long sentence 'the world will have moved on' but you are going to be expected to live independently (for example, money management, cooking, living skills and establishing routine). Some prisons have kitchens on the wings, which provide you with invaluable experience for learning to cook and gaining different skills and recipes from peers, lessons that are transferable to the outside. More needs to be done in relation to money management, there is a strong link to offending but there is limited support for people leaving about how to manage bills, pay rent, budget. Education and employment skills: a lot of the time you'll have been kicked out of school and you won't have your qualifications when you enter prison. Education in prison needs to put you on an equal footing to the education you'd get outside. The skills that jobs require today: what if your family couldn't afford a computer at home, where will you have gotten IT skills from? Prison needs to be upskilling you to make it easier to find work on the outside. You also need to be prepared to go from having a completely structured day to having no routine at all and therefore be able to establish one for yourself, such as volunteering in your community, doing exercise, socialising.

Family is a priority: they provide much needed support and it is highly important for services to see them as a resource to a young person. Keeping families involved whilst a young person is in prison, especially when they are going through a difficult time, is crucial.

Housing is a priority: you have to come out with a roof over your head. There can be major problems in coming out of prison and being placed in the same area where nothing has changed. Wanting to make changes doesn't stop old rivals still associating you with an area, police remembering your face and relentlessly stopping and searching you and locals still knowing you as the 'drug dealer'. You need money and you can't get a job, so when the offer of dealing remains the only viable way of getting money you're going to do it.

Money is a priority: there needs to be a legitimate way of making enough money. It's very hard to get a job on the outside. How do you get past the criminal record on job applications when people won't give you a chance. We need to get employers to think differently, it might be that they have 20 applicants and you might be the best person for the job but they won't even look at you because of your criminal record. On the occasion that you get an interview as soon as you're asked that question, 'what have you been doing for the past year?' How do you answer that? When you say you've been in prison, they say 'No thanks'.

In general, there is limited support for young people as they leave prison. There are fantastic probation workers who provide invaluable practical and emotional support, but the issue is that it can be a lottery and not all experiences of probation are positive. Professionals, working with young people leaving prison need to remember that they are working with a person not just a criminal, who has faced and survived so many stresses and traumas and who needs a second chance. Professionals need to recognise the multiple and positive stories about each young man they work with: as a loving father, a committed community member, a talented cook. Recognising and building these strengths and resilience would help you in transitioning back into the outside world.

What society, commissioners and services need to learn is that to prevent young people from going back to prison there has to be more support. The transition can be hugely stressful: you have to mend family relationships, find a way of making money and get a roof over your head. This support is exactly what Project Future is about. It is a holistic well-being service in Haringey, which is co-produced with local young men, psychologists, and youth workers to design a service, shaped around what young people identified as 'offenders' need. It supports you to use the skills and strengths you have and to develop a sense of agency in navigating the outside world. The employment support helps you overcome barriers to work, in 're-storying' your life, for example, thinking about how you talk about past offences and time in prison with potential employers. Project Future supports you to consider the skills and resources you have demonstrated through your life experiences and helps you to see the different side to your story – as resilient, as resourceful, as community-minded, which can be transformative in fostering a sense of confidence and self-worth when applying for a job.

The kind of work being done at Project Future needs to be in place in prison so that you are supported on that journey before you leave. When you leave prison, you need someone who isn't going to judge you and who can be there to talk through difficult times with you. For young people leaving prison, there can be multiple stresses that affect your mental health and wellbeing and Project Future has provided a safe space to talk things through without feeling judged. Young men who have recently left prison say that all young people being released need something like Project Future to support with the emotional and practical transition back to the outside world.

So, what has to be learnt? These are young people, like any other, with dreams, hopes and goals for their life; they are not just criminals. As society, we need to remember to see the human in the being.

SOCIAL ENTREPRENEURSHIP FOR EX-OFFENDERS:
'everybody has the capacity to be remarkable' – Michael Young

SHEENA LEAF
Founder/Director, The Entrepreneur Inside CIC;
Fellow of School of Social Entrepreneurs

'Not to commit crime', would be a flippant response to the question. As a society, we are nowhere near achieving that aim or there wouldn't have been a rise in the prison population of 82 per cent over the last 30 years, with nearly 68,000 people sent to prison in 2016. (*Bromley Briefings*, summer 2017)

Many arrive in the criminal justice system pre-programmed by their learned life experience. But when we have these people in our sights (or in our prisons) why are current teaching and learning initiatives falling short? Around £145m is spent each year on prison education. Jonathan Robinson, a former prisoner who campaigns for education in prisons, speaking to BBC Radio 4's Today programme in July 2015 commented, "During a totally deserved prison sentence I saw missed opportunity, after missed opportunity, after missed opportunity for rehabilitation in prison via education."

There's plenty of formal learning on offer, so what's being missed? For a start, over half (57 per cent) of people entering prison are assessed as having the literacy skills expected of an 11-year old, so may struggle to access education. Regarding purposeful activity, Inspectors routinely conclude that in too many prisons work remains mundane, repetitive and is rarely linked to learning or resettlement objectives.

What about the personal learning and development that arises from thinking and behaviour programmes? Often delivered by charities but, with recent economic austerity and an inability to compete for contracts, many are no longer operating.

Entrepreneurship as a platform for effective learning

The solution to offering some helpful learning may be closer than we think. Are we imposing traditional learning platforms and styles on offenders, but missing their potential; ignoring the abilities they already possess?

Take entrepreneurship: many people find themselves in offending 'hot water' due to the illegitimate use of their considerable entrepreneurial skills. Does the criminal justice system embrace, encourage and build on those skills? Mostly, people are consciously steered away from any former activity, concerned that it could compromise their rehabilitation. Better an NVQ1 in something practical, as a safer bet? Suppose a person with entrepreneurial potential could be supported to develop a legitimate business, which could lead him, or her, out of criminality and on to a sustainable future.

What if learning embraced such broad thinking, was solutions focused, sustainable and offered a pathway back to society? Well it can be, through the vehicle of entrepreneurship and social entrepreneurship. This different take on learning utilises the skills and talents that are latent and doesn't rely on 'teaching' to impose and embed knowledge.

Those whose lives have unravelled due to their convictions often lack confidence, self-esteem and a sense of self-worth. Many are experts in their field, but it hasn't served them well because their fixed mindset prevents them from reaching their true goals. Their skills can be underplayed, in a bid to 'reduce reoffending' and their former life of rejecting challenge, operating in a closed network, promotes a stereotypical view of their ability.

Social entrepreneurship and School for Social Entrepreneurs

Since 1997, School for Social Entrepreneurs has been supporting social entrepreneurs: people who create social and environmental change by starting, scaling and sustaining organisations. Ranging in age from 17 to 74, participants come from diverse cultural and ethnic backgrounds. SSE believes that a passion for change is what matters most, not where you come from: one in four Fellows have direct experience of the social issue they aim to address; fifty per cent of all Fellows are working in the 20 per cent most deprived geographical communities in the UK.

It is not what SSE does, but *how*: its network of 11 schools run practical learning programmes to help people realise their potential. Learning focuses on developing individuals' emotional resourcefulness and confidence, as well as their business skills and impact. Bringing social entrepreneurs together in cohorts allows them to build networks and diverse connections. A jargon-free, purposefully non-academic approach allows a variety of people access to the programmes. Learning is not theoretical or abstract – instead it centres on taking action on live problems the entrepreneur faces. Because SSE welcomes people from all backgrounds, its approach sings to the learning needs of offenders. How life-affirming to come to a place of authenticity, validation, constructive challenge and acceptance, all wrapped around by a network of similar souls and successful role models who have gone before. A place where your educational background is of little relevance and which embraces a wide variety of multiple intelligences and learning styles. The familiar activity of 'trading' is also a natural fit for many former offenders, providing a sustainable and growing income model rather than just a re-distribution of wealth.

A restorative approach can be carefully woven into this business model, which provides a person with criminal convictions the opportunity of 'paying back'. The power of this mechanism is much under-rated and successful social entrepreneurs often become effective agents for change.

One programme, the Lloyds Bank and Bank of Scotland Social Entrepreneurs Programme, run by SSE and jointly funded by Big Lottery Fund, will have already supported 1,300 social entrepreneurs over five years by October 2017. Participants received a fully funded place on a year-long SSE course, a grant from the Big Lottery Fund, and a Lloyds Banking Group mentor. Some of the impact measured during this period includes:

- Twelve per cent of the social entrepreneurs taking part in the programme were people living with a mental illness, recovering from substance abuse, formerly homeless or ex-offenders
- Forecasts suggest over 7,000 jobs will be created during the five-year programme.
- Many fellows will have a longer-term influence on how society is organised and the opportunities available to people: 64 per cent are changing people's attitudes; 28 per cent are changing practice in the public or private sector; 10 per cent are influencing national government policy.

Example 1:

Simon Short
Managing Director, Intelligence Project Ltd, Grimsby

What does your social enterprise do? "We deliver 'through the gate' services to those convicted by the courts. We train and empower offenders to deliver case management and floating support whilst also delivering thinking skills programmes, delivering contracts in the Yorkshire and Humberside."

Why are you passionate about this cause? "As Founder/CEO of this company, my life began a little differently. I spent 16 years in and out of the care system, young offender's institutes and ultimately adult prison, having been involved with serious crime. The Open University saved me but although I completed a degree, I left prison with only £47 after an eight-year sentence. I was sick of being forgotten. When I came home from prison, I thought I could do better. After 16 years of being a service user I believed that I was best placed to bring wider social change and leadership within the criminal justice market."

What was your biggest challenge in starting your social enterprise? "The first 18 months, being on licence from prison and working with others also on licences, proved complex for partners like the Probation Service and Police to grasp. The biggest challenge was getting people to see the enterprise, not the offender. Winning my first regional contract with Sodexo justice services was hard and my biggest commercial challenge was at the due diligence stage."

How has SSE helped to support your development? "SSE was instrumental in my own rehabilitation process. Being on SSE Yorkshire & Humber's Lloyds Bank Start Up programme when first released, then later on SSE London's Lloyds Bank Scale Up programme, I matured as a man, father and leader of my organisation. The acceptance I got from SSE staff and participants unlocked my future. Due to the tools I have been given, my HR structure, and our management mantra, we see our service users as humans and people who can change. We use our platform to talk about the need for change and our voice is getting louder."

What difference have you made? "Many offenders have been supported with about £10 million SROI (social return on investment) since our start date, seven years ago. We have employed 40 offenders so far and have generated tens of thousands of 1-2-1 contact hours with service users. Hundreds of benefits in place and hundreds of homeless people housed, with more than 200 into employment. To contain a prisoner for one year is around £45k and we have kept 40 out of custody, with a potential saving of £1.8 million."

What are your plans for the future? "To become an organisation that commissions the criminal justice system budget; carries out the procurement process and identifies who wins contracts. We would audit the work and service delivered via our due diligence team of ex-offenders.

In the short to medium term we are in the process of purchasing housing stock for people who are on release from long sentences."

Example 2:

Junior Smart
Team Leader at SOS Project, St. Giles Trust, London

What does your social enterprise do? "SOS Project was founded in 2006 and provides tailor-made support to young people aged 15 to 30 at risk of involvement in gang-related activity and negative lifestyle choices. Critically the support is from staff with lived experience and are best placed to help and give advice."

Why are you passionate about this cause? "While I was in prison I could see systemic failures in the penal system. My cellmate had become so institutionalised that he seemed to enjoy prison. He was repeatedly serving short sentences and the underlying issues for his troubles were ignored by the authorities. I couldn't understand why I was the only one to see this and I started to think about what would be needed in order to break the cycle. I am motivated by the young people I work with and their cause, pure and simple. I never want to be distant from their plight as I like to be hands-on and practical in the way I deal with things. I remember reading about the life of Mahatma Gandhi in prison and my favourite quote of his was 'be the change you want to see in the world'. Every day gives me an opportunity to make a positive difference to others."

What was your biggest challenge in starting your social enterprise? "It was the lack of belief that ex-offenders could be used to support other offenders. People said we would fail and that it shouldn't be done. My dream was for ex-offenders to be seen as professionals. Despite the ongoing struggle, we now find ourselves welcomed around tables where key decisions are made."

How has SSE helped to support your development? "School for Social Entrepreneurs was a great learning experience for me. When I first came to SSE I had a very limited understanding of how businesses and charities worked. Due to my previous life experiences I also had very constrained ideas about my own leadership ability and what could be possible. Having previously dropped out of formal education I had felt education was not for me, but SSE's atypical approach to learning really worked for me. It also brought me together with other social entrepreneurs who I could listen to and understand their difficulties and learning experiences, as well as who I could bounce my own ideas off."

What difference have you made? "We have achieved some incredible outcomes, smashing reoffending rates for our clients down from an average of 75 per cent to just 12 per cent."

What are your plans for the future? "We have plans to scale the project up. One of the key areas is to pursue the gangs that proliferate out of London and provide services which support young people at risk of their exploitative recruitment tactics. We hope to reach more young people than ever before."

Barriers and benefits

What prevents the implementation of such a key driver for learning and success? Can we acknowledge the positive 'by-products' of criminal activity? Do we believe that the offender can be an expert, who holds many of the answers? Is the hierarchy and bureaucracy of our criminal justice system ready and open to a different way of doing things? How invested are we in an offender's innate ability to broker their own solutions, with support? How willing are we to slacken or let go the reins, in order to challenge our own risk aversion and that of our institutions? Of course, it's a riskier strategy and may also be politically unpopular.

By addressing learning for this cohort, through the model of social entrepreneurship, many of the core barriers to reducing reoffending can be tackled. By honing existing skills and talents, there is an opportunity for both personal and societal re-entry. Focussing on personal sustainability, and on the product or service, a platform is created to foster legitimate income; reducing the reliance on a benefit culture for both them and their families.

The lived experience of those caught up in criminality, and their ability to identify solutions, trumps many traditional public sector-based approaches, which are often bureaucratic and cumbersome. A social entrepreneur, by comparison, is innovative, agile and flexible. Ground-up solutions are predictably lighter on resources and management, but rely on a different, more open, relationship with traditional agencies.

The value that is uncovered plays to the person's personal development, and those self-esteem and confidence issues. It validates their thinking and skills, offering a pathway of contribution and acceptance.

References And Endnotes

PETER NEYROUD / Pre-court Diversion of Offenders

Blakeborough, L. and Pierpont, H. (2007). *Conditional cautions: An examination of the early implementation of the scheme.* London: Ministry of Justice.

Britton, S. (2014). *Improving Responses to Young Adults: A Checklist for Police and Crime Commissioners.* Transition to Adulthood Alliance. www.barrowcadbury.org.uk/wp-content/uploads/2014/03/T2A_PCC_Improving_responses_final4web.pdf Downloaded 17.11.2014.

Campbell, E. (1997). Two Futures for Police Cautioning. In Francis, P., Davies, P. and Jupp, V. (Eds). *Policing Futures.* Basingstoke: MacMillan: pp. 51–79.

Easton, H., Slivestri, M., Evans, K., Matthews, R. and Walklate, S. (2010). *Conditional Cautions: Evaluation of the women specific condition pilot.* London: Ministry of Justice Research Series 14/10.

Jones, J.M. (1982). Young Offender Policy in Hampshire and the Isle of Wight. *Police, 55,* 279–285.

Neyroud. P.W. and Slothower, M.P. (2013). *Operation Turning Point: second interim report.* Interim report to West Midlands Police: Cambridge: Institute of Criminology, University of Cambridge.

Petrosino, A., Turpin-Petrosino, C. and Guckenburg, S. (2010). *Formal System Processing of Juveniles: effects on delinquency.* Campbell Crime and Justice Systematic Review: www.campbellcollaboration.org/lib/project/81/: Downloaded 17.11.2014.

Rice, L. (2010). *Conditional Cautions: lessons learnt from the unpaid reparative work pilot implementation.* London: Ministry of Justice Research Summary 5/10.

Rose, G. and Hamilton, R.A. (1970). Effects of a Juvenile Liaison Scheme. *British Journal of Criminology,* 10(1), 2–20.

Steer, D. (1970). *Police Cautions – a study in the exercise of police discretion.* Oxford: Blackwells.

Slothower, M.P., Sherman, L.W. and Neyroud, P.W. (2015) 'Tracking Quality of Police Actions in a Victim Contact Program: A Case Study in Training, Tracking and Feedback (TTF) in Evidence-based Policing', *International Criminal Justice Review,* 25(1): 98-116.

Strang, H., Sherman, L.W., Mayo-Wilson, E., Woods, D. and Ariel, B. (2013). *Restorative Justice Conferencing: Effects of Face-to-Face Meetings of Offenders and Victims.* www.campbellcollaboration.org/lib/project/63/: Downloaded 17.11.2014.

Weisburd, D. and Neyroud, P.W. (2011). *Police Science: a new paradigm.* Cambridge, Mass.: Harvard, Kennedy School of Government.

GREG PARSTON / Transition to Adulthood

1. *Lost in Transition: A Report of the Barrow Cadbury Commission on Young Adults and the Criminal Justice System*, Barrow Cadbury Trust, September 2005, p.23.

2. www.t2a.org.uk

3. www.t2a.org.uk/t2a-evidence/project-evaluation/

4. Parston G., Timmins, *Joined-Up Management*, Public Management Foundation, October 1998.

5. Wilson S., Davison N., Clarke M., Casebourne J., *Joining up Public Services Around Local, Citizen Needs*, Institute for Government, November 2015.

6. Sullivan C.J., Piquero A.R., Cullen F.T., 'Like Before, but Better: The Lessons of Developmental, Life-Course Criminology for Contemporary Juvenile Justice' in *Victims and Offenders*, 7:4:2012

7. Kippin H., Adebowale V., "The Collaborative Citizen", research report, Collaborate CIC, 2014.

8. Kippin H., Adebowale V., p 19.

9. House of Commons Work and Pensions Committee, 'Support for ex-offenders, Fifth Report of Session 2016–17', December 2016, p 4.

10. www.stgilestrust.org.uk

11. england.shelter.org.uk/get_advice/prisoners/help_and_advice_for_prisoners

12. www.gold.ac.uk/open-book/

CAROLINE DRUMMOND / Essential Elements for Providing Education and Skills to Young People Involved with the Criminal Justice System

1. IPPR (2016) *Education, education mental health: supporting secondary schools to play a central role in early intervention mental health services*

2. Beyond Youth Custody (2016) *Young offenders and trauma: experience and impact – A practitioners guide*

LIZ DIXON / Reflections on 30 Years
Working in Probation and Criminal Justice

Shadd Maruna (2001) *Making Good: how ex-convicts reform and rebuild their lives.*

Paulo Friere (1970) *Pedagogy of the Oppressed.*

Erwin James (2005) *A Life Inside: a Prisoners Notebook.*

A. Underdown (1998) *Strategies for Effective Offender Supervision: Report of the H.M.I.P. What Works Project.*

J. McGuire and P. Priestley (1985) *Offending Behaviour: Skills and Strategies for Going Straight.*

PHILIP EMERY / An Educator's Reflections

(David Hillson (ed.) (2011) *The Failure Files: perspectives on failure.*

McNeill et al (2011) *Inspiring Desistence? Arts projects and 'what works?*

CORIN MORGAN-ARMSTRONG / 'Parenting is Not For Cowards'

1. Ministry of Justice Resettlement Survey 2008 stated that prisoners receiving visits are 39 per cent less likely to reoffend

2. H.M. Inspection Team September 2014 states, "an offender's family are the most effective resettlement agency." See the Barnardo's run and Department of Education funded website www.i-hop.org.uk/ for an ever-expanding resource of research/evidence and practical help, ideas and support for professionals working with children and families of prisoners. See also, "HMP Parc worked with families to ensure that they were involved in the rehabilitation and resettlement of prisoners. The approach was radical and innovative and probably the best we have seen in any prison." HM Inspection Team report, June 2016.)

3. Lord Michael Farmer (2017) *The Importance of Strengthening Prisoners' Family Ties to Prevent Reoffending and Reduce Intergenerational Crime.* Ministry of Justice

CLAIRE O'SULLIVAN / Experiences of Learning and Growth in a High Security Prison

1. Liebling, A. and Maruna, S. (Eds.) (2005) *The Effects of Imprisonment.* Cullompton:Willan.

2. Liebling, A. with Arnold, H. (2004) *Prisons and Their Moral Performance: A study of values, quality and prison life.* Clarendon Studies in Criminology, Oxford: Oxford University Press.

3. Liebling, A. with Arnold, H. (2004) *Prisons and Their Moral Performance: A study of values, quality and prison life.* Clarendon Studies in Criminology, Oxford: Oxford University Press

4. Barron, A. (2016) 'Ticket to re-entry: Understanding the journey of the Hardman Trust award winners'. *Prison Service Journal*, May 2016: issue 225: 39–44.

5. Dweck, C. (2012) *Mindset: How you can fulfil your potential.* Great Britain: Robinson.

6. Blyth, C. (2008) *The Art of Conversation.* London: John Murray.

7. Liebling, A. with Arnold, H. (2004) *Prisons and Their Moral Performance: A study of values, quality and prison life.* Clarendon Studies in Criminology, Oxford: Oxford University Press.

JANE SLATER / Prison Education for Prisoners Convicted of a Sexual Offence

Allison, E. and Sloan, A. (2015) Prison education still at the back of the class, as Gove takes new course, Guardian online www.theguardian.com/education/2015/aug/04/michael-gove-prison-education-justice-secretary-jail

Allen, G. and Dempsey, N. (2016) Prison Population statistics. House of Commons Library. researchbriefings.files.parliament.uk/documents/SN04334/SN04334.pdf accessed 31st October 2016

CfBT Education Trust and YouGov. (2011) Employers Perception of Best Practice in Prison Education

Clark, R. (2016) How education transforms: Evidence from the experience of Prisoners' Education Trust on how education supports prisoner journeys, Prison Service Journal, 225, 3–8

Coates, S. (2016) Unlocking potential: A review of education in prison. www.gov.uk/government/uploads/system/uploads/attachment_data/file/524013/education-review-report.pdf (Accessed 31st October 2016)

Darke, S. and Aresti, A. (2016) Connecting Prisons and Universities through Higher Education, Prison Service Journal, 225, 26-32

Government. UK (2015) Sex offender sentences hit record levels www.gov.uk/government/news/sex-offender-sentences-hit-record-levels (Accessed 31st October 2016)

Hawley, J. Murphy, I. and Souto-Otero. (2013) Prison Education and Training in Europe: Current State of Play and Challenges. GHK Consulting

Hudson, K. (2005) Offending Identities: Sex Offenders Perspective of their Treatment and Management. Cullompton: Willan Publishing

Manza, J. Brooks, C. and Uggen, C. (2004) Public attitudes toward felon disenfranchisement in the United States. Public Opinion Quarterly, 68(2), 275-286

Ministry of Justice. (2014) Experimental Statistics from the MoJ/DWP/HMRC data share: Linking data on offenders with benefits, employment and income date, London: Ministry of Justice

NOMS, (2005) The Government's National Reducing Re-Offending Delivery Plan

Offender Management Statistics, (2016) https://www.gov.uk/government/uploads/system/uploads/attachment_data/file/585870/omsq-bulletin-q3-2016.pdf (Accessed 15/02/2017)

Office for National Statistics, (2017) https://www.ons.gov.uk/peoplepopulationandcommunity/crimeandjustice/datasets/crimeinenglandandwalesappendixtables (Accessed on 02/05/2017)

Owen-Evans, S. And McNeill, P. (2006) Paving the Way: from Key Skills to Functional Skills. London: DfES

Schuller, T. and Watson, D. (2009) Learning through life: Inquiry into the future of Lifelong Leaning (NIACE)

Skills Funding Agency. (2016) Further Education and Skills: Learner Participation, Outcomes and Highest Qualification Held. Statistical First Release, London: SFA

Stickland, N. (2016) Transforming rehabilitation? Prison education: Analysis and options. Education Policy Institute. https://epi.org.uk/wp-content/uploads/2016/03/transforming-rehabilitation-epi.pdf (Accessed on 02/05/2017)

Taylor, C. (2014) Brain Cells: Third Edition, Surrey: Prisoners' Education Trust

Terry, L. and Cardwell, V. (2015) Understanding the Whole Person: Part One of a Series of Literature Reviews on Severe and Multiple Disadvantage. Revolving Door Agency

Tofte, S. (2007) No easy answer, sex offender laws in the US. Human Rights Watch, 19 (4), 1–146

West, T. (1997) Prisons of Promise. Winchester: Waterside Press

Wilson, D. and Reuss, A. (2000) Prions(er) Education. Stories of change and transformation. Waterside Press

KIRSTINE SZIFRIS / Philosophical Dialogue

1. I was trained in Sheffield by an organisation called SAPERE, www.sapere.org.uk

Lipman, M., Sharp, A. M., & Oscanyan, F. S. (1980). *Philosophy in the Classroom*. Philadelphia: Temple University Press.

Murris, K. S. (2000). 'Can Children Do Philosophy?' *Journal of Philosophy of Education*, 34 (2), 261–279.

Robinson, D., & Garratt, C. (1996). *Introducing Ethics*. Cambridge: Icon Books Ltd.

Warburton, N. (2004). *Philosophy: The Basics* (4th edition). Oxfordshire: Routledge.

Worley, P. (2011). The *'if' machine: Philosophical enquiry in the classroom*. London: Continuum.

ROGER READER / The Man of Sorrows and the Dignity of the Prisoner

* Matthew 25 verses 35–46

For I was hungry and you gave me food, I was thirsty and you gave me drink, a stranger and you welcomed me,

Naked and you clothed me, ill and you cared for me, in prison and you visited me.

Then the righteous will answer him and say, 'Lord, when did we see you hungry and feed you, or thirsty and give you drink?

When did we see you a stranger and welcome you, or naked and clothe you?

When did we see you ill or in prison, and visit you?'

And the king will say to them in reply, 'Amen, I say to you, whatever you did for one of these least brothers of mine, you did for me.'

Then he will say to those on his left, 'Depart from me, you accursed, into the eternal fire prepared for the devil and his angels.

For I was hungry and you gave me no food, I was thirsty and you gave me no drink,

A stranger and you gave me no welcome, naked and you gave me no clothing, ill and in prison, and you did not care for me.'

Then they will answer and say, 'Lord, when did we see you hungry or thirsty or a stranger or naked or ill or in prison, and not minister to your needs?'

He will answer them, 'Amen, I say to you, what you did not do for one of these least ones, you did not do for me.'

And these will go off to eternal punishment, but the righteous to eternal life.

ANNE O'GRADY and PAUL HAMILTON / Re-imagining the Prison Education Paradigm

Coates, S., (2016) *Unlocking Potential: A Review of education in prison,* London: Ministry of Justice.

Forster, W., (1998) *Education behind bars, international comparisons,* Leicester: NIACE.

Freire, P., (1996) *Pedagogy of the oppressed*, Rev. Ed, Harmondsworth: Penguin.

Griffiths, M., (1998) *Educational Research for Social Justice: getting off the fence,* Buckingham: Open University Press.

Hodgson, A., and Spours, K., (1999) *New Labour's Educational Agenda*, London: Kogan Page.

Loeber, R., Stouthamer-Loeber, M. Van Kammen, W. and Farrington, D.P. (1991) 'Initiation, Escalation and Desistance in Juvenile Offending and Their Correlates', *Journal of Criminal Law and Criminology*, Vol. 82, 36–82.

Maruna, S., Lebel, T.P., Mitchell, N., and Naples, M., (2004).'Pygmalion in the Reintegration Process: Desistance from Crime Through the Looking Glass', *Psychology, Crime & Law*, 10(3), pp. 271–281

Newman, A. P., Lewis, W., and Beverstock, C., (1993) *Prison Literacy*. Philadelphia, PA: National Center on Adult Literacy (ED 363 729).

Rogers, A., (2003) *What is the Difference?* Leicester, NIACE.

Schmitt, J., and Warner, K., (2010). Ex-Offenders and the Labor Market, Washington: CEPR.

Vaughan, B., (2007). 'The Internal Narrative of Desistance', British Journal of Criminology, 47, 390-404.

Wilshaw, M., (2015) *The Annual Report of Her Majesty's Chief Inspector of Education, Children's Services and Skills*, Ofsted, Available at: 2014/15 www.gov.uk/government/uploads/system/uploads/attachment_data/file/483347/Ofsted_annual_report_education_and_skills.pdf, Accessed: May 2017.

Yeaxlee, B. A., (1929) *Lifelong Education*, London: Cassell.

KATE O'BRIEN, FIONA MEASHAM and HANNAH KING / University Students and Prisoners Learning Collaboratively

Note that there are a growing number of Inside-Out programmes running in the US and elsewhere that cover non-criminological subjects such as history, women's studies and philosophy.

Braggins, J. and Talbot, J. (2006) *Wings of Learning: the role of the prison officer in supporting prisoner education* London: Centre for Crime and Justice Studies

Cohen, S and Talyor, L (1972) *Psychological Survival: The Experience of Long-term Imprisonment* London: Penguin Books

Crewe, B., Warr, J., Bennett, P. and Smith, A. (2014) 'The emotional geography of prison life' *Theoretical Criminology*, 18(1), 56–74.

Freire, P. (1996) *Pedagogy of the Oppressed*, London: Penguin.

bell hooks (1994) *Teaching to Transgress: Education as the Practice of Freedom*, London: Routledge.

O'Sullivan, C. (2017) *Prisoner experiences of learning and growth within a high security prison*, Masters Dissertation (unpublished), University of Cambridge.

Palmer, P. (2007) *The Courage to Teach: Exploring the Inner Landscape of a Teacher's Life*, San Francisco: Jossey-Bass.

Piche, J. and Walby, K. (2012) 'Carceral tours and the need for reflexivity: a response to Wilson, Spina and Canaan', *The Howard Journal of Crime and Justice*, 51(4): 411–418

Pompa, L. (2013) 'One brick at a time: the power and possibility of dialogue across the prison wall', *The Prison Journal*, 93(2): 127–134.

Ridley, L. (2014) 'No substitute for the real thing: the impact of prison-based work experience on students' thinking about imprisonment', *The Howard Journal of Crime and Justice*, 53(1): 16–30.

GARETH EVANS / Learning Your Value in Society

1. Farrington, David P. (1961-1981) Cambridge Study In Delinquent Development

2. Bottoms, A., Shapland, J., Costello, A., Holmes, D., and Muir, G., (2004) Towards Desistance: Theoretical Underpinnings for an Empirical Study The Howard Journal Vol 43 No 4. September 2004 ISSN 0265-5527, pp. 368–389.

3. Allport, G. W., (1954). See also, Valentine, G. (2013) Living with difference: Proximity and encounter in urban life. Geography 98 (1):4-9

4. Sapouna, M., Bisset, C., Conlong, A. M., and Matthews, B., (2015) Justice Analytical Services Scottish Government www.gov.scot/Publications/2015/05/2480/3. ISBN 978 1 78544 333 6 (Web only)

KATE DAVEY / Art and Creativity

1. www.artsevidence.org.uk/media/uploads/re-imagining-futures-research-report-final.pdf

2. The Melting Pot, Year One Evaluation (2009) www.artsevidence.org.uk/media/uploads/20090075-melting-pot---year-one-evaluation-report.pdf

3. www.artsincriminaljustice.org.uk/write-to-be-heard/

4. www.gov.uk/government/uploads/system/uploads/attachment_data/file/524013/education-review-report.pdf

ELAINE KNIBBS and MOLLY WRIGHT / Overcoming Trauma, Building Emotional Resilience

Abram, K.M., Teplin, L.A., McClelland, G.M., and Dulcan, M.K. (2003). 'Comorbid psychiatric disorders in youth in juvenile detention'. *Archives of General Psychiatry*, 61(11):403–410.

Ardino, V. 'Post-traumatic stress in antisocial youth: A multifaceted reality'. In: Ardino V, editor. *Post-traumatic syndromes in children and adolescents*. Chichester, UK: Wiley/Blackwell Publishers; 2011. pp. 211–229.

Becker-Blease, K. A. (2017). 'As the world becomes trauma–informed, work to do'. *Journal of Trauma & Dissociation, 18*(2), 131–138.

Benedict, A., (no date), *Using Trauma Informed Practices to Enhance Safety and Security in Women's Correctional Facilities*, National Resource Center on Justice Involved Women, CORE Associates

Beyond Youth Custody (2014). *Young offenders and trauma: experience and impact. A practitioner's guide.* Retrieved from www.beyondyouthcustody.net/

Boswell, G. R. (1996). 'The needs of children who commit serious offences'. *Health and Social Care in the community, 4*(1), 21–29.

Clark, L., Tyler, N., & Gannon, T. A. (2014). 'Eye movement de-sensitisation and reprocessing (EMDR) for offence-related trauma in a mentally disordered sexual offender'. *Journal of Sexual Aggression, 20*(2), 240–249.

Foy D. W, Furrow J, McManus S. 'Exposure to violence, post-traumatic symptomatology, and criminal behaviors'. In: Ardino V, editor. *Post-traumatic syndromes in children and adolescents.* Chichester, UK: Wiley/Blackwell Publishers; 2011. pp. 199–210.

McGue, H. (2016). 'Trauma hiding in plain view: the case for trauma informed practice in women's prisons'. *Practice: The New Zealand Corrections Journal, 4*(2). Retrieved from http://www.corrections.govt.nz/index.html

Miller, N., and Najavits, L., (2012) Creating trauma informed correctional care: a balance of goals and environment, *European Journal of Psychotraumatology, 3*(1). Retrieved from www.tandfonline.com/

Ministry of Justice (2017). Criminal Justice System statistics quarterly: December 2016. London, UK: Ministry of Justice.

Wright, S. and Liddle, M. (2014) *Developing Trauma-Informed Resettlement for Young Custody Leavers. A Practitioner's Guide.* Beyond Youth Custody.

NATHAN DICK / The Voluntary Sector Approach

1. Clinks has published a range of good practice guidance and examples on service user involvement, www.clinks.org/criminal-justice/service-user-involvement

2. Clinks, state of the sector reports, www.clinks.org/eco-downturn

3. Making Every Adult Matter, Solutions from the frontline (2015), meam.org.uk/wp-content/uploads/2013/04/Solutions-from-the-Frontline-WEB.pdf

4. Revolving Doors Agency, www.revolving-doors.org.uk/

5. Agenda, http://weareagenda.org/

6. Lankelly Chase Foundation, https://lankellychase.org.uk/

7. Calouste Gulbenkian, https://gulbenkian.pt/uk-branch/

8. Samaritans, Listener scheme, www.samaritans.org/your-community/our-work-prisons/listener-scheme

9. User Voice, www.uservoice.org/

10. Shannon Trust, Reading Scheme, www.shannontrust.org.uk/our-work/the-reading-plan

11. St Giles Trust, Peer Advisor Programme, site.stgilestrust.org.uk/what-we-do/peer-advisor-programme

12. Clean Break, www.cleanbreak.org.uk/

13. Samaritans, case study, www.samaritans.org/your-community/our-work-prisons/listener-scheme/lynn-samaritans-listener

14. RECOOP, www.recoop.org.uk/pages/home

15. Transitions to Adulthood Alliance, www.t2a.org.uk/

16. The Young Review,www.youngreview.org/

17. Clinks, Introducing desistance theory: a guide for voluntary, community and social enterprise sector organisations (2013), www.clinks.org/sites/default/files/null/Introducing%20Desistance%20-%20 August%202013.pdf

GERARD LEMOS / Race Against Crime, Crime Against Race

1. Keith, B., Hon. Justice (2006) *Report of the Zahid Mubarek Inquiry*. London. The Stationery Office.

ANNE PIKE and RUTH McFARLANE / Experience of Post-Secondary Learning After Prison

Pike, A. (2014) 'Prison-based transformative learning and its role in life after release', The Open University.

PET (2017) Prison University Partnerships in Learning (PUPiL) www.prisonerseducation.org.uk/PUPiL

Index